Defining God

Athanasius, Nicaea and the Trinitarian Controversy of the Fourth Century

— PATRICK WHITWORTH —

Sacristy Press

Sacristy Press
PO Box 612, Durham, DH1 9HT

www.sacristy.co.uk

First published in 2023 by Sacristy Press, Durham

Sacristy Limited, registered in England & Wales, number 7565667

British Library Cataloguing-in-Publication Data
A catalogue record for the book is available from the British Library

Paperback ISBN 978-1-78959-267-2
Hardback ISBN 978-1-78959-128-6

Contents

Black Sea
Constantinople
Thessalonica
Calchedon
Nicomedia
Nicaea
Sinope
Annisa
Neocaesarea
Nicopolis
Sebaste
Pergamum
Smyrna
Ephesus
Iconium
Nyssa
Caesarea
Nazianzus
Tyana
Athens
Miletus
Samosata
Antioch
CRETE
CYPRUS
Salamis
N
Mediterranean Sea
Damascus
Alexandria
Jerusalem

Foreword

As we approach the 1700th anniversary of the Council of Nicaea and the Nicene Creed, we do well to remember the struggle involved in establishing the Trinitarian Creed which lies at the heart of our faith.

A bitter struggle took place in the fourth century to maintain that the Son and the Holy Spirit were of *the same substance as* the Father and equally co-eternal (without beginning or end) and con-substantial. What the Church might take for granted today involved a century of struggle involving councils, creeds, emperors and church leaders. Principal among these and contending for orthodoxy was the Coptic Pope Athanasius, the leader of the Coptic church for much of the fourth century, to whom we all owe so much.

Patrick Whitworth, in this timely reminder of the course and nature of the controversy, shows us the twists and turns, both doctrinal and historical, which defined this struggle. At times in this struggle, until others took up the cause, Athanasius stood *Contra Mundum* (against the world). In an age where the Church struggles with new foes, the resoluteness of a leader like Athanasius gives us both a star to steer by and an anchor in stormy seas. If you wish to understand both the issues at stake and the cross currents of this controversy you could not do better than start with Whitworth's faithful and vivid account of its theology and history, deftly woven together. It should provide an invaluable guide to the church as we approach the important anniversary of Nicaea, learn its lessons for today and strengthen our desire to remain faithful to the biblical revelation.

The Most Reverend Dr Mouneer H. Anis
Archbishop Emeritus
Anglican Province of Alexandria

Preface

As we approach 2025 and the 1700th anniversary of the First Ecumenical Council of Nicaea called by Constantine the Great in 325, Christians may want to once again, or for the first time, understand the issues behind that Council and the deep truths about the nature of the Godhead at stake. It was probably almost inevitable that the reality and truth of the Triune God, each sharing the same substance of the Godhead, but each also being defined by their own actions and identity, should stretch the understanding of Christians. In a world then in which Aristotelian logic and Platonic concepts often reigned, it was more plausible to believe in a single Godhead with various emanations rather than three divine beings consubstantial and coeternal with identifiable roles. It may even have made the mission of the Church easier to go for the idea of a single divine Godhead, but it would have been a travesty of Christianity. The glory of the Christian faith is the existence and action of the Trinity.

To uphold the Trinity required two things: theologians who could show from the Bible the truth of what they were saying and, secondly, an agreeable language which represented biblical truth without twisting it. This process took the best part of a century from the time when Arius proclaimed that there was a time *when the Son was not*; in other words that he, the Son, was a created being. The reason why it took so long to establish the doctrine of the Trinity was because of the interplay of other factors: the need to find an agreeable way of describing what is in the end still a mystery to human minds and souls; the establishment of a settled vocabulary in Greek and Latin which was complementary to each other—and so give universal or catholic understanding to what is orthodox; the interjections of emperors who wanted to settle the issues themselves and had their own favourites (and their bêtes noires for that matter); the rivalries between East and West and between great cities of the empire like Rome, Alexandria and Constantinople; and finally local difficulties and prejudices. All of these came into play. Creeds were being written and rejected at the rate of several a year at some points. Indeed, creed-making was a positive industry.

This book attempts to explain, I hope reasonably clearly, the essence and the development of the controversy. It has been well charted by greater minds and theologians over the years. Some are necessarily very lengthy; others are better suited to the university than to the marketplace. The book shows the stages of the controversy and that Nicaea was a marker along the way. The greatest advocate, in his day, of the Trinity and so of the equality of Father, Son and Spirit in the Godhead was Athanasius. For his pains he went into exile five times, but there he often wrote seminal works on the Incarnation (*Contra Gentes: De Incarnatione*), on the Spirit (*Letters to Serapion*), on the controversy itself (*Apologia contra Arianos* and *De Synodis*) and on ascetism (*Life of Antony*). He was single-minded and stubborn, but most of all a pastor to his flock, the Egyptian or Coptic Church to whom he wrote a Festal Letter every year before Lent. By the end of the fourth century, others like the Cappadocian Fathers in the East, and Hilary and later Augustine of Hippo in the West (writing in Latin as opposed to Greek) had taken up the task. Their combined work laid the foundation to the Church's Trinitarian understanding of the Scriptures.

Why is this controversy more than just history? More than anything else it was the tortuous process by which the Church established its orthodoxy about the Trinity, and in particular the consubstantial nature of Christ, the Son of God whose divine nature enabled an eternal redemption which was secure, and who revealed to humankind the likeness of God. Within the struggle there were well-meaning theologians with false ideas, there were sinister plotters, there were wilful ecclesiastics who wanted influence more than truth, there were the misleading and the misled. The Church has never in its entire history been without struggle; you could say it was born to it. By reviewing this controversy, probably the greatest of all struggles about the very nature of God, there may be lessons for struggles today.

In writing this book I would like to thank Professor Mark Edwards for his many helpful corrections, The Most Reverend Dr Mouneer H. Anis, Archbishop Emeritus of the Anglican Province of Alexandria, for his generous Foreword, Dr Natalie K. Watson, my editor at Sacristy Press, and the team there for taking on another of my books, Marian Aird for the excellent index, and Kevin Sheehan for the map. And the shortcomings of such a mind-stretching endeavour as writing on the debates of the Church on the reality of the Trinity are entirely mine. I could not have attempted it without the support of my family, and especially Olivia.

CHAPTER 1

Church and state at the beginning of the fourth century

When Constantine was acclaimed *augustus* (emperor) of the West by his father's troops in York, England, on 25 July 306, Athanasius was approximately ten years old.[1] Their paths would not cross for nearly 20 years, but thereafter they would do so quite often until Constantine's death in 337. Outside York Minster today, a statue records Constantine's accession to power, although he would have to fight to gain it fully in the following years. The statue is of a seated Constantine, languid of limb and athletic in appearance: a young man in his thirties at the height of his military powers. Across his knees lies a sword in the form of a cross, and below it an inscription in English, "Constantine, by this sword conquer." A few years later, on 28 October 312, at the Battle of Milvian Bridge across the Tiber in Rome, Constantine defeated his rival Maxentius and became the *augustus* of the western half of the Roman empire, bringing Christianity with him.

If Constantine was to become the dominant force in the shaping of the empire after 306, establishing Christianity as the imperial religion and supplanting paganism, Athanasius would become the chief spokesperson for orthodoxy, based on the creed hammered out at Nicaea, a council which Constantine himself called in 325, when at the peak of his political power. Yet although Constantine and Athanasius both had interests in upholding the divinity of Christ, they were not friends. Indeed, in the context of this narrative, their uneasy relationship lay some way in the future. Nevertheless, the two men, with differing responsibilities towards state and Church, would profoundly shape the future: Constantine in establishing a model of Christian government which, with its strengths and weaknesses, would be the pattern for Christendom for over 1,700 years of western government; and Athanasius in preserving the central tenet of Christianity: that Christ is fully God. Although there was a real overlap in their objectives, there would be times when Constantine would see Athanasius as a "turbulent priest" (the phrase supposedly used by Henry II of Thomas Becket when that archbishop would not do his bidding). Relationships between kings and archbishops were often fraught, each believing himself superior to the other. But before we see both their common interests and their occasional conflicts, we must trace their respective ascents to leadership.

The empire at the beginning of the fourth century

It would not be an exaggeration to say that in the fourth century, the Roman empire in both West and East proceeded by way of one crisis after another. Following the reign of Hadrian, emperor from AD 117–38, the borders of the empire had been reached: Hadrian's Wall in the north, the Rhine and Danube in the east, Spain in the west, and the Euphrates in the south-east, with the North African littoral forming the natural boundary on the south side of the Mediterranean. Having established this vast empire by AD 138 through force of arms, the next two and a half centuries would be spent maintaining its borders against incursions from the east, either from beyond the Rhine or the Danube in the north, or from the Persian or Sassanian empire beyond the Euphrates in the south. The so called "Five Good Emperors": Nerva (96–8), Trajan (98–117), Hadrian, Antoninus Pius (138–61) and Marcus Aurelius (161–80), represented the zenith of imperial Rome following the rule of Augustus (27 BC–AD 14); at least until Constantine himself became sole emperor and the empire shone briefly before its division among his sons.

Following the assassination of Commodus, who was strangled on the evening of 31 December 192, the empire once again became vulnerable.[2] Commodus's successor Pertinax was proclaimed emperor but was promptly murdered on 28 March 193. In a single year, five emperors took office and were ousted until a powerful new general and emperor emerged from North Africa, Septimus Severus.

Born in Lepcis Magna in AD 145, near present-day Al-Khums in Libya, Severus was from the aristocratic and ruling class of North Africa. Cassius Dio said that he was a "man of few words but many ideas".[3] He became emperor in 193 and would remain in office until 211. His was a life of permanent campaigning, initially around Byzantium, Syria,[4] and against the Parthians, shoring up his position against a rival Niger, and later against a usurper governor of Britain called Albinus, whom he defeated near Lyons. Finally campaigning in Britain against the Picts, Severus died in York on 4 February 211, aged 66, with his sons Caracalla and Geta succeeding him. Severus had ruled in the manner of Marcus Aurelius, and according to the author Aelius Spartianus, his dying words in York were, "I took over the republic in a disturbed condition everywhere, and I leave it pacified even among the Britons. Now an old man crippled in the feet, I bequeath to my Antonines, a stable empire if they will be good, a weak one if bad." And finally, before dying, he gave the watchword for his troops: "Let us work".[5]

Ruling in the style of Marcus Aurelius also entailed suppressing anything which was anti-Roman, and this meant the Church. He supported the traditional Roman ruling classes of senatorial rank, kept legions permanently installed in Italy, and was not an innovator or reformer. His advice to others was, "be harmonious, enrich soldiers and despise all the rest".[6] For all his beautifying of North Africa, and in particular his birthplace of Lepcis Magna, Severus began an unrelenting persecution of the Church in Africa to which we shall return.

Severus was succeeded by his oldest son Caracalla, famous for building the largest baths in Rome, and who ordered the murder of his younger brother Geta. Like his father, much of his time was spent campaigning firstly against the Alamanni on the Rhine, defeating them in August 213, and then later from 214 in the east, where he was accompanied by his mother Julian Domna. Having established his headquarters in Antioch and then having moved to Alexandria, he perpetrated a bloody massacre on a recalcitrant population of that city for showing him little respect.[7] Thereafter, he shored up Armenia by appointing a client king, invaded Parthia, having been refused marriage to King Artababus of Parthia's daughter. His eastern campaign came to an abrupt end, however, when he was murdered by a praetorian prefect, Macrinus, while visiting the temple of Carrhae on the upper Euphrates, in present-day northern Syria.

As an emperor, Caracalla was less effective than Severus, for he failed to foster the senatorial classes of Italy. While absent in the east, Caracalla had appointed a eunuch, Sempronius Rufus, to take charge of Rome. Rufus specialized in juggling and sorcery, and his appointment was tantamount to a slur on Rome.[8] Caracalla had visions of being a second Alexander the Great, but his leadership was more that of showman than a professional soldier. His murder ended the Severan dynasty; two emperors, Elagabalus and Severus Alexander, followed in relatively swift succession, but by the mid third century the Roman empire was entering its most unstable and vulnerable stage.

The empire was threatened by a growing number of incursions across the Rhine and Danube from the Alamanni and Goths respectively, and by a more confident and aggressive Persian empire under Ardashir (208–40), and then Shapur I (r. 240–70) in the mid third century AD. Between AD 235 and 260, 51 people received the title of emperor of Rome or *augustus*.[9] Some were killed, like Aemilianus, proclaimed emperor on the Danube in 253, but murdered by his troops only four months later near Spoletium.[10] Rome became in part dependent on client kings, such as Tiridates of Armenia, until he was overwhelmed by neighbouring Persia, and King Odaenathus (260–7) of Palmyra, who offered successful resistance to the Persians after the defeat and capture of Emperor Valerian by Shapur. Indeed, the capture of the Emperor Valerian in 260, whose back was then used by Shapur as a mounting block for his horse, was a low-water mark of Rome's fortunes. Rome nevertheless appeared able to produce military leaders to reverse such setbacks. Aurelian (270–5) was able to surmount many of Rome's reverses in the east and contain the Persian threat, also subjugating the widow of Odaenathus, the brilliant Queen Zenobia of Palmyra, and establishing Roman hegemony in Gaul and the north-western part of the empire.

Despite these years of vulnerability, the empire held together. There were many weaknesses: the need for constant taxation to sustain almost continual warfare, difficulty in paying for major campaigns, recourse to debasing the silver coinage, and the conviction that setbacks were due to neglect of traditional pagan gods—hence the persecution of the Church under several emperors like Decius and Valerian—and too frequent political intrigue. At the same time, the empire had enormous resilience born of its underlying structures, its military heritage, and a system that continually threw up leaders wanting to take on the risk of leadership. The empire was able to adapt. It became multi-centred, with Rome no longer playing a central role. Instead, there were regional centres, as in Trier on the Moselle, Milan just south of the Alps, Sirmium north-east of Belgrade on the River Sava, Antioch, and later Constantinople. New centres of administration arose to meet the strategic needs of the empire.

The *cursus honorum* (or career structure) of the empire became less centred on a senatorial class based in Rome, and instead related more to the army and civil administration throughout the territory. Indeed, military success and cultivating a regional base were often the stepping stones to becoming emperor. All this provided the background to the substantial changes promulgated by the Emperor Diocletian, whose reign as *augustus*, a little before Constantine, precipitated the greatest reform of the empire, and the gravest threat to the Church since Marcus Aurelius.

Diocletian

Diocletian, whose birth name was Diocles, was probably born in Salona near present-day Split, Dalmatia, in 243.[11] Representing the soldiery tradition of Illyricum, the Latin name for the area, he too joined the army in *c.*270.[12] He soon rose through the ranks, becoming part of an elite group called the *Protectores* and then *Dux Moesia*. He was "masterful, ambitious with a naturally shrewd and calculating nature".[13] He left nothing to chance and planned tirelessly. Something of a loner, and keeping his own counsel, he avoided extravagant shows of largesse, or joshing and drinking with his men. Following the assassination of the Emperor Gallienus in 268, a succession of emperors followed. In 283, Emperor Carus died, survived by his sons Numerianus and Carinus.[14] Numerianus was murdered by his praetorian prefect and father-in-law Apter, whereupon the army called for Diocles to become *augustus*. He accepted, donning the scarlet cape, and his first act was to summon Apter to the platform on which he stood covered with the insignia of emperor, whereupon he promptly stabbed Apter to death. Diocletian started as he meant to go on.

Unlike any emperor that century, Diocletian ruled for over two decades, from 284–305. He would be responsible for the re-establishment of political, military and economic stability after half a century of crisis and the swift recycling of emperors who failed to hold the support of the army for long or were defeated in battle. In Egypt, Diocletian was praised as follows, "The whole land takes delight in its joy as at the light of a golden age, and the iron, drawn back from the slaughter of men, lies bloodlessly in the scabbard".[15] He appointed Maximian as *augustus* in the west, and each *augustus* identified himself with a particular deity. Maximian defeated the Bagaudae in Gaul, but one of his officers, Carausius, began to enrich himself with booty and to establish himself among the British legions as a probable usurper. By 286, Carausius had declared himself *augustus* in Britain.

By now, the pattern of rule was set, with Diocletian for the most part campaigning in the east and based in Nicomedia. He made peace with the Persians under Vahran II (or Bahram II) in 287 and restored Tiridates III as ruler of Armenia. Peace reigned in Syria and Palestine. In the west, Maximian, ruling from Milan and Trier, sought to bring stability to the Rhine region and to Gaul. But a new model of leadership in the empire arose from the need for incessant military engagement. This plan became known as the tetrarchy.

On 1 March 293, two further *caesars* were appointed to serve alongside each of the two *augustii*. In the west, Flavius Constantius, a former governor of Dalmatia, an experienced soldier who had campaigned with Aurelian against Zenobia, was appointed Caesar to Maximian. To strengthen blood ties with the imperial family, Constantius married Maximian's daughter, Theodora, in 289. However, Constantius already had a son from a previous marriage with a woman of humble extraction called Helena: Constantine—the future Constantine the Great.

Likewise, in either Philippopolis (present-day Plovdiv in Bulgaria) or Sirmium, Galerius was appointed Caesar to Diocletian. He too married the daughter, here Diocletian's daughter Valeria.[16] Galerius would once again be engaged in warfare with the Persians. He was initially defeated by King Narses at Callinicum in 296, but he reversed that defeat the following year and captured the king's harem and treasury. It was this victory that Galerius would commemorate with a triumphal arch still visible in Thessaloniki today. Meanwhile, Constantius was sent to re-establish Roman control of Britain, carefully planning an invasion from Boulougne to wrest control of the island from Allectus, who had murdered the usurper Carausius. By 296, Constantius had recovered Britain for Rome, and by 303 both *augustii* were celebrating their *vicennalia*, twenty-year anniversaries since their accession in Rome. All seemed set fair.

The tetrarchy was not all about military success, however. There were also many administrative and legal reforms of the empire. Furthermore, there was a strengthening of traditional Roman piety, with the result of a sudden and very sharp persecution of Christians, who were seen as weakening traditional Roman piety towards the pagan gods, and also unwilling to recognize the divine claims of the emperors. The empire was reconfigured into 12 administrative dioceses, effectively groups of previous provinces. They were led by *vicarii*, that is, prefects or governors who stood (vicariously) in place of the emperor as ruler in that region. (It is evident from whence the Church got its administrative names.) The coinage was strengthened. An abortive attempt was made at fixing prices of goods throughout the empire, in what was a salutary lesson in the weakness of central planning. A census was taken of all wealth—a kind of early Domesday Book.[17] A new dating system was adopted, starting with the beginning of Diocletian's reign. Many years later Athanasius would date his annual Festal pre-Easter Letters using this dating system, so the Letter of 329 was dated the forty-fifth year since Diocletian's accession. The Edict of Marriages of 295 banished incestuous relationships and encouraged the birth of children.[18] Deviant religious practices such as those of the Manichees (see the Epistle to the Manichees of 297) were proscribed, with their books burnt and their leaders executed. From this it was only a short step to such enforcement of Roman pagan orthodoxy on Christians, which began with their banning from the army in 297.

Then in 305 a unique event took place: the abdications of both *augustii*, both Diocletian and Maximian. They were succeeded by Galerius in the east and Constantius Chlorus in the west. At the same time, two new Caesars were announced, Severus and Maximinus, although their succession was anything but smooth. Constantine, the son of Constantius Chlorus, present at this announcement in the court of Diocletian, was shocked to have been overlooked.[19] It was not a state of affairs with which he could live. Two years before this event, and quite suddenly on 23 February 303, the Great Persecution against the Church began. Before tracing the development of the Church through the third century and the impact of this persecution, we must complete the story of the rise of Constantine, however. There had been two events in close order, both of which Constantine was instrumental in reversing.

The rise of Constantine

When Constantine heard that his father was gravely ill in Bononia (Boulogne), and with Severus in Milan wanting to take the emperor's purple, he knew his succession was in jeopardy. Soon after 1 May 305, as the Great Persecution was getting underway in the east, Constantine slipped out of the court of Galerius at Serdica (Sofia)—Galerius himself had ambitions to take over the western empire—and joined his father at Boulogne. His father conducted one last campaign, against the Picts beyond Hadrian's Wall, and died on 25 July 306 in York. Constantine was acclaimed emperor or *augustus* by his troops, but he had no shortage of rivals: Severus the newly appointed *caesar* in the west; Maxentius the oldest son of the former emperor Maximian; and Maximian himself, the old emperor, showing signs of restlessness in retirement, having initially taken an oath of allegiance to Constantine at Carnuntum in 308, but then thinking better of it and rebelling, only to be forced to commit suicide.

Constantine, now 35 years old, knew that he must act if he wanted to secure his rule. In Gaul he married Fausta, Maximian's young daughter, who was just seven years old. In his wedding speech, he seemed committed to the sun-god, *Sol Invictus*, who had been invoked by Aurelian.[20] Constantine certainly showed himself invincible as a soldier while based at Trier, defeating the Franks and executing two of their kings by throwing them to the wild beasts in the amphitheatre in Trier. Constantine remained a skilled and resolute general throughout his life. He showed little mercy to his opponents or to anyone who crossed him:

as his wife Fausta, and his older son Crispus (by a previous wife), would later discover.

To be truly *augustus* in the west, Constantine needed to defeat his rival Maxentius, based in Rome, and take the capital city. Rome was well defended with new walls built by Aurelian and further strengthened by Maxentius. Indeed, Maxentius had gone in for a building spree in Rome, creating a massive basilica in the Forum, two halls on the Lateran Hill, and a suburban palace on the Via Appia complete with its own circus.[21] Maxentius was also more accommodating towards the Church during the Great Persecution, exiling its leaders, but not persecuting its members.[22] By 311, Constantine was moving east and south towards Italy, stopping at Autun en route for Rome with an army possibly as large as 40,000 men. It was a campaign that demonstrated Constantine's ability as a commander: anticipating the constraints and opportunities of his opponent and supervising the enormous amount of detail involved in moving an army of that size through the Alps.[23] Soon Constantine had taken Turin and Verona, employing his heavy cavalry to devastating effect. By now, Maxentius's authority in Rome was weakening: Christians resented the exile of their bishops; the people remembered the bloody suppression of city riots; and senatorial leaders were considering their options.[24] Constantine arrived at the entrance to Rome near the Milvian Bridge. He was at the culmination of his campaign. A victory would give him Rome, the ancient capital of the empire, and with it rule in the western empire. It was a time when any commander would look to the gods for the outcome of the battle ahead. It was also to be the most defining moment of his own spiritual journey.

The exact nature of the epiphany Constantine received that led him to his commitment to the Christian faith is well documented, but it is still hard to piece together. Some, like the Roman author and Christian Apologist Lactantius (240–320), believed that during the night before the battle the emperor was commanded in a dream to place the sign of Christ on the shields of his soldiers.[25] Much later Constantine gave Eusebius of Caesarea, bishop, Church historian and scholar (265–339), an account of his own conversion. In Eusebius's biography of Constantine, he recalls the emperor's account that, "about midday when the day was beginning to decline, he saw with his own eyes the trophy of a cross of light in the heavens, above the sun, and bearing the inscription, 'Conquer by this'. At this sight he himself was struck with amazement, and his whole army also, which followed him on this expedition, and witnessed the miracle."[26] Whether this happened the day before the Battle of Milvian Bridge or at some earlier point in the campaign we cannot be sure. In any event, he replaced the pagan standards of his legionnaires with a new sign consisting of the Greek letters *chi* and *rho*, the first two letters of Christ's name. This sign came to be called a *labarum*, a Gallic word that befitted the largely Gallic and German army Constantine commanded. Thus, either before, during or soon after the battle, Constantine came to the conviction that he was the servant of the living and divine Christ and on that day of 28 October 312, "he was entrusted with the divine mission to convert the Roman empire to Christianity".[27] The battle was quickly won, most of Maxentius's forces fled knowing they faced a superior enemy and Maxentius died, drowning in full armour in the Tiber. Constantine was truly the *augustus* in the west, and quickly proclaimed the chief *augustus* in the empire. He was nearly 40 years old and would reign for a further 25 years, eventually over both west and east.

The rule of Constantine would be marked both by continuity and fundamental change. Although he would turn the empire in an unmistakeably Christian direction, he did not abolish paganism so much as discourage it, nor did he remove from office those who would not call themselves Christians. The suppression of paganism, its buildings, liturgies and personnel, did not fully arrive till the fifth century when legislation was enacted and persecution of paganism became ruling policy. But in February 313, a landmark edict was made by both *augustii*, Constantine and Licinius, when they met in Milan, to the effect that all governors of provinces were to recognize the legitimacy of Christian worship and tolerate the Church. The Edict of Milan officially ended the persecution of the Church, which had taken hold from 303, especially in the east, and which had become known as the Great Persecution. In the same year, Licinius defeated Maximinus Daia, who as the *caesar* (or *augustus* as he claimed) in the east had continued the persecution of Christians undertaken by Diocletian and Galerius, both of whom died in 311.

Having made this immediate and fundamental change to imperial policy, Constantine pushed ahead with his own policies of establishing the Church and enacting new legislation by edict. Exiled bishops and clergy were welcomed back. They were excused taxes or the necessity of taking part in civic duties (*patria potestas*) and liturgies.[28] Priests could release slaves in a legal act performed in church.[29] Church courts were set up with the bishop presiding over cases between Christians. Crucifixion and disfigurement of the face were ended, as was gladiatorial combat. Divination was regulated. Divorce was made more difficult. And a great programme of church building was begun. A new basilica called Constantiniana was started off the Caelian Hill in Rome, on property previously owned by the Laterani family, and this become the site of St John Lateran. Further churches were dedicated to St Peter and St Marcellinus, with a mausoleum attached for Helena, Constantine's mother; a basilica of the Apostles (now San Sebastiano) on the Via Appia; a basilica of St Lawrence (now San Lorenzo outside the city walls); a basilica to St Agnes; and lastly basilicas dedicated to St Peter and St Paul. These churches, along with the edicts of Constantine, his great arch commemorating his victory over Maxentius (standing by the Colosseum) and the colossal statue of himself (see remains, including the head, in the Musei Capitolini, Rome) must, taken together, have changed the built landscape of Rome irrevocably, especially along the main roads into the city.[30]

By 315, Constantine's imprint on Rome was unmistakeable. Yet it would be another nine years before he was able to unite the empire, west and east, with the defeat of the eastern emperor or Augustus Licinius, firstly in the Balkans at Cibalae (316) in a hard-fought battle which he only narrowly won, and at Adrianople on 3 July 317 when Licinius suffered a near fatal defeat.[31] Licinius's rule limped on, but eventually, through the encouragement of his wife Constantia, the half-sister of Constantine, he gave himself up, having being outmanoeuvred by superior forces led by Constantine on land and sea along the Bosporus.[32] In 324, Constantine took control of the east and began building a new capital at Constantinople, a city which would remain Christian, and the capital of the eastern empire or Byzantium, for over a thousand years.

Constantine had united the empire under his single command. His marriage to Fausta had been fruitful, giving him three sons, although in 326, and in a shadowy event, she was removed from public life, and Crispus, his son by a previous marriage, already declared *caesar*, was executed. It is thought that the pair may have been having an affair.

More difficult to unite than the empire was the Church itself, split as it was in North Africa by its response to persecution, which led to the Donatist schism, and also by its understanding of the Trinity and the divinity of Christ. Much of Constantine's time was spent attempting to heal the divisions in the Church along these lines.

The Church at the start of the fourth century

By the start of the third century, Christianity was widely disseminated throughout the empire. The apostolic mission recorded in the New Testament had founded churches (groups of Christians in particular communities with appointed leaders) in the provinces of Palestine, Syria, Cappadocia, Galatia, Pontus and Bithynia, Macedonia, Achaea (Greece), Dalmatia, and Italia, and in the principal cities of the empire, such as Antioch, Caesarea, Ephesus, Alexandria, Athens and Rome. These churches were gathered around the apostolic teaching, such as they possessed, and the conduct of the sacraments of baptism and eucharist. The Church had survived its early persecutions under Nero, Domitian and Trajan (98–117), whose governor of Bithynia, Pliny the Younger, had asked for specific guidance on how to treat those Christians who would not sacrifice to the emperor. He was advised not to hunt them down and to give them time in the courtroom to recant. If they persisted, he was to imprison or flog them. Trajan did not want a scourge of all Christians, but he did want to punish those who refused to burn incense to the image of the divine emperor, such as a bust in a courtroom.

Despite this early opposition from AD 60, the Church grew and became established in new provinces, such as Britanniae. At the centre of church life was fellowship—including sharing material resources, prayer and teaching (see Acts 2:42–7). Access to written texts of Scripture was rare, and the canon of the New Testament (as we now know it) was not yet finalized. But we do know that by the late second century, Irenaeus, Bishop of Lyons (Lugdunum), had listed the four Gospels and the 13 Pauline epistles circulating among the churches. Likewise, a list of New Testament books, which came to be called the Muratorian Canon, and discovered in a monastery founded by the Irish monk Columbanus in Bobbio, also affirms the circulation of the Gospels and the Pauline epistles by the late second century. The letter to the Hebrews, James and Jude, 2 and 3 John, 2 Peter and Revelation were affirmed later. The New Testament was rapidly being assembled. Baptisms in rivers, lakes and pools took place, especially around Easter, and the Eucharist was celebrated regularly, if not weekly. In his *First Apology*, Justin Martyr records a moving account of a weekly Eucharist:

> Having ended the prayers (following a Baptism), we salute one another with a kiss. There is then brought to the president of the brethren (meaning the one presiding) bread and a cup of wine mixed with water; and he taking them, gives praise and glory to the Father of the universe, through the name of the Son and of the Holy Spirit, and offers thanks at considerable length for being counted worthy to receive these things at His hands. And when he has concluded the prayers and thanksgivings, all the people present express their assent by saying Amen. And when the President (the presiding presbyter) has given thanks, and all the people expressed their assent, those who are called by us deacons give to each present to partake of the bread and wine mixed with water over which thanksgiving was pronounced, and to those who are absent they carry away a portion.[33]

This apology was a defence of Christianity by Justin addressed to the Emperor Antoninus Pius in *c.*155–7, but Justin was nevertheless martyred with some of his colleagues in 165. His plea that Christians be accepted as reliable members of the community fell on deaf pagan ears.

The Church had a similar structure throughout the empire: congregations would be led by presbyters; groups of churches in a city or region would be led by an elected bishop, and in addition there would be deacons and deaconesses. Ignatius, the martyr and Bishop of Antioch, had a high view of the need for unity around the bishop, writing, "we are clearly to look upon the bishop as the Lord himself".[34] Furthermore, the early Church text called the *Didache*, found in Jerusalem in the library of the Church of the Holy Sepulchre in 1873, set out a path of moral purity and the peaceful conduct of ministry which was incumbent on Church life.[35] Famously, according to Eusebius of Caesarea, by 251, one church in Rome had one bishop, 46 presbyters, seven deacons, seven subdeacons, 42 acolytes, and 52 exorcists, traders and door keepers.[36] But it was also responsible for feeding 1,500 needy persons and widows.[37] They were fed "by the grace and kindness of the Lord".

What is clear is that these communities of care and mutual support—governed and led by a clear structure of leadership settled around apostolic teaching and the sacraments—provided a human fellowship quite unlike anything else in the pagan world except the synagogue. Furthermore, the hope of resurrection, the forgiveness of sins and the presence of the Spirit in the life and community of believers also constituted a real difference from the synagogue. And indeed, the dissolution of human difference in the bonds of fellowship created a community radically different from the stratified communities of the pagan, and even Jewish, world. As Paul wrote, "There is no longer Jew or Greek, there is no longer slave or free, there is no longer male and female, for all of you are one in Christ Jesus" (Galatians 3:28). It is *this truth* that cut through the pagan world and gave extraordinary growth to the Church.

If the growth of the Church was mostly due to its gospel message of forgiveness and resurrection and the presence of the Spirit illuminating the world, its growth also resulted from its social dynamic. In particular, a number of facets of Christianity facilitated its growth in the ancient world. It gave hope to slaves, who numbered a third to a quarter of the population of the ancient world, and who after Constantine could be freed; and indeed teaching as in Paul's letter to Philemon about a runaway slave encouraged this. Women had an entirely different status. In the Christian community, adultery was a grave sin, divorce was not to be practised, and infanticide and abortion were to be banned.[38] Men were to be the husband of one wife (Titus 1:6), and although "just concubinage" (the right to live with a man who was not your husband) might be allowed for a while under Pope Callistus (217–22), it was a controversial concession to concubinage.[39] In time, the disproportionate number of women in the Church led, in part, to the establishment of serving orders and the call to virginity among both women and men. Interestingly this sexual revolution was a springboard to growth.

Not only were freedom from slavery after Constantine, the new status of women, and greater protection for children reasons for church growth, but so too was the care offered by the Church for the poor and the disadvantaged. The ancient world faced serious pandemics. Epidemics in 180 and 251 and in the surrounding years carried off as much as a third of the population.[40] Cyprian, Bishop of Carthage, and Dionysius of Alexandria both saw the epidemics as opportunities to show care and fortitude.[41] Indeed, in his apology, Tertullian wrote, "It is our care of the helpless, our practice of loving kindness that brands us in the eyes of many opponents. 'Only look,' they say 'look how they love one another.'"[42] In both the worst and the best of times, mutual care fulfilled the teaching of Jesus, that in so far "as you did it to one of the least of these who are members of my family, you did it to me" (Matthew 25:40). If these were all reasons for growth, it came at great cost, sometimes sharp and sustained.

The persecution of the Church

The Church was born to persecution. Jesus told his disciples, "If the world hates you, be aware that it hated me before it hated you" (John 15:18). In the early days after Pentecost, the apostles Peter and John were arrested (Acts 4:3), Stephen was martyred (Acts 7:54ff.) and "a severe persecution began against the church in Jerusalem" (Acts 8:1). Most of the Church was scattered, finding a new centre at Antioch, where the disciples were first known as "Christians" (Acts 11:19ff., especially 26b).

If persecution of the Church came first from the Jewish authorities, seeking to stamp out this deviant Jewish sect as they saw it, called "The Way", that believed Jesus was the Messiah and Son of God (Mark 1:1), more sustained persecution would come from Rome. The reasons for this persecution were severalfold: the refusal of Christians to recognize the emperor's title of *divi filius*; the recognition that only Jesus was truly the Son of God and Lord; the refusal to offer worship to the emperor; and the abandonment of the pagan gods. The resulting persecution of the Church by Rome was given further fuel by political events, which the emperors used. Emperor Claudius expelled Christians from Rome after some riots in about 48 (see Acts 18:2). Nero used Christians as scapegoats for the great fire in Rome in 64, and it is quite possible that both Peter and Paul were executed at this time.[43] And we do know that Christians were used in gladiatorial shows as prey for wild animals. Not only that, but some were deliberately set on fire to become human torches at receptions in Nero's Golden House. Christians had become the collective whipping boy of the Roman state, as Tertullian makes clear in his *Apology* in around 200, writing, "If the Tiber rises as high as the city walls, if the Nile does not send its waters over the fields, if the heavens give no rain, if there is an earthquake, if there is a famine or pestilence, straightway the cry is 'Away with the Christians to the lion!'"[44]

Persecution would continue intermittently, but with some peaks throughout the second and third centuries, with complicating results for the Church itself. At the beginning of the second century, we find Bishop Ignatius of Antioch being escorted by soldiers from Antioch to Rome to await certain death there. In his letter to the Roman Church, Ignatius writes:

> I am writing all the churches and giving instruction to all, that I am willingly dying for good, unless you hinder me. I urge you do not become an untimely kindness to me. Allow me to be breads for the wild beasts: through them I am able to attain to God.[45]

Later in the second century, a new wave of persecution began in Smyrna, where Polycarp, Bishop of Smyrna, was martyred around 165. The proconsul there urged Polycarp to take the oath to the emperor, proclaim him a divinity, and make a sacrifice to him. "'Take the oath,' he said, 'and I will release you. Revile Christ', But Polycarp responded, 'For eighty-six years I have served him, and he has done me no wrong. How can I blaspheme my king who has saved me?'"[46]

Conservative emperors, intent on restoring pagan worship, were often the most energetic persecutors of the Church. This was true of Marcus Aurelius, under whom there was sharp persecution in the Vienne region of Gaul, and of Septimus Severus from Lepcis Magna. In March *c.*203, four youthful Christians were tried and condemned to fight wild beasts in the arena in Carthage during games celebrating the birthday of Geta, the Emperor Severus's younger son. They were the young, high born, breastfeeding mother Perpetua and her companions, and this happened because Perpetua could not be persuaded by her father to "take the oath". While in prison awaiting her end, she had a number of visions of paradise, of spiritual superiority and heavenly tranquillity.[47] She died bravely in the arena, and although objecting to her scantily dressed appearance, the crowd were nonetheless ready to see her devoured by beasts. Mercifully her life was ended by a centurion's sword thrust. There were further years of sharp persecution against Christians before the middle of the third century, under Emperors Decius (249–51) and Valerian (253–60). Not only was this a scourge in itself, but the response opened up a rift within the Church.

The issue the Church faced by the middle of the third century was how to treat those who, unlike Perpetua and her companions, did not win the martyrs' crown, but either "took the oath" or handed over church property, including prayer books and Scriptures, thus becoming *traditores* (the origin of our word traitor). In other words, they denied their faith. In the Decian persecution, the authorities required all Christians to obtain a *libelli* (certificate) to avoid prosecution, torture, imprisonment or death. Some agreed to "take the oath" or burn incense outright; others bought the certificate (they paid a bribe) without taking the oath. At the same time, others suffered imprisonment, torture, confiscation of property and death. How should the Church respond? There were two options: refusing such *traditores* fellowship in the Church and hence excommunicating them, or incorporating them after a suitable penance. The hard line that split the Church was taken by Novatian (the anti-pope of 251) in Rome, by Donatus in North Africa, and by Melitius, Bishop of Lycopolis. In Rome, there was a split between the more moderate Cornelius—elected Bishop of Rome or Pope in 251 and who had the support of Cyprian of Carthage—and the more rigorous and noted theologian, Novatian. Likewise, the Great Persecution, which began on 23 February 303, precipitated the same split between Caecilian of Carthage and Donatus, a presbyter of Casae Nigre, Numidia (present-day

Algeria). These splits or schisms would last until the coming of Islam and the Arabs, especially in North Africa, despite Constantine's efforts to reconcile or suppress them at the Council of Rome in 312 and at Arles in 314. These were Constantine's first attempts at peace-making in the Church, and he would find repeatedly that winning a military campaign was easier than reconciling such differences.

The final severe twist to the life of the Church, just before the arrival of Constantine as emperor—the Great Persecution that began in 303—was pursued mostly in the eastern part of the empire by the Augustus Galerius until 311 and the Milan Edict of Tolerance, and then until 313 by Maximinus Daia, his Caesar. Licinius (308–24), who Constantine defeated in 324 to take the east, seemed to have a more ambivalent attitude towards Christianity, having co-authored the Edict of Milan.

The Great Persecution began suddenly and unexpectedly, and in an unusual way. The inability of pagan priests and haruspices to read the entrails of a sacrifice because of the presence of Christians at the shrine and oracle of Apollo at Didyma appears to have been the last straw. Although Diocletian had been emperor or *augustus* for 18 years by then, and there had been a growing persecution of the Manichees from 276, and more recently a purge of Christians from the army, the extent and ferocity of this persecution broke from a seemingly cloudless sky.[48] Diocletian issued an edict in 303, the first of several, banning assembly for worship, and calling for the destruction of places of worship, and the handing over of Scriptures, prayer books and liturgies. Christians in imperial service were stripped of their office.[49] When an enthusiastic Christian tore down the edict posted in the imperial city of Nicomedia, the persecution developed from an attack on services, worship and property to one requiring sacrifice to the emperor on pain of torture, imprisonment and death. The arrests of bishops, presbyters and other church workers soon followed. Many were killed in Nicomedia after suffering excruciating torture.[50] Likewise, there were martyrs in Egypt, Phrygia, Syria and Antioch,[51] and many in Palestine also.[52] Persecution in the east would continue until the Edict of Tolerance in 311. Despite this edict, Maximin, the *caesar* in the east, continued the persecution against Christians almost until his death in 313. Then, in that same year, the Edict of Milan brought to an end this last violent ten-year persecution of Christians and destruction of their property. However, it left the issue, discussed above, of dealing with the lapsed, which split the Church into two. Nowhere was this more acute than in Carthage and Alexandria by the second decade of the fourth century.

Notes

1 Averil Cameron, "The Reign of Constantine", in Alan K. Bowman, Peter Garnsey and Averil Cameron (eds), *The Cambridge Ancient History, second edition, Vol. XII: The Crisis of Empire, A.D. 193–337* (Cambridge: Cambridge University Press, 2005), pp. 90–109, here at p. 90.

2 Brian Campbell, "The Severan Dynasty", in Alan K. Bowman, Peter Garnsey and Averil Cameron (eds), *The Cambridge Ancient History, second edition, Vol. XII: The Crisis of Empire, A.D. 193–337* (Cambridge: Cambridge University Press, 2005), pp. 1–27, here at p. 1.

3 Campbell, "The Severan Dynasty", p. 3.

4 Campbell, "The Severan Dynasty", p. 5.

5 Aelius Spartianus, "Severus", in *Lives of the Later Caesars, the first part of the Augustan history: with newly compiled Lives of Nerva and Trajan*, tr. and intr. Anthony Birley (Harmondsworth: Penguin, 1976), p. 201.

6 Spartianus, "Severus", p. 17.

7 Spartianus, "Severus", p. 19.

8 Spartianus, "Severus", p. 16.

9 Spartianus, "Severus", p. 28.

10 Spartianus, "Severus", p. 41.

11 Stephen Williams, *Diocletian and the Roman Recovery* (London: Routledge, 1997), p. 22.

12 Williams, *Diocletian and the Roman Recovery*, p. 24.

13 Williams, *Diocletian and the Roman Recovery*, p. 26.

14 Alan Bowman, "Diocletian and the First Tetrarchy", in Alan K. Bowman, Peter Garnsey and Averil Cameron (eds), *The Cambridge Ancient History, second edition, Vol. XII: The Crisis of Empire, A.D. 193–337* (Cambridge: Cambridge University Press, 2005), p. 68.

15 Bowman, "Diocletian and the First Tetrarchy", p. 67, citing a poem from Oxyrhynchus, lxiii, 4352.

16 Bowman, "Diocletian and the First Tetrarchy", pp. 74–5.

17 Williams, *Diocletian and the Roman Recovery*, p. 141.

18 Bowman, "Diocletian and the First Tetrarchy", pp. 80–1.

19 Timothy D. Barnes, *Constantine and Eusebius* (Cambridge, MA: Harvard University Press, 1981), p. 26.

20 David Potter, *Constantine the Emperor* (Oxford: Oxford University Press, 2013), p. 116.

21 Potter, *Constantine the Emperor*, p. 133.

22 Potter, *Constantine the Emperor*, p. 134.

23 Potter, *Constantine the Emperor*, p. 139.

24 Barnes, *Constantine and Eusebius*, p. 42.

25 See Lactantius, *De Mortibus Persecutorum* 44:4ff.

26 Eusebius, *Vita Constantini* I.28 (Limovia, 2013), p. 33.

27 Barnes, *Constantine and Eusebius*, p. 43.

28 Barnes, *Constantine and Eusebius*, p. 50.

29 Barnes, *Constantine and Eusebius*, p. 50.

30 See Jonathan Bardill, *Constantine, Divine Emperor of the Christian Golden Age* (Cambridge: Cambridge University Press, 2015), pp. 208–16, 240–50.

31 Potter, *Constantine*, p. 212.

32 Potter, *Constantine*, p. 213.

33 Justin Martyr, *First Apology*, Section LXV, in *Ante-Nicene Fathers: Vol. I. Apostolic Fathers with Justin Martyr and Irenaeus*, ed. Philip Schaff et al. (Grand Rapids, MI: Eerdmans, 1975), p. 185.

34 Ignatius, "Letter to The Ephesians 6", in *Apostolic Fathers I*, ed. Bart Ehrman, Loeb Classical Library, Vol. 24 (Cambridge, MA: Harvard University Press, 2003), p. 225.

35 *Didache*, in *Apostolic Fathers I*, ed. Bart Ehrman, Loeb Classical Library, Vol. 24 (Cambridge, MA: Harvard University Press, 2003), pp. 405ff.

36 Henry Chadwick, *The Early Church* (Harmondsworth: Penguin, 1993), p. 57.

37 Chadwick, *Early Church*, p. 58.

38 Rodney Stark, *The Rise of Christianity* (London: HarperCollins, 1997), pp. 105, 119.

39 Stark, *Rise of Christianity*, p. 111.

40 Stark, *Rise of Christianity*, pp. 73ff.

41 Stark, *Rise of Christianity*, pp. 80ff.

[42] Tertullian, *Apology* 39, cited in Stark, *Rise of Christianity*, p. 87.

[43] Eusebius, *Historia ecclesiastica* II.19,20, tr. G. A. Williamson (London: Penguin, 1989), pp. 55–6.

[44] Tertullian, *Apology* 40, in *The Ante-Nicene Fathers: The Writings of the Fathers Down to A.D. 325, Vol. III Latin Christianity: Its Founder, Tertullian*, ed. Alexander Robertson (New York: Cosimo, 2007), p. 47.

[45] Ignatius, "To the Romans", in *Apostolic Fathers I*, ed. Bart Ehrman, Loeb Classical Library, Vol. 24 (Cambridge, MA: Harvard University Press, 2003), p. 275. Later Pliny the Younger writes to the Emperor Trajan.

[46] "The Martyrdom of Polycarp", in *Apostolic Fathers I*, ed. Bart Ehrman, Loeb Classical Library, Vol. 24 (Cambridge, MA: Harvard University Press, 2003), p. 381.

[47] B. D. Shaw, "Rebels and Outsiders", in Alan K. Bowman, Peter Garnsey, Dominic Rathbone (eds), *Cambridge Ancient History, second edition, Vol. XI: The High Empire,* AD *70–192*, pp. 361–414, citing B. D. Shaw, *The Passion of St Perpetua* (Cambridge: Cambridge University Press, 1993), p. 139.

[48] Graeme Clarke, "Third-Century Christianity", in Alan K. Bowman, Peter Garnsey and Averil Cameron (eds), *The Cambridge Ancient History, second edition, Vol. XII: The Crisis of Empire, A.D. 193–337* (Cambridge: Cambridge University Press, 2005), pp. 589–671, here at p. 647.

[49] Barnes, *Constantine and Eusebius*, pp. 148ff.

[50] Eusebius, *Historia ecclesiastica* VIII, op. cit., p. 261ff.

[51] Eusebius, *Historia ecclesiastica* VIII, op. cit., p. 269.

[52] See Eusebius's *Martyrs of Palestine*.

CHAPTER 2

Alexandria

Alexandria was one of the great cities of the ancient world. At the beginning of the fourth century, it joined Ephesus, Byzantium (soon to be Constantinople), Carthage, Syracuse, Athens and Rome as leading centres of culture and commerce in the late classical world.

Alexandria was founded by Alexander the Great in 332 BC, before he turned east to take on the Persians in revenge for their attacks on Greece in the fifth century BC. After Alexander's death in 323 BC, Alexandria and its Egyptian territories passed to the Ptolemy family. Lying on the western edge of the Nile Delta and close to Lake Mareotis, the site seemed favourable for a new metropolis and harbour. A limestone shelf just below the surface provided a stable foundation for the city's great buildings. Out in the bay was the island of Pharos, base for one of the greatest lighthouses in the ancient world, reaching slightly higher than the Statue of Liberty.[1] A road to the island called the Heptastadion was built by one of the early Ptolomies, thereby creating two harbours: the Great Harbour to the east and the Eunostos Harbour to the west. Situated near the estuary of the Nile and in the eastern Mediterranean, trading corn (83,000 tons were exported to Rome each year), cotton and papyrus to the empire, it was not long before Alexandria became a thriving city, and a strategic cultural and commercial centre.

The city's strategic value was quickly grasped by leading Roman generals and further enhanced by the mesmeric appeal of Cleopatra. Pompey was killed on a vessel in the harbour on 28 September 48 BC when fleeing there, following his defeat at the Battle of Pharsalus during the civil war with Julius Caesar. Julius Caesar fell for the charms of Cleopatra, taking her to Rome and having a son by her named Caesarion in 47 BC. Three years later Caesar was assassinated, and Octavian, his heir, tracked down Mark Antony and Cleopatra to Alexandria where they both died by suicide. Alexandria had become the backdrop to some of the greatest political events of the late Republic. It was to Alexandria and Egypt that the Emperor Hadrian, aesthete and soldier as he was, went with his lover Antinous in August 130 and where he restored the tomb of Pompey. Antinous drowned in an accident on the Nile and Hadrian was overwhelmed by grief. More ominously, in 215 Caracalla massacred many of Alexandria's citizens for possibly supporting his brother Geta's bid for power,[2] and in 298 Diocletian marched on Alexandria to end a serious disturbance.[3] Because of its strategic position and potential wealth, Alexandria was never placid for long.

If Alexandria was recognized by Rome for its strategic and commercial importance, it was also, by virtue of its diverse communities, an intellectual centre: a place of ideas, exercising a gravitational pull on some of the greatest minds of the late ancient world. By the end of the third century BC, its population was approximately 300,000, rising to nearly half a million by the fourth century AD, before decline set in.[4] If, unlike Athens, it could not boast the greatest philosophers, such as Socrates, Plato (428–348 BC) and Aristotle (384–322 BC), it did nurture their heirs and intellectual successors. Alexandria became a place of Jewish, pagan and Christian study, at least on a par with Antioch and Rome, and in some respects surpassing them. It was a polyglot city, not only ethnically, but also intellectually, and it was to take up that role again in the nineteenth and early twentieth centuries, when it became one of the great Levant cities, boasting a mix of English, French and Egyptian communities, known for their commercial skill and intellectual ferment.[5]

The Jewish community

From its inception, the city had been divided into five districts, each designated by one of the first five letters of the Greek alphabet. The section occupied by the Greeks and Romans was the Brucheion district. This lay in the vicinity of the Great Harbour and was the central section of the city. Here could be found the palace of the Ptolemaic rulers, and later of the prefect of Egypt in the Roman empire, the state buildings and the temples, as well as the residential quarter of the Greeks and Romans.[6] The Jewish quarter was to the north and east of the Brucheion. In fact, in two of the five sections of the city, one of which was called Delta, the Jews made up the majority of the population. They had their own ruler or ethnarch responsible to the prefect and emperor and were a vibrant commercial and intellectual community.

Jews had settled in Alexandria by the third century BC, in the Intertestamental Period (that is, the historical period between the Old and New Testaments). They had been made welcome by Ptolemy II, Philadelphus, 284–246 BC. Philadelphus sought with mixed success to expand the city militarily into Syria, Nubia and Cyrene (Libya), but in taking on the Seleucids, he made a friend of the Jewish nation, which was increasingly oppressed by the Seleucids and their government of Syria, as well as by their ominous encroachment into Palestine itself. This would come to a climax a century later with the revolt of the Jews under the Maccabees in 167 BC, the establishment of the Hasmonean Dynasty, which lasted until 37 BC, and the appointment by Rome of Herod the Great. Philadelphus, however, not only welcomed Jews to Alexandria, but commissioned 70 Jewish scholars to translate the Old Testament into Greek, which became the Septuagint. This ground-breaking project anticipated by 300 years the inclusion of the Old Testament Scriptures into the Christian Bible after the life of Christ and the writing of the Gospels and Epistles (60–90). In time, Alexandria's linguistic bent would make it the principal city for biblical studies in the empire, reaching new heights with Origen (to whom we shall return).

If Philadelphus triggered this seminal event of translating the Hebrew Old Testament into Greek, there were other scholars who took the Hebrew-Greek interface into new fields, in particular Philo (*c.*20 BC–*c.* AD 50). Philo lived at the beginning of the Christian era, but his aim was to reconcile Greek philosophical thinking, particularly that of the Stoics, with Hebrew thought, especially as evidenced by Moses and the Torah. He therefore made a bridge, which, although not always convincing, was just waiting to be made and which would be further strengthened by Christian apologists in the second century, notably Justin (*c.*100–165). The idea, simply put, is that God's wisdom (the *Logos*) was revealed through Moses in the Torah, then hinted at in some of the Greek philosophers, and finally and fully in Christ, such that a line of revelation can be drawn through each. Furthermore, the Church historian Eusebius maintained that Philo's *On the Contemplative Life*, which was about the *theraputae* (healing and philosophic communities) on and around Lake Mareotis near Alexandria, in fact described early Christian communities of the first century. Others are not as sure as Eusebius was.[7] Indeed, they think that Eusebius mistook these Greek philosophical communities for Christian ones. What Eusebius does make clear is how wide-ranging an author Philo was, writing, among many other themes, on *Farming, Drunkenness, Three Cardinal Virtues Proposed by Moses, Emigration* and *The Immutability of the Godhead*.[8]

It is sobering to recall that these promising intellectual bridges fostered by Philo were ruptured by a more intransigent Church in Alexandria in the fifth century, when violence between Christians and Jews was frequent, and when Jews were roundly condemned for the death of Christ. An equal intransigence was shown towards Greek philosophy, as when Hypatia lost her life to a group of violent monks. Jewish and Greek thought were clearly held in creative tension in Alexandria at the start of the first century AD.

Greek thought in Alexandria

It is fair to say that the Ptolemies sought to forge a syncretistic blend of Egyptian religion and Greek culture and philosophy. This was evident in the cult of Sarapis, which Tacitus said was associated with the Greek healing god Asclepius, with Zeus, and with Pluto, the god of the underworld. Sarapis was also associated with the Egyptian gods Osiris and Apis. Hence Osor-Apis or Sarapis was an amalgamation of these Egyptian deities.[9] There were shrines to Sarapis both in Alexandria and Memphis, and the cult quickly grew outside Egypt.

Alongside this cult, the Ptolemies—and in particular Cleopatra and then Augustus—patronized the Caesarion and the museum. The Caesarion was another shrine constructed by Cleopatra in memory of Julius Caesar, and was completed by Augustus, and became the home of the Roman Imperial cult. The museum, which was located in a very central position near the Great Harbour in the Bruchium district, was a shrine to the Muses, contained the great library and had an official resident priest. It was set up like Plato's school in Athens, and in the early days the Ptolemies lured scholars to the museum to teach and research, as well as collect by all means, honest and underhanded, countless Greek manuscripts for the library. Both the library and the philosophical school would grow to become among the most influential in the ancient world. The library itself eventually held 400,000 volumes, making it the largest in the ancient world.[10] A further library was established at the Serapeon. It is no wonder that, given this patronage and such resources, the school together with the library became an inspiration to Greek philosophy and to a significant neo-Platonist movement, which in turn gave way to influential Christian studies. The library, partially ransacked by Julius Caesar, was further destroyed by fire during the Emperor Aurelian's confrontation with the uprising inspired by Queen Zenobia of Palmyra before being finally destroyed in 495.

The museum would become home to the teaching of the neo-Platonists and in particular Ammonius Saccas (175–242) and his pupil Plotinus (204–70), who would in turn exercise considerable influence on the Alexandrian theologian and teacher, Origen. Both Plotinus and Saccas were written about by the pagan philosopher, Porphyry, and both were to exert a powerful influence on Christian theology in the late third and fourth centuries.

Plotinus was educated in Alexandria for about 11 years, having arrived there as a student from elsewhere in Egypt. He remained in Alexandria until 243, when he joined the army of the luckless Emperor Gordian III with the goal of acquainting himself with the wisdom of the Chaldeans and the Indians.[11] Gordian, who had emerged in the Year of the Six Emperors in 238, was defeated by the Sassanids at the town of Fallujah in present-day Iraq, and Plotinus never realized his aim, ending up first at Antioch and then in Rome from 263–8. Our knowledge of Plotinus comes mostly from Porphyry's *On the Life of Plotinus and the Arrangements of his Works*, but also from Porphyry's assembly of the six volumes of the *Enneads*.

Plotinus's god was divided into three separate beings: firstly, there was the One or the Good, who transcends all being and is pre-eminent.

Secondly, the Nous, who represents the mind or the spirit of god, which some liken to an intellectual principle, and others, like Dean Inge, to the Spirit.[12] And thirdly, the soul, which is the author of all living things and indeed the essence of life and being in matter and living beings. It does not take a great leap of imagination to see that Plotinus's thought, together with that of his teacher Ammonius Saccas, would eventually have important, if contentious, influence on a city and church, which, perhaps more than any other, was at the heart of the Trinitarian storm of the fourth century. The Gnostic threat, which had been very strong in Egypt (witness the great cache of Gnostic Gospels found at Nag Hammadi by the Nile in the second century), was a further spur in defining the essence of the Godhead in opposition to the notions of semi-divine emanations of Gnostic and Middle Platonic characterizations.

If Plotinus was influential in conceptualizations of the Trinity and the roles of each member, so too were his Platonic formulations on the soul, being, ideas or knowledge, and prayer. In other words, Plotinus, like his master Plato, sought to categorize and enquire into the essence of being: what makes a table a table, or what makes justice justice, for instance. The Platonic answer is that it is a table if it approximates to the perfect single, universal idea of a table, and equally true justice must conform to the universal idea of justice. Plato argued this idea of forms in his *Phaedo, Republic and Phaedrus.* Following him, and in an attempted reconciliation with Aristotle, Porphyry argued (in Enneads 6:1–3) that something may be described according to its five voices (*Quinque Voces*), that is, its genus, species, substance, accident, and property.[13] One of these five descriptions, that of substance or *ousia*, was to become an all-important concept in describing the Trinity.

Furthermore, the notion of the progress of the soul and the soul's immortality developed into a particular form of spirituality, which was thereafter closely associated with Christian pilgrimage and formation and the ascent of the soul. For the Platonist, progress of the soul means the harmonization of passions with the intellect, the discipline of bodily appetites, and abstinence from food, sex and comfort. In fact, the search for virtue and happiness becomes coterminous. Real happiness is dependent on the metaphysical level and the use of human reason. From the practice of such abstinence, Plotinus had times of ecstasy which led to the *henosis* or mystical oneness with the divine in which great happiness could be found. Once again, these ideas fed into disciplines of contemplation, meditation and prayer, linked to the ascent of the soul which was also present in the writings of Gregory of Nyssa, mediated in part by Origen. Without defining the borders between Christianity and Platonism, it is enough at present to say that such was the intellectual and spiritual milieu in Alexandria, come the middle of the third century. This would be the intellectual background to the great controversy over describing the Godhead in the fourth century, but it would also be the background out of which the critical teachers of the Alexandrian Church would come in the third and fourth centuries, teachers such as Clement, Origen and Athanasius.

Alexandria was thus a melting pot of ideas: it had a syncretistic cult blending Greek and Egyptian paganism, based on worship of Serapion, and begun by the Ptolemies; and it had a vibrant and creative Jewish community, which was itself exploring the borders of Greek philosophy and the Hebrew Torah, exemplified by Philo. And early in the first century, it also had the beginnings of a Christian community, which would be later buffeted by Gnosticism, with its greatest teachers developing a theology centred on the *Logos* and the relationship between the different persons of the Godhead.

With a tradition of scholarship centred on the city's museum, and boasting Plotinus and Saccas, Alexandria would always be attractive to the intellectually curious. One such figure in the fourth century was Gregory of Nazianzus (329–90), one of the Cappadocian Fathers. He came to Alexandria, according to his autobiographical poem, *De Vita Sua*, to "cull a few fruits of learning".[14] It was during a storm on the way from Alexandria to Athens that Gregory had his own "spiritual baptism in the purifying waters" of a violent storm and offered his life and learning to God.[15] This Christian community and its learning would be the fourth part of the intellectual and spiritual life of the city.

Christianity in Alexandria

Tradition has it that Christianity came to Alexandria with St Mark the Evangelist, author of the second Gospel. Eusebius of Caesarea (260–339), writing in his *Ecclesiastical History* in the fourth century, tells us that "Mark is said to have been the first man to set out for Egypt and preach there the gospel which he had himself written down, and the first to establish churches in Alexandria itself".[16] However, never entirely reliable, and as previously mentioned, Eusebius went on to confuse the therapeutic communities then living in the Nile Delta with Christian communities. In a separate work called the *Chronicle*, which was reworked by Jerome, it is said that Mark arrived in Alexandria in the third year of Claudius's reign or 43.[17] This may fit in with what we know of Mark's life from the Acts of the Apostles, and could have come after Mark's mission to Cyprus with Barnabas, when the Apostle Paul refused to take him on his second missionary journey (see Acts 15:36–41), and after he turned back from the first missionary journey into Galatia. Other sources, such as a purported letter from Clement of Alexandria (150–*c.*215), the so-called *Acts of Mark*, written in the fourth century, include an account of his martyrdom.[18] Although these documents record a growing tradition in the Alexandrian records of Mark's ministry there, the documents themselves are as much indicative of that tradition as clear about the historical narrative which undergirds it. However, in his *History*, Eusebius goes on to chart the development of the Church in Alexandria, incidentally giving his readers the names of ten bishops who were successors to Mark, from Anianus to Julian in the twelfth year of the Emperor Commodus (176–92).[19] Apart from these names we know "next to nothing" about the Alexandrian Church, or indeed about the Church in Egypt.[20]

In fact, a protracted struggle with Gnosticism in the second century may also account for this silence. We know that many Gnostic Gospels were circulating in Egypt, among them the *Gospel of the Egyptians* and the *Gospel of the Hebrews*.[21] The Church in Alexandria, as in Rome and elsewhere, was in a life-and-death struggle with Gnosticism, as indicated by the circulation of the classic work *Against Heresies* by Irenaeus (*c.*130–202) during that period. One of the main leaders of the Gnostic movement in the Alexandrian Church was Valentinus, along with his colleague Basilides, who was nurtured in Alexandria, and who later went to Rome in *c.*140. Such was his plausibility that Valentinus was very nearly made Bishop of Rome.

Having survived and emerged from this struggle with Gnosticism, the Egyptian Church was to be marked by two characteristics: more powerful episcopal oversight of the Church with the election of Bishop Demetrius in 189, and the spontaneous growth of a school of theology which drew on the influence of neo-Platonism in the museum, through the teaching of Saccas and Plotinus, as well as influence from the Jewish community. This would result in a mix of speculative theology with strong Platonic tendencies, the advocacy of a *Logos* theology in response to Gnosticism, and a very strong exegetical and philological tradition based on the Scriptures. It was a unique blend resulting from the influences in the city and the struggles of the Church. The two theologians who came to represent it especially were Clement of Alexandria and Origen, who led the catechetical school in Alexandria, producing many influential pupils, such as Didymus the Blind, to whose work on the Holy Spirit we will return.

Clement of Alexandria and Origen

Clement of Alexandria (*c.*150–215) lived through the reigns of Emperors Marcus Aurelius, his son Commodus (*c.*180–92), and Severus and Caracalla: for the most part powerful and persecuting emperors. Clement was educated in Athens and at some point moved to Alexandria and joined the catechetical school established by Pantaenus.[22] Eusebius describes Pantaenus as a philosophical theologian influenced by Stoic thought,[23] although the precise relationship between each is hard to ascertain. Although philosophical in bent, Pantaenus was nonetheless missionary in outlook and left (and possibly returned to) the catechetical school to go to India, where he found a church already in existence, with the tradition that the Apostle Bartholomew had started it.[24] Succeeding Pantaenus, Clement became the principal of the catechetical school until the persecution by Severus.

Clement's teaching and influence appears in the main to be threefold: a refutation of Gnosticism through an appeal to find true knowledge in Christ and the Word, who is the "Instructor" (the title of one of Clement's three books); a debunking of the pagan gods, showing their immorality and ineptitude; and, thirdly, a call to eschew the seamier side of Alexandrian life, especially overindulgence in food and promiscuity.[25] He was influenced by several of the main intellectual movements in Alexandria, notably the writings of Philo, the teachings of Platonism, and the *Logos* theology so prevalent in the city. Clement's emphasis is more on the virtuous life than on a theology of the Trinity. Thus, he emphasizes the example and power of the *Logos* when embraced as the Instructor. "Our Instructor is the holy God Jesus, the Word, who is the guide of all humanity."[26] At the same time, he appears to hold to the Platonic view that God did not create matter *ex nihilo*, and that in some sense the *Logos* was created by God the Father, and so in some sense he is a precursor to the Arians. Later Orthodox Christians would, however, settle for the idea that the Son was begotten (not created) by the Father. In other words, his emphasis is not so much a theology of the Trinity, which would become the focus by the mid third century in Alexandria, as the way men and women can become holy children of God. In that sense, in terms of the economy of God's salvation, Clement is similar to Irenaeus, although with less of Irenaeus's overarching goal for humanity: becoming the glory of God. For Clement, salvation meant "growth towards perfect humanity", which is the true image of God,[27] but the means was not so much the need for redemption and the power of the Spirit, as a yielding to the Instructor or *Logos*, and a concomitant eschewing of the world.

Clement was succeeded by the unwitting troubler of early Church theology, Origen (*c*.184–253). Although his Egyptian name means "descendant from Horus", there is no certainty that he was Egyptian himself. His "education, privileges and connections suggest that he was Greek",[28] and certainly Porphyry, the biographer of Plotinus, refers to him as Greek, and probably from Athens. Origen's family may well have been part of the considerable Greek community of Alexandria in the Brucheion, which included satirist Lucian of Samosata, Aristarchus, Herodian and the teacher, Ammonius Saccas. Origen's father was martyred during the persecution of Severus in 202, having already begun to teach his son the Scriptures, but Origen's mother persuaded him not to present himself to the authorities as a Christian and thus avoid martyrdom. From early on, Origen's intellectual talent was noticed by a number of wealthy individuals who became his patrons. These included an Alexandrian called Ambrose and a woman who Eusebius describes as "extremely wealthy and very distinguished in other ways", who gave Origen lodging, and another man called Paul, who proved a heretic.[29] Origen's shining gifts earned him rapid promotion and by the age of 17 he was principal of the elementary or grammar school. He broke with his classical studies, however, and gave himself entirely to personal theological study, living an immensely frugal and self-disciplined life, not dissimilar to that of an ascetic monk. He devoted most of the night to study of Scripture, went about without shoes and fasted to the point of damaging his health.[30] Not content with these deprivations, Eusebius reports that Origen castrated himself in a literal interpretation of Christ's metaphorical teaching of Matthew 19:12 about making oneself a eunuch for the kingdom of God, for which action he was reproved.[31]

Nevertheless, Origen pressed on with his own studies and with teaching at the catechetical school, where he succeeded Clement. His teaching at the school probably lasted from *c.*210–31, when he moved to Caesarea after a dispute with the bishop in Alexandria, having received a warm invitation from the bishop in Palestine, who ordained him. While in Alexandria, Origen was taken up not only with teaching, but also with writing a number of commentaries on the Old and New Testaments at the request of his patron, Ambrose, while also assembling an exhaustive study of the text of the Old Testament called the *Hexapla*. The *Hexapla* was a massive compilation of six entire Old Testament texts. It is estimated that the complete work would have comprised a minimum of 6,500 pages.[32] The first column contained the Hebrew text, the second a transcription of the Hebrew in Greek letters, the third the translation of Aquila of Sinope, the fourth the translation of Symmachus the Ebionite, the fifth a recension of the Septuagint, and the sixth the translation of Theodotion. As a committed philologist, Origen was seeking to establish a reliable text of the Old Testament, especially because of the variant readings in different editions of the Septuagint itself. There was something in his mind that sought to standardize and tidy up textual inconsistencies. He would apply the same terrier-like philological attitude to his commentaries on Matthew and John which he also started on at this time.

If biblical studies were a central part of Origen's work, linking him strongly to the catechetical school in Alexandria, it was his speculative theology, especially relating to the nature of God as Trinity, and his teaching about creation, the incarnation, the soul and judgement, which later landed him in theological hot water for being too Platonist. Eventually, this would mean that his teaching was anathematized in the fifth century—so much so that most of his works were destroyed and only those reproduced by others survived. His theological work *On First Principles*, conveyed to us in an incomplete Latin translation by Rufinus, was his most systematic theological statement on the nature of the Trinity. "He is said to be the first Christian systematic theologian, even if no agreed view has yet been reached in his theology."[33] Of supreme interest to Origen in his Christology, and arising from his Platonic emphasis on the soul, was the mediacy of the soul between the *Logos* of God and the flesh of humanity.[34] For Origen, "one soul had never turned away from God when the rest fell, this soul was chosen to be united to the divine *Logos* in a union as close as that of human body and soul".[35] The degree to which the divinity of Christ was perceived depended on the spiritual capacity of the recipient. Someone with eyes to see would discern the *ousia* or substance of God. Elsewhere Origen would speak of the *ousia* or essence of God in his teaching on prayer and likewise in his commentary on John.[36] But how the *Logos* proceeds from God the Father was not yet fully formulated. For Origen, the *Logos* was both eternally begotten and the source of all *sapientia* (divine wisdom) and human *ratio* (reason).[37] It was these questions Origen left unclarified, although using terms that would become familiar, and which the Trinitarian debates would enter in the fourth century. In other words, Origen laid out the bricks which others would later assemble.

Perhaps Origen's most thoughtful description of the Father begetting the Son comes in Book 1 of *On First Principles*, where he wrote:

> Whereas the offspring of men or of other animals whom we see around us correspond to the seed of those by whom they were begotten, or of the mothers in whose womb they are formed

> and nourished, drawing from these parents whatever it is that they take and bring into the light of day when they are born, it is impious and shocking to regard God the Father in the begetting of his only-begotten Son and in the Son's subsistence as being similar to any human being or other animal in the act of begetting; but there must needs be some exceptional process, worthy of God, to which we can find no comparison whatever, not merely in things, but even in thought and imagination, such that by its aid human thought could apprehend how the unbegotten God becomes Father of the only-begotten Son. This is an eternal and everlasting begetting, as the brightness is begotten from the light (Wisdom 7:26; Hebrews 7:25).[38]

The issue that Origen raises here and which would be further debated, wrangled over and pronounced upon, is the mystery of "the exceptional process" by which the Father begat the Son in such a way that the Son remained eternally God and not created (sharing the divine substance), whilst at the same time being individuated or distinct from the Father. Origen began this speculation using terms that did not yet have well-established meanings. And he did so in a world where terminology was used loosely, where communication was cumbersome and infrequent, and where suspicions quickly grew. It would take a long time for there to be a settled vocabulary to describe the Trinity.[39] There was an earlier testing ground for some of these ideas in the early third century in the western Church centred in Rome, however, and in *c.*215 Origen visited Rome at the height of the so-called Monarchian Controversy, in which the western Church was itself struggling to both comprehend and describe the Trinity.

The main theologians of the Trinity in the western Church, centred on Rome and North Africa, were Justin, the Apologist and martyr (*c.*100–65), Hippolytus (*c.*170–235) and Tertullian (*c.*155–220). Justin lived shortly after the end of the apostolic age and came to Rome from Nablus in Samaria, and, having taken the philosopher's garb or *pallium* sought to win acceptance for Christianity from the powers in Rome as an Apologist. His appeals to the Senate and emperor were turned down, however, and he and his colleagues were martyred. Justin clearly stated that Jesus was not a mere man, but God, and that this was strongly proven by John's Gospel and by the open statements about Jesus's divinity both in the Prologue and by Jesus himself (see John 1:14,18; 14:9). Against this clear assertion of Jesus's divinity, there was also a subordinationist theology advanced by some, in which Jesus appears inferior in status to the Father. Here Jesus is regarded as a man like other men, but "differentiated in being indwelt by the Spirit of God to an absolute and unique degree".[40] The alternative way of retaining a sense of the "monarchy of the Father" while still acknowledging the uniqueness of Jesus was to advocate, as did Sabellius, about whom we will hear more, that Jesus was in fact the Father on earth in human form. This was called modalism, or in the west, Patripassianism (i.e., the Father himself suffered in the Son). In early third-century Rome, this Monarchian Controversy became heated, with Sabellius advocating modalism, and Hippolytus (*c.*170–235) *Logos* theology, also familiar in Alexandria, which emphasized the distinct persons or *prosopa* of Jesus and the Father. Hippolytus advocated a two-stage procession of the *Logos*, firstly as being without flesh and begotten (*asarkos*), and then incarnate through the Spirit and Mary (*ensarkos*).[41] It was Hippolytus's teaching that Origen heard as a young man in Rome around 215, and which confirmed for him the distinctness of the Father and the Son and hence *Logos* theology. As a strong Platonist, the link between the pre-existent *Logos* and the human Jesus was for Origen the soul.

Tertullian would take up the cause of defining the Trinity in the west in his long work *Against Praxeas*, in which he maintained that the Trinity was one substance consisting in three persons, although the precise meaning of *substantia* (substance) and *persona* (persons) remained unclear. It is fair to say that the Greek or eastern Church would ultimately spend the best part of 170 years working this question out.

The Alexandrian Church in the late third century

Origen returned from Rome to Alexandria, and then, after falling out with Bishop Demetrius, who began consolidating episcopal power over the catechetical school, left for Caesarea in Palestine in 234, eventually dying following torture and imprisonment during the Decian persecution. His pupil Gregory Thaumaturgus (the Wonderworker), who (probably) wrote an encomium to Origen, carried forward and further clarified his teaching on the Trinity in his *Expositio Fidei*.[42]

Back in Alexandria, Heraclas, the recently installed head of the catechetical school, by then a bishop's appointment, succeeded Demetrius in 231 as bishop and remained in office until 247.[43] Heraclas was succeeded in turn by Dionysius, who was Bishop of Alexandria from 247–64. First called the *papas* (pope) of the Egyptian Church—a title which remains to this day—he faced two challenges. The first was handling the Decian persecution, which, although short, was vehement, and the second was formulating the doctrine of the Trinity. Both challenges were problematic for Dionysius.

The Decian persecution began with an edict in 250 and would last for two years. It was systematic and intense. Many Christians lapsed, either sacrificing to the gods or the emperor to obtain the necessary *libelli* or certificate saying they had fulfilled the requirement to sacrifice to the emperor, or asking a slave to do so on their behalf, and then bribe the official to issue the *libelli* to his master. Bishop Dionysius went into hiding. The fate of others who held their witness was horrific: some had their flesh dissolved in quick lime, others were disembowelled with a sharp instrument, one was beheaded, others burnt or torn in pieces.[44] The sheer horror of the violence is testimony to the brutality of the age.

Still others, called confessors (rather than martyrs) were put into prison, where they awaited death and often experienced torture. Dionysius, like his fellow bishop from Carthage, Cyprian (*c.*210–58), remained in hiding from where he hoped to run his diocese. But whereas Cyprian took the view that he was better able to lead the Church alive (he was later executed in a subsequent persecution under Valerian in 258) and so remained in hiding, Dionysius fully expected to be martyred. By an act of providence, he said, he was never found, and hence spared.

He tells the story of one police agent sent to find him who had been smitten with blindness when nearing the house in which Dionysius was hiding.[45] Later Dionysius was captured but then rescued. However, it was important for Dionysius to stress that he fully expected and wanted martyrdom, and was miraculously spared, given the schism that resulted in the Church between those who had suffered and those who had either lapsed or gone into hiding.

Whether someone who had lapsed or apostasized could be readmitted to the Church became a dominant issue that would continue to divide the Church thereafter. Cyprian, the confessors (those who had been imprisoned), and Dionysius were willing to readmit the lapsed after penance and a period of waiting, others were adamantly opposed, leaving the lapsed in a permanent state of excommunication. It was people in this latter camp who would form the Donatist Church around Carthage and the Melitian Church in Egypt. This sore would run and run, and be fuelled by renewed persecution. Both Cyprian and Dionysius were caught up in successive waves of persecution under Valerian (253–60) and Diocletian. Cyprian would embrace martyrdom by execution (258), while Dionysius would go into exile in Libya, but die peacefully in 264.[46] Yet if Dionysius's episcopacy was forged in the white heat of persecution, he also faced the fallout from the ongoing controversy over defining the Trinity.

Dionysius had a rather uncertain grasp of the doctrine of the Trinity, and how to express it. He was later considered an early Arian, but in response, Athanasius defended him in a pamphlet entitled *De sententia Dionysii*.[47] In truth, Dionysius only came to a more orthodox expression of the Trinity after a rather public conflict with Sabellians in Libya, and a correspondence with Pope Dionysius (260–8), in which the Pope rebuked him for false teaching. In response to the Sabellian teaching, which maintained in essence that Jesus was a further emanation of the Father, and therefore not a distinct and eternal member of the Trinity, Dionysius had conceded, in correspondence with Euphranor and Ammonius, that "the Son of God is a creature and generate, and he is not by nature belonging to but is alien in *ousia* from the Father".[48] No one denies that Dionysius wrote this, although Athanasius argued there were extenuating circumstances and that later, in his response to the Pope, Dionysius reasserted his orthodox views. According to Athanasius, he replied to the Pope, "Thus we extend the Monad into an inseparable Triad, and we pack up the undiminished Triad again into the Monad."[49] He went on to use analogies for the Trinity, such as the relationship of thought and word, and the sun and its rays, thereby illustrating the connectedness and distinctness of the Father and the Son.

Much later in 361, and with no disposition to defend the See of Alexandria as Athanasius held, Basil of Caesarea was more candid about Dionysius. He wrote rather charmingly, "I am wont to compare Dionysius with a gardener who, in trying to correct the bent of a young plant, by a miscalculation of the counterstain, misses the mean, and draws the stem to the opposite side."[50] What this episode shows is that the nature of the Trinity was far from settled, and Church leaders did not have a commonly agreed vocabulary ready to hand. It would take the best part of 200 years to define the Trinity.

The final years of the third century and the early years of the fourth were marked by steady growth in the Church in Alexandria. With the advent of Gallienus, Valerian's successor, edicts were issued restoring Church property. Two bishops, Maximus (264–82) and Theonas (283–300), built up the powers of the Alexandrian see. Then, in 303, unexpectedly and suddenly, through the edicts of Diocletian and Galerius of that year, the Great Persecution began. It was a concerted move to return to the pagan gods so as to seek their blessing on the empire. This would have far-reaching effects on the province of Egypt and the Pentapolis, as indeed throughout the east; while in the west the persecution was never prosecuted with the same consistency or vehemence. The Bishop of Alexandria at the time of this renewed persecution was Peter, who was bishop from 300–11.

The Great Persecution unleashed against the Church by Diocletian was vehement. It mandated the handing over and burning of Scriptures, the demolition of churches, the stripping of social rank from Christians working for the empire, and the imprisonment, torture and martyrdom of many. This persecution would continue at varying levels of intensity for the next ten years, not only rocking the Church, but also producing a schism, already seen in earlier persecutions. Peter, like Dionysius before him (and Athanasius later) went into hiding, justifying this not so much as an outcome of divine providence as Dionysius had done, but as an action of obedience to Christ's teaching: "When they persecute you in one town, flee to the next" (Matthew 10:23).

When other bishops, like Hesychius, Pachomius, Theodorus and Phileas, were imprisoned, some questioned the validity of Peter's rationale, with Bishop Melitius of Lycopolis in Upper Egypt standing his ground and consecrating other bishops in the place of the four who had been imprisoned so as to provide ongoing pastoral and liturgical leadership in Peter's absence. In so doing, however, Melitius created the beginnings of a schism in the Church, which would later play into the Arian controversy in Egypt.[51] At first, the imprisoned and later martyred bishops objected that these consecrations were uncanonical. They wrote asking Melitius to desist. Bishop Peter issued a canonical letter doing the same, but Melitius would not cease consecrating other bishops while Peter remained in hiding.

The incipient schism was further widened by a growing division between Peter and Melitius over the grounds for readmitting the lapsed into the Church, with Melitius taking a hard-line stance, and insisting on longer penance. What had happened in Rome between Novatian and Bishop Stephen of Rome, and would happen between Augustine of Hippo and the Donatian Church in North Africa, was now underway in Egypt. An unexpected twist was to alter the perspective of many, however, for after years of persecution, Diocletian and Galerius recognized the ineffectiveness of their policy against the Church, and in 311, Galerius, now sole emperor in the east, rescinded the Edict of Persecution. Peter emerged from hiding, only to find that the new Caesar in the east, Maximin, had reimposed the persecution. Peter was arrested and in November 311 was executed at the shrine to St Mark at Baucalis (Boukolu) in the east of Alexandria.[52] Despite all his care to remain at large, Peter thus joined the ranks of Ignatius and Cyprian as a martyr bishop. He was succeeded by Achillas and then by Alexander (312–28), to be followed by Athanasius (328–73).

Between them, Alexander and Athanasius would lead the Church of Alexandria for 61 years (312–73), but not without many interruptions and the breakout of fresh controversy. For in 318, Arius emerged as a popular presbyter in Alexandria, preaching that there was a time when the *Logos* was not, and that the Son was not fully divine. The Arian controversy had begun and would run beyond the end of the century.

Notes

1 Ronald E. Heine, *Origen: Scholarship in the Service of the Church* (Oxford: Oxford University Press, 2010).

2 Garth Fowden, "Public religion", in Alan K. Bowman, Peter Garnsey and Averil Cameron (eds), *The Cambridge Ancient History, second edition, Vol. XII: The Crisis of Empire, A.D. 193–337* (Cambridge: Cambridge University Press, 2005), p. 546.

3 Bowman, "Diocletian and the First Tetrarchy", in Alan K. Bowman, Peter Garnsey and Averil Cameron (eds), *The Cambridge Ancient History, second edition, Vol. XII: The Crisis of Empire, A.D. 193–337* (Cambridge: Cambridge University Press, 2005), p. 81.

4 Heine, *Origen*, p. 2.

5 Philip Mansell, *The Levant: Splendour and Catastrophe on the Mediterranean* (London: John Murray, 2011), pp. 56ff.

6 Heine, *Origen*, p. 3.

7 Eusebius, *Historia ecclesiastica* II.16–17, 24, op. cit., pp. 50ff.

8 Eusebius, *Historia ecclesiastica* II.18, op. cit., p. 54.

9 Heine, *Origen*, p. 10.

10 Heine, *Origen*, p. 15.

11 Mark J. Edwards, *Culture and Philosophy in the Age of Plotinus* (Cambridge: Duckworth, 2006), p. 31.

12 Bertrand Russell, *The History of Western Philosophy* (London: Routledge, 2007), p. 273.

13 Edwards, *Culture and Philosophy in the Age of Plotinus*, p. 60.

14 Gregory Nazianzus, *Autobiographical Poems*, tr. Caroline White (Cambridge: Cambridge University Press, 1996), p. 19, line 129.

15 Nazianzus, *Autobiographical Poems*, p. 23, line 165.

16 Eusebius, *Historia ecclesiastica* II:16, op. cit., p. 50

17 Stephen J. Davis, *The Early Coptic Church* (Cairo: The American University in Cairo Press, 2017), p. 6.

18 Davis, *The Early Coptic Church*, pp. 8–12.

19 Eusebius, *Historia ecclesiastica* V.22, op. cit., p. 170.

20 Davis, *The Early Coptic Church*, p. 16.

21 Davis, *The Early Coptic Church*, p. 16.

22 Davis, *The Early Coptic Church*, p. 23.

[23] Eusebius, *Historia ecclesiastica* V.10.1, op. cit., p. 156.

[24] Eusebius, *Historia ecclesiastica* V.10.13, op. cit., pp. 156–7.

[25] For a fuller description of Clement's teaching, both theological and pastoral, see Patrick Whitworth, *Suffering and Glory: The Church from the Apostles to Constantine* (Durham: Sacristy Press, 2018), pp. 129ff.

[26] Clement of Alexandria, *The Instructor* (Lighthouse Christian Publishing, 2014), p. 45.

[27] Eric Osborn, *Clement of Alexandria* (Cambridge: Cambridge University Press, 2005), p. 273.

[28] Heine, *Origen*, p. 20.

[29] Eusebius, *Historia ecclesiastica* VI.2, op. cit., p. 181.

[30] Eusebius, *Historia ecclesiastica* VI.3, op. cit., p. 183.

[31] Eusebius, *Historia ecclesiastica* VI.8, op. cit., p. 186.

[32] Heine, *Origen*, p. 73.

[33] Aloys Grillmeier, *From the Apostolic Age to Chalcedon*, tr. John Bowden, Vol. 1 of *Christ in the Christian Tradition* (London: Mowbray's, 1975), p. 139.

[34] Grillmeier, *From the Apostolic Age to Chalcedon*, p. 146.

[35] Henry Chadwick, *The Early Church* (Harmondsworth: Penguin, 1993), p. 105.

[36] Origen, *On Prayer* 25:3 and *Comm. John* 13.25, op. cit., p. 153.

[37] Grillmeier, *From the Apostolic Age to Chalcedon*, p. 140.

[38] Origen, *First Principles* I.2 (Notre Dame, IN: Ave Maria Press, 2013), pp. 24–5.

[39] Grillmeier, *From the Apostolic Age to Chalcedon*, p. 148.

[40] Chadwick, *Early Church*, p. 86.

[41] Grillmeier, *From the Apostolic Age to Chalcedon*, pp. 114–15.

[42] Grillmeier, *From the Apostolic Age to Chalcedon*, pp. 232ff.

[43] Davis, *Early Coptic Church*, p. 27.

[44] Davis, *Early Coptic Church*, p. 29, and Eusebius, *Historia ecclesiastica* VI.41, op. cit., pp. 210ff.

[45] Davis, *Early Coptic Church*, pp. 30–1.

[46] Davis, *Early Coptic Church*, p. 34.

[47] Athanasius, *De sententia Dionysii*, in *Nicene and Post-Nicene Fathers: Second Series, Vol. IV: Athanasius: Select Works and Letters*, ed. Philip Schaff (Edinburgh: T&T Clark, 1987), pp. 172ff.

48 R. P. C. Hanson, *The Search for the Christian Doctrine of God: The Arian Controversy 318–381* (Edinburgh: T&T Clark, 1988), p. 73.

49 Athanasius, *De sententia Dionysii* 17, p. 182.

50 Basil, Letter 9, in Basil of Caesarea, *Letters* I, tr. Roy Deferrari, Loeb Classical Library, Vol. 190 (Cambridge, MA: Harvard University Press, 1926), p. 93.

51 Davis, *Early Coptic Church*, pp. 35ff.

52 Davis, *Early Coptic Church*, p. 41.

CHAPTER 3

The origins of a controversy: Personalities and terms

The understanding of God as Triune is latent in the Scriptures: implicit, if shadowy, in the Old Testament, and explicit and more defined in the New Testament. In the Old Testament, God is shown in many roles: as the creator (Genesis 1:1) and as the redeemer (Isaiah 44:6); as creating the world and liberating his covenant people from the slavery of Egypt. God is also shown as the personification of wisdom (Proverbs 8:22,23). He appears mysteriously as the Ancient of Days, the all-powerful Son of Man (Daniel 7:9–14; 10:4–11) as well as the Suffering Servant (Isaiah 52:13–53:12). But it would take the coming of the Son of Man in person to fill out the meaning of these titles. God too is the Spirit brooding over the waters (Genesis 1:2) and reviving fallen Israel (Ezekiel 37:1–14). The Spirit will come with apparent power in the New Testament, both around the birth of Jesus and on the day of Pentecost. Yet despite these several distinct roles and activities, God is still unmistakeably one, as declared in the Hebrew prayer of the *Shema* in Deuteronomy 6:1–25.

Likewise in the New Testament, God is one. As Paul writes in Ephesians 4:6, there is "one God and Father of all". And yet both in the teaching of Jesus and in the exposition of the Apostles, God is also Father, Son and Holy Spirit. Thus, Jesus commands his Apostles to baptize new disciples in the name (singular) of the Father, Son, and Holy Spirit (Matthew 28:19). Mark's Gospel begins with the declaration that Jesus is both Messiah and Son of God (Mark 1:1) and ends with the exclamation by a Roman centurion: "Truly this man was God's Son" (Mark 15:39). In St John's Gospel, Jesus, speaking to his disciple Philip who has requested, "Lord, show us the Father, and we will be satisfied", says, "Have I been with you all this time, Philip, and you still do not know me? Whoever has seen me has seen the Father. How can you say 'Show us the Father?' Do you not believe that I am in the Father, and the Father is in me?" (John 14:8,9–11).

Also, the Apostle Paul consistently uses the formula of Father, Son and Holy Spirit: in prayer (2 Corinthians 13:13), in the preaching of the gospel (Romans 15:17–19a; 1 Thessalonians 1:2–5), and even in his travel plans (Romans 15:30). It seems his expression of the Triune God, one and yet three, had become as plain to Paul as breathing. His reliance upon Father, Son and Holy Spirit, as members of the Godhead, was entire in his life, prayer, worship and ministry.

The question must arise, therefore, that since the New Testament draws out teaching about the Trinity that was implicit in the Old Testament—and more explicit after the coming of the Son and the Spirit (see Luke 1:26–38; Acts 2:14–39)—why did a controversy rage over the status of the Son and the Spirit more than 200 years later? Or, to put it another way, if the churches established by the Apostles around the Mediterranean, in say Antioch, Ephesus, Thessalonica, Corinth, Philippi and Rome, had accepted the teaching about the Trinity and experienced this triune reality at their inception, why was there such dissension, uproar, and controversy about the Trinity in the fourth century?

The answer, in broad terms, is that the debate over the nature of the Trinity began much earlier, and certainly by the end of the second century. It was then that Praxeas, who probably taught in North Africa, put forward his monarchist views of the Trinity—expressing the monarchy of the Father at the expense of the divinity of the Son and the Spirit, only to be roundly condemned by Tertullian in his lengthy work *Adversus Praxean*. It was also at the end of the second century that Sabellius, a presbyter in Rome, advocated his theory that the Trinity was simply the Father taking on existence in different forms (i.e., as Son and Spirit), modalism, in other words. If we were to further question why earlier confidence over the Trinity should be so diminished in some places, the answer most probably is that the Church had been buffeted by the twin gales of Gnosticism and neo-Platonism by the late second and mid third centuries respectively, and a restatement of the reality of the Trinity was needed.

Both Gnosticism and neo-Platonism had in successive centuries seriously affected and challenged the Church. In the second century, Gnosticism took hold both in Rome and in Alexandria, providing a substantial threat. Gnosticism was a complicated system in which a Supreme Being operated through a Demi-urge, Ialdabaoth, who had provoked the fall of Adam and Eve. Their bodies became corrupted and darkened, thus requiring enlightenment. The only way out of this darkened state of bodies subject to selfish passions was through illumination, enlightenment or *gnosis*. The Jewish Law could help in this process, as could Jesus, a further emanation of the Supreme Being, bringing Gnosis or illumination and saving knowledge. Yet the whole system, complicated as it was, is a distortion of biblical Christianity.[1] It is a travesty of Jesus's divinity; it distances God from his creation *ex nihilo* (which he made from nothing), and it denies the necessity for Jesus's death and resurrection as the means of redeeming humankind. It would take Irenaeus, Bishop of Lyons (*c*.130–202), to unmask Gnosticism and express biblical Christianity in his ground-breaking work *Against Heresies*. Against the backdrop of Gnosticism, and the near successful bid for the bishopric of Rome by the leading Gnostic, Valentinus, it is not altogether surprising that there was a reaction to Gnosticism with its incipient muddying of Christian teaching about the Godhead. Thus Sabellius, from the Pentapolis in present-day Libya, taught in Rome that there was one God, who as Father expressed himself in three forms or emanations, Father, Son and Spirit, thus ensuring the monarchy of God at the cost of the reality of the three Persons.

If Gnosticism had the effect of producing a more monotheistic response from a teacher like Sabellius early in the second century, then neo-Platonism, so prevalent in Alexandria, had a similar effect, albeit through a different solution. Neo-Platonism posited the notion of a Supreme Being, who, according to Plato's *Timaeus*, was responsible not just for the ordering of pre-existing eternal matter (as Aristotle supposed) but in creating everything *ex nihilo*.[2] In Plotinus's system, this Supreme Being was known as the One, and the being who communicated his existence and ideas, at least in part, was the *nous*. In Alexandria, and through the teaching of Philo, *nous* would come to be identified with the *Logos*.[3] For Philo, humans were capable of union with *Logos* or *nous*, but certainly not with the One, whose being could not be known and who was unapproachable and incomprehensible by humans.[4] Here then was the background of thought present in Alexandria and elsewhere, and which became influential in Christian communities. These categories of thought were also a tool used in describing the relations between Father, Son and Spirit. The effect was to raise the supremacy of the One or the Father, and render all else, including the Son, dependent upon him as a creature. The earlier confusion of Gnosticism and Middle Platonism, which also relied on many emanations (intermediaries between God and humans), was thus being replaced by an idea with intellectual traction in the schools of Alexandria, and to which the notion of *Logos* might be accommodated, in which the Supreme Being or One, was exactly that: supreme. All else was secondary. In a different way this would also be taken up by Paul of Samosata, the Bishop of Antioch (260–8), who would be deposed for his view that Jesus was adopted by the Father as a unique human.

If Sabellius's response to Gnosticism, and to the other swirling philosophical and theological movements of the day, was to create the Modalist idea of the Father *becoming* the Son and the Spirit in differing effusions, in order to substantiate the monarchy or supremacy of the Father, Paul of Samosata and Arius, as we shall see, emphasized the supremacy of the Father in other ways. Arius would approximate to the theories of neo-Platonism and Philo—in which the *Logos* was equated more with *nous*, the second strata of Platonic being—while Paul of Samosata taught that the Father adopted the human Jesus, giving him a new status, but leaving him far short of the status given in the New Testament. All three, Sabellius, Arius and Paul of Samosata, made attempts, with greater or lesser integrity, to uphold the monarchy of God, while at the same time reconciling the revelation of Father, Son and Spirit as presented in the Scriptures with Greek philosophy. If this is to state the issues at their crudest, as the controversy over defining God and the Trinity took shape, there were genuine disputes about how to render the relationship of Father, Son and Spirit and the precise terminology and language to use. It was a controversy in which most of Christendom, east and west, would be involved, and was to consume almost interminable Church councils over 60 years and result in Creed-making such as there has never been since. It would also involve the exertions of the Emperor Constantine and his heirs in trying to bring about solutions or to push a particular line. The spark who would set alight the tinder-dry theological brush which had been building up over the years was Arius.

Arius: background and theology

Epiphanius, the Bishop of Salamis in Cyprus and heresy hunter of the fourth century, tells us that Arius was born in Libya, sometimes known as the Pentapolis, from which he drew much support. In later years, Bishops Secundus of Ptolemais (the chief city of "upper" Libya) and Theonas of Marmarica especially supported him. In fact, it seems that to be a friend of the Bishop of Alexandria was to be at odds with the Church of the Pentapolis, and vice versa. There was in effect a regional stand-off between Alexandria and Libya that widened the doctrinal divide between the bishops of Alexandria and the Libyans.[5]

The date of Arius's birth is unknown, although often assumed to be in the 250s, which means that at the height of the controversy in Alexandria (*c.*318), Arius was already in his early sixties. Alternatively, a much later birth date, but still before 280, allows Arius to be ordained by Bishop Achillas of Alexandria (bishop for only one year in 312) at the age of 30, the minimum age for ordinations as a presbyter according to Nicene regulations, which in turn probably reflected earlier practice. If so, Arius was in his mid-thirties at the height of the controversy in Alexandria.

Arius's education is likewise shrouded in mystery. We have only a single word in the scant records to go on, which describes his educational stance, *sulloukianista*, in his letter to Eusebius, Bishop of Nicomedia, when appealing for help in the first years of the controversy. The word simply means "fellow-Lucian". Lucian was a martyr and teacher in Antioch, of whom, likewise, little is known. He was known to Eusebius of Caesarea, who describes him as "a man of the highest character, self-disciplined and steeped in divinity, a presbyter of the Antioch Diocese". Lucian was arrested and taken to Nicomedia, where he was executed on the orders of the Emperor Maximinus.[6] It seems therefore that although originating from Libya and probably schooled in Alexandria, Arius completed his education in Antioch, where he learnt from Lucian and quite possibly from a neo-Platonist teacher and dialectician called Iamblichus, who taught in both Antioch and Apamea.[7] By the latter part of the second decade of the fourth century, Arius was clearly back in Alexandria and had become a presbyter. He was a popular and persuasive preacher and had a reputation for asceticism. Taken together, these attributes would make him a compelling spiritual force in the city. At this point Epiphanius (*c*.310–403), who wrote to expose heresies in the Church, gives us a vivid portrait of Arius:

> He was very tall in stature, with downcast countenance—counterfeited like a guileful serpent, and well able to deceive any unsuspecting heart through its cleverly designed appearance. For he was always garbed in a short cloak, and sleeveless tunic; he spoke gently, and people found him persuasive and flattering.[8]

There is little doubt that by 315 Arius had become a significant figure in the Church life of Alexandria. It seems that by then he had become a respected cleric attached to the church called Baucalis, one of nine substantial churches in the city, and had supervision of some 70 women living an ascetic life having taken a vow of virginity.[9] The Church in Alexandria was divided by the Melitian schism and by the question of whether rebaptism was a valid way of re-entering the Church having lapsed. And it seems from the later development of Arianism that Arius was closer to the hard-line reaction to lapsed Christians, and hence to the Melitian part of the Church. The Church in Alexandria was similarly conflicted in its response to an ascetic movement led by Hieracas, who had a clutch of heretical views including questions over the resurrection of the body.[10] In this theological and spiritual melee, Arius may have even stood for election for the bishopric or papacy of Alexandria, although withdrawing in favour of Alexander.[11] But in 312, after the brief episcopacy of Achillas, Alexander was elected bishop and the lines were drawn for the doctrinal conflict that would dominate the fourth century. Indeed, Alexander faced "a spectacularly fissiparous Christian body",[12] but it was about to get a whole lot worse.

At some point before 318, the Arian controversy got underway. The German Church historian Hans-Georg Opitz (1905–41) undertook the publication of the definitive collection of works in relation to Arius and Athanasius. However, it is important to stress from the outset that the documents that we have concerning the early stages of the controversy are very fragmentary, and we can only piece together a tentative narrative of those years, which initially involves parties in Alexandria, before drawing in others from much further afield.

Between 313 and 318, Arius began to promulgate his views on the status of Christ in relation to the Godhead in Alexandria. These views were driven by the intellectual and doctrinal movements existing at the time, which came in part from an accommodation to neo-Platonism, as well as a more general response to the ongoing debate about the Trinity, as we have seen in Sabellianism and the adoptionism proposed by Paul of Samosata. Furthermore, the general confusion about the Godhead, following the legacy of Gnosticism in the Church, created conditions in which some thought the related issues would be best settled by the simple construct of one, single eternal Godhead, or Father, from whom came two emanations of the Son and the Spirit. What Arius was offering was a "plausible" construct, given the intellectual climate of the day, but one which denied the full divinity of the Son and the Spirit, and as such, was not in keeping with the witness of the Scriptures, although plenty of individual texts were quoted in support.

The opening theological salvos from Arius are only partially recorded, since the extant manuscript record is extremely sparse. In fact, there are only three texts that can be directly ascribed to Arius.[13] These are the confession of faith presented to Bishop Alexander and signed by Arius and 11 supporters; a letter from Arius to Eusebius of Nicomedia; and a confession submitted by Arius and Euzoius to the emperor much later in either 327 or 335 (i.e., after Nicaea). Without becoming involved in a word-by-word textual and theological critique of these documents, we can safely give the following summary of their conclusions. They affirm that God (the Father) alone is *agennētos* (without beginning). He is immaterial and is subject to no emanation or diffusion of his substance. Furthermore, God is entirely free, rational and purposive. The Father or God freely brings into being the Son, who is a subsistent individual truly distinct (*alēthōs*—truly) from himself. This creation of the Son was before all ages, so the Son was not timelessly self-subsistent. Rather the Son is a perfect creature, not one among others, and is the recipient of all God's gifts and glories. The role of the Holy Spirit is not spelt out, however.[14]

What is clear from these documents, which stake out the ground of the controversy, is that Arius and his supporters maintain that the Son was not without a beginning. Or to put it the other way round, there was a time when he was not and was then brought into existence. He did not exist from eternity, and the Father existed before him. This very assertion made by Arius, for whatever reason, compromises the Son's full divinity. The Spirit's status, although acknowledged, is not defined, and like the Son, the Spirit does not have an eternal existence.

If these are the conclusions we may draw from works *directly* attributable to Arius, other parts of his teaching in the work called the *Thalia* (meaning "feast") were reproduced and published by Athanasius in his narrative of the Arian controversy. The *Thalia* appears in two places in Athanasius's record of the controversy: in the *Oratio Contra Arians* (*c*.339–46) and *De Synodis* (359). As you can see, both these records of Arius's *Thalia* were reproduced well after the Council of Nicaea of 325, a time when the controversy was still raging and Athanasius was seeking to show both the root cause and the course of the controversy. Of the two accounts of the *Thalia* recorded by Athanasius, the second in *De Synodis* is more complete. In *De Synodis*, Athanasius summarizes Arius's teaching as follows: "God made the Son out of nothing, and called him his Son; The Word of God is one of the creatures"; "Once he was not and he is alterable, capable, when it is his will, of altering".[15] Athanasius goes on to record Arius saying the following:

> Thus, there is a Triad, but not equal in glories. Not intermingling with each other are their subsistences. One more glorious than the other in their glories unto immensity. Foreign from the Son in essence is the Father, for He is without beginning. Understand that the Monad was; but the Dyad was not, before it was in existence. It follows at once that, though the Son was not, the Father was God. Hence the Son, not being (for He existed at the will of the Father), is God only-begotten, and He is alien from either.[16]

Thus, in this and other parts of his quoted writings, Arius was making the following assertions: there was a time when God was not a Father, since the Son had not yet been created or begotten. There was a time when the Son did not exist, although to be fair to Arius, he was cautious about committing himself to the concept of time in the emanation of the Son from the Godhead saying, "there was when he was not "(but surely the "when" indicates or implies time). For a time, therefore, God existed alone before creating Wisdom, then the Son, and finally humanity. God's own wisdom produced a distinct entity of Wisdom expressed in the Word. Unlike the Father, this Word may be subject to change and is not true God (*theos alēthinos*). The *substance* (a word we must soon define) of the Son and the Spirit is separate from the Father, and the Father is invisible to the Son.[17] In these views, Arius was attempting to define the relationship of Father, Son and Spirit, in which he was not very far removed from the views of an earlier bishop of Alexandria, Dionysius, who was corrected by his namesake the Bishop of Rome. Nor was he far from Origen, who also taught that the Son was not of the same substance as the Father, because of having a human soul.[18]

These then were the views proposed by Arius, as expressed in the *Thalia*, itself passed on by Athanasius as the only source of these views, and deeply influenced by Platonist thinking. It was a gauntlet thrown down to the Church in Alexandria and indeed to all teachers of the nature of God throughout Christendom. Arius was summoned by Alexander, Bishop of Alexandria, and urged to modify his views. When he refused, Alexander convened a council of some hundred bishops from Egypt and Libya, which drew up a creed repudiating Arius's views. When Arius refused to accept this document, he was excommunicated and banished from Alexandria.[19] Arius then sought allies outside Egypt and wrote to Eusebius of Nicomedia, who was close to the imperial court, having a relation who was the praetorian prefect.

The controversy was beginning to widen and deepen. Arius claimed that he had been unjustly banished from Alexandria for failing to agree publicly that the Son is coeternal with the Father. He began to gather support from various bishops, including Eusebius of Caesarea, the scholar and great Church historian, Theodotus of Laodicea, Paulinus of Tyre, Athanasius of Anazarbus, Gregorius of Beryta, and Aelius of

Lydda.[20] All of these individuals asserted the prior existence of God before the begetting or creation of the Son. What is clear is that from the outset Arius was not a lone voice in the wilderness of the Egyptian desert, but part of an intellectual and spiritual movement throughout the Church in the east devoted to raising the doctrine of the monarchy of God and his prior existence above all others. They genuinely sought to elevate the unique authority of God, but in so doing impaled the teaching of the Trinity, the greatest glory of the Christian faith, and put at risk, as Athanasius would show, the redemptive work of the Son and the status of the Spirit. The issue of how the Godhead might be expressed in terms of both unity and individuation became the theological conundrum of the fourth century. The task was on to find a vocabulary that adequately expressed the mystery of the Godhead.

The key terms in the debate

There appear to be four fundamental terms around which the Trinitarian debate revolved, and about which the Church needed to make up its mind in its understanding of Father, Son and Spirit, their status and interrelationship. These terms were part of the lexicon that sought to clarify whether each member of the Trinity was coeternal, having no beginning and no end; whether the *Logos* was fully God whilst undergoing suffering, and therefore changed during the incarnation; whether members of the Godhead were of the same substance or *ousia*; and finally, whether each member of the Trinity was individuated or a separate *hypostasis*. These questions were, of course, deeply interrelated, and their answers would determine the nature of the Trinity. The theological outcome of these issues would depend on the degree to which Greek philosophy rather than the biblical witness would be used to settle them, although as we shall see, it was not quite as simple as that.

The first of these interrelated issues to highlight is whether each member of the Godhead is coeternal or, to use the expression of the time, whether each is without beginning (or end), *agėnētos*. Arius and Arians argued that the *Logos* or the Son was not without beginning; he was created, in other words.

The way the Son was created by the Father was itself a matter of considerable theological speculation among the Arians, however. Asterius of Cappadocia (*c.*280–341), also a pupil of Lucian of Antioch, took the view that such was the sovereignty of God that, without contact with anything material, the Father formed himself into the Son, whom he then taught to create in obedience to his will, as though the Son were a pupil and the Father an instructor and architect.[21] In his commentary on Job, the Arian biblical commentator known simply as Julian called the Almighty the only ingenerate being with the Son subservient to him.[22] The Son was created from nothing material, neither from the *ousia* (being) of the Father, nor from anything already in existence; the *Logos* is simply brought into being by the *fiat* of the Father. Thus, Julian comments in his exposition of Job:

> When God generates, he does not generate by *pathos* (his own need or desire, as if creation was to satisfy some unfulfilled need) or division of his own *ousia* and when he creates he does not need material or movement nor natural nor artificial instruments, but he generates and creates by will and power, for he is not dependent upon material nor does he use his own *ousia* instead of some material (for he has no need of anything), nor is he who is wholly independent dependent on himself. He is alone omnipotent and unapproachable and greater than any cause or origin; immutable, unchangeable, he does not generate in the same way as fathers do with us nor create in the same way as craftsmen do with us, but as One who is authentic and wholly independent, he generates by his authority without any intermediate and by his authority creates and by his authority controls his own products.[23]

Julian's intention, along with other Arian authors, was to defend or annunciate the absolute monarchy of God. The presupposition from which they wrote was derived from both the monotheism suggested in the Scriptures and the Greek neo-Platonic idea of the complete sovereignty of the One. What could not be conceived was that such sovereignty might be shared by other members of the Godhead, who were also God, but with distinct roles and energy. If one starts from the premise that supremacy can never be several, one is hard pushed to accommodate any notion of Trinity.

Much of the debate over the coming years would revolve around the idea that only God the Father can be ingenerate; that all other beings must be contingent on his being, formed by his authority and power. The upshot of this teaching of the Arians, whilst well motivated, was a way of restricting God, and more than that, of demonstrating the inferiority of the *Logos* and the imperfection of his being. Arians were to draw on texts from the Bible, such as John 20:17, where the resurrected Jesus says to Mary Magdalene that he is returning to "my God and your God", and Proverbs 8:22, where Wisdom (the *Logos*) says that "the Lord brought me forth as the first of his works" (NIV), to argue that Jesus or the *Logos* as the personification of Wisdom were in some way God's creation.

The second area of dispute between Arians and non-Arians concerned the understanding that God is *impassible.* Impassibility is not a concept with which many are familiar. It means *incapable of change, suffering or alteration.* This understanding of God's being, which was partly based on Scripture and partly shaped by Greek philosophy, meant that God did not vary (James 1:17; Hebrews 13:8). God cannot change, and God cannot not suffer pain or pleasure. This view was later strongly supported by Augustine of Hippo (354–430) and Theodoret of Antioch (*c.*393–458) and the Bishop of Cyrrhus in Syria, and was to be held equally by Roman Catholic teaching and by the Reformers, Luther and Calvin. In light of this doctrine of the impassibility of God, what are we to make of those phrases in Scripture which indicate the possibility of change in God's emotional state: delight, anger, hatred etc. (e.g. Exodus 4:14; Psalm 5:5b; Isaiah 30:27; Romans 9:13)? Expressions of different emotions implicitly indicate the possibility of change. The answer often given is that these descriptions do not violate God's immutability or impassibility, since they are anthropomorphic descriptions to explain God's attitude in terms of human emotions. Such expressions do not necessarily mean that God was *not* impassible; they simply impute to him responses expressed in human terms.

The Arians maintained that since Jesus patently suffered, he could no longer be impassible, and if not impassible, he could not be God. At the same time, several of the exponents of Arianism speculated about the structure of Jesus's incarnate being. Indeed, they posited a construction of his divine and human nature that would anticipate the debate in the fifth century over how Jesus could be both human and divine. Lucian of Antioch and Arius both believed that Jesus did not have a human soul,[24] whereas Origen had believed he did. Asterius, a contemporary of Arius who combined the roles of "theologian, scientist, and journalist",[25] and who reflected on Arianism in his *Syntagmation*, maintained that the division of Christ into a divine *Logos-inhabited mind* and *human body* allowed Arians to maintain that, while the human body of Jesus and his emotions suffered, as inhabited by the *Logos*, his mind and soul remained impassible. Here was a clear example of what would later be both Apollinarianism and Nestorianism (see glossary of terms on page 218) and a creeping rationalism. Indeed, the debate over how to describe the divinity and humanity in Jesus would run for at least another 150 years, and over that description the Coptic (Egyptian) Church would split from the orthodox or remaining catholic Church at the Council of Chalcedon in 451. At its simplest, the suffering of Christ put at risk *his divine and impassible status*, giving Arians further reasons for saying that he could not be of the same nature or being as the Father. It is to that question of divine *being* or *ousia* we must now turn.

Of all the terms that reverberated around the Trinitarian debates of the fourth century, none received more attention or spilt ink than *ousia* and its several variations. The idea of the *ousia* of a thing is derived from both Aristotle and the Stoics, and reflects an understanding of the essence of a thing rather than its properties. To further complicate matters, there were two forms of *ousia* the thing itself and the property or the essence of a thing in a class or species which defines them. Plato preferred the former while Aristotle preferred the latter. In Aristotelian thought, a distinction was made between the substance of a thing and its accidents or properties (and this would have a momentous effect when applied to the sacraments of bread and wine in the medieval period). A further complication was that some writers or theologians used another word, *hypostasis* (to which we will come), almost interchangeably with *ousia*.[26] *Ousia* is a Greek word and means the substance or the essence of a thing, or simply its being.

In his book *Divine Substance*, Christopher Stead gives a broad definition of *ousia* as existence, category, status, substance, stuff, form, definition and truth. Both Origen and Athanasius used the word *ousia* when speaking of God's being. Then, later in the fourth century, the Cappadocian Fathers in particular made a distinction between the *ousia* of the Godhead, *which could not be known*, and the energies of each member of the Trinity, which *could be* experienced. The Nicene Creed was to place the concept of *ousia* central to an understanding of the Godhead. Nicaea would pin its colours to the mast of *homoousios*, meaning that the Father and the Son were deemed of the *same substance*, and this would become the benchmark. The term *homoousios* had had a relatively short history in Christian theology, being used only in the second half of the third century.[27] Dionysius, Bishop of Rome, had been shy about using it in his controversy with Dionysius of Alexandria, because it was not a biblical word. Yet the concept would come to be used in various forms, reflecting the degrees to which people held that members of the Trinity were equal. *Ousia* means the defining substance of something. Thus, *homoousios* means of the same substance. *Homoiousian*, however, means being like in substance, and was taken up by Basil of Ancyra. *Homoios kat' oùsian* also means like in substance and was preferred by Alexander of Alexandria. *Homoian* (not an *ousia* word), meaning like in will but not in substance, was a further variation. It was between these definitions that the debate raged in the fourth century, until the Church collectively decided which word best represented the truth found in the Scriptures to describe the triune Godhead. Hence, there were many options for describing the closeness of Father and Son.

To make things more complex, another word was used, and sometimes preferred, by many of the Church leaders to describe the nature of God: i.e., *hypostasis*, which has the advantage, unlike *ousia*, of being a biblical word. It is used in the Letter to the Hebrews to describe the Son in relation to the Father: "He is the reflection of God's glory and the exact imprint of God's very being (*hypostasis*), and he sustains all things by his powerful word" (Hebrews 1:3). The precise way in which *hypostasis* was used, both by itself and in relation to *ousia*, was hardly consistent, however. Sometimes it was used synonymously with *ousia*, and sometimes to delineate the "distinct existence" of a member of the Trinity. Origen, who avoided using *homoousios*, taught that there were three *hypostases* within the Godhead, whereas Eusebius of Caesarea appears to have accepted that *hypostasis* and *ousia* are interchangeable.[28] Nor is any of this surprising at a time when the more precise way of describing the relationship of the Trinity was still in the melting pot, and as yet there was no settled vocabulary for expressing the mystery of the Godhead.

The lead-up to Nicaea

After Arius had stirred up controversy in Alexandria over the status of the Son or Christ, maintaining that he was a created being, Bishop Alexander initially called on him to recant. Arius remained adamant in his views, however, replying to Alexander in an open letter:

> For the Father did not, in giving to Him the inheritance of all things deprive himself of what he has ingenerately in himself; for he is the fountain of all things. Thus, there are three substances (*hypostases*). And God, being the cause of all things, is unbegun and altogether sole, but the Son being begotten apart from time by the Father, and being created and founded before all ages, was not before his generation, but being begotten apart from time before all things, alone was made to subsist by the Father. For he the Son is not eternal or co-eternal or co-originate with the Father, nor has he his being together with the Father, as some speak of relations, introducing two ingenerate beginnings, but God is before all things as monad and beginning of all.[29]

With Arius and his supporters remaining firm in their convictions, Alexander summoned about a hundred bishops to the council at Alexandria, spoken of earlier, and Arius was condemned. He went into exile, where he began to gather supporters from across Asia Minor and Palestine.[30] Among them were two heavyweights: Bishop Eusebius of Caesarea and Bishop Eusebius of Nicomedia—the former a well-respected theologian and Church historian, the latter virtually the bishop in residence at the imperial court of Licinius, and then of Constantine.

By this time, Alexander had taken onto his staff a young aspiring secretary, Athanasius, whom he had known since he was a boy playing on the beach of Alexandria (as described by Rufinus).[31] Up to the point of working for Alexander, Athanasius had had an unusual upbringing. His father had died, and his mother was a pagan and sought to make him marry against his will. She "used to take beautiful girls, adorn them and perfume them and make them enter to him in his chamber, and sleep near him and solicit him; but when he awoke, he beat them and drove them away".[32] Having failed with this strategy, and realizing that he was already a Christian, she took him instead to Bishop Alexander and both of them were baptized.

Meanwhile, much larger changes were afoot across the empire. In July 324, fighting once more under the banner of the *labarum* with its *Chi-Rho* symbol and having spent time in his tent praying, Constantine defeated the eastern emperor, Licinius, at Adrianople, although not fatally. Indeed, a symbol of the cross had become a heavenly standard on the battlefield and was moved around by 50 hand-picked men like "some triumphant charm against disasters".[33] Furthermore, Constantine's young son, Crispus, later to be executed by Constantine for an unrecorded misdemeanour, went on to defeat Licinius's navy in the Dardenelles. Constantine then crossed the Bosphorus and faced Licinius's now weakened army once again in Asia, near Chalcedon at Chrysopolis. This time Licinius suffered fatal losses, with over 25,000 soldiers killed. Constantine was now in control. He entered Byzantium and renamed it Constantinople, and began to issue edicts rescinding Licinius's policies around taxation and civic services (or liturgies), as well as restoring to Christians property that had been confiscated.[34]

Constantine was now emperor over the entire empire from Hadrian's Wall in the north to the Euphrates in the south-east, and he would have a further 13 years of rule. He saw himself as liberator of the empire from oppressive and mismanaged government, and as saviour of the Christian population. He issued a substantial letter to be published in the east, detailing his policies, warning that those who oppressed the Church would perish, restoring all confiscated property to Christians and the Church, and freeing Christians from prison, exile and servitude. The latter included having to work in menial occupations, such as laundry workers in women's apartments.[35] A further letter was issued in his own handwriting, in which he condemned idolatry, and praised the Supreme God, writing, "It is your power which removes our guilt, and makes us faithful. The solid fabric of the earth was established by your word. . . . Were it not so, were not all regulated by the determination of your will, so great a diversity, so manifold a division of power, would unquestionably have brought ruin on the whole race and its affairs."[36]

If Constantine saw himself as the unifier of the empire, he also saw himself as the unifier of the Church. He had already given himself to this task in the west, seeking to defuse the Donatist controversy in North Africa and bringing the combatants to two conferences in Rome and then in Arles, but without success. With this desire for unity in mind, Constantine then wrote to the Alexandrian Church, and in particular to Bishop Alexander and Arius. According to Eusebius "the churches everywhere were distracted by divisions".[37] The letter urging unity was taken personally to Alexandria by Constantine's closest ecclesiastical adviser, Bishop Ossius of Cordoba, who would remain part of the imperial court and close to the controversy for years to come. The essence of Constantine's letter, no doubt advised by Ossius, was that Arius's speculations upon the nature of the Godhead should not be brought into public assembly, and that they should be met with forbearance. Indeed, "very few are able either accurately to comprehend or adequately to explain subjects so sublime and abstruse in their nature".[38] To Constantine's mind, subjects of such complexity should not be publicly aired or speculated upon, nor should they become matters for public debate. Although there is more than a grain of sense in this position, the controversy in Alexandria had gone too far for this admonition to be heeded. Furthermore, a fundamental question about the nature of the Godhead had been raised and had to be settled; it could not be swept under an imperial carpet for the sake of a spurious unity. Ossius then presided over a synod in Alexandria as the emperor's envoy. A further council was proposed at Ancyra, where Marcellus, an extreme opponent of Arius, was bishop. But it would never take place, for other events would intervene.

Notes

1 Patrick Whitworth, *Suffering and Glory: The Church from the Apostles to Constantine* (Durham: Sacristy Press, 2018), pp. 160ff.

2 Rowan Williams, *Arius* (London: SCM Press, 2001), pp. 202ff.

3 Williams, *Arius*, p. 184.

4 Williams, *Arius*, p. 203.

5 Williams, *Arius*, p. 29.

6 Eusebius, *Historia ecclesiastica* IX, 6.3, op. cit., p. 286.

7 Williams, *Arius*, p. 31.

8 Williams, *Arius*, p. 32, citing Epiphanius, *Panarion/Adversus haereses* 69.

9 Williams, *Arius*, p. 42.

10 Williams, *Arius*, p. 41.

11 Williams, *Arius*, p. 40.

12 Williams, *Arius*, p. 46.

13 Williams, *Arius*, p. 95.

14 Williams, *Arius*, p. 98.

15 Athanasius, *De Synodis*, in *Nicene and Post-Nicene Fathers: Second Series, Vol. IV Athanasius: Selected Works and Letters*, ed. Philip Schaff (Edinburgh: T&T Clark, 1987), p. 457.

16 Athanasius, *De Synodis*, op. cit., pp. 457–8.

17 Williams, *Arius*, pp. 98ff.

18 Timothy Barnes, *Constantine and Eusebius* (Cambridge, MA: Harvard University Press, 1981), p. 204; and Origen, *On First Principles*, IV.8, tr. G. W. Butterworth (Notre Dame, IN: Ave Maria Press, 2013), p. 421.

19 Barnes, *Constantine and Eusebius*, p. 204; and Opitz, *Urkunden zur Geschichte des Arianischen Streites* (Berlin/Leipzig: De Gruyter, 1939), p. 4b.

20 Barnes, *Constantine and Eusebius*, p. 204.

21 Hanson, *The Search for the Christian Doctrine of God*, pp. 100–1.

22 Hanson, *The Search for the Christian Doctrine of God*, p. 102.

23 Julian on Job, 205.14–206.3, cited in Hanson, *The Search for the Christian Doctrine of God*, p. 101.

24 Hanson, *The Search for the Christian Doctrine of God*, p. 111.

25 Hanson, *The Search for the Christian Doctrine of God*, p. 32.

26 Hanson, *The Search for the Christian Doctrine of God*, pp. 182ff.

27 Hanson, *The Search for the Christian Doctrine of God*, p. 191.

[28] Hanson, *The Search for the Christian Doctrine of God*, p. 185.

[29] Athanasius, *De Synodis* II.16, op. cit., p. 458.

[30] David M. Gwynn, *Athanasius of Alexandria: Bishop, Theologian, Ascetic, Father* (Oxford: Oxford University Press, 2012), p. 24.

[31] Rufinus, *Historia ecclesiastica* X.15, cited by Gwynn, *Athanasius of Alexandria*, p. 1.

[32] *History of the Patriarchs* PO 1:1407, cited by Gwynn, *Athanasius of Alexandria*, p. 1.

[33] Eusebius, *Vita Constantini* II (Limovia, 2013), p. 62.

[34] Barnes, *Constantine and Eusebius*, pp. 208–9.

[35] Barnes, *Constantine and Eusebius*, p. 209, and Eusebius, *Vita Constantini* II, op. cit., pp. 73–86.

[36] Eusebius, *Vita Constantini* II, op. cit., p. 89.

[37] Eusebius, *Vita Constantini* II, op. cit., p. 98.

[38] Eusebius, *Vita Constantini* II, op. cit., p. 103.

CHAPTER 4

Nicaea: An imperial call to order

The build-up to the Council of Nicaea had been going on for some time. Since *c.*314, the dispute over the teaching of Arius had been deepening, both in Alexandria and then in Palestine.

Alexander, Bishop of Alexandria, had written a long encyclical letter to the bishops and Church of Egypt. It was called *henos sōmatos* and had an extensive list of signatories denouncing Arius and his teaching.[1] It is quite possible that this letter was written by Athanasius himself, in his role as Alexander's secretary.[2] Later in *c.*324, as recorded by Athanasius, Alexander wrote another immensely long letter, called *hē philarchos*, to his namesake Bishop Alexander of Byzantium, in which he stressed the coeternity of Father and Son and denounced several Syrian bishops who had given their support to Arius, although he was silent about that given by Eusebius of Nicomedia.[3] What is clear is that through those five years the Church was becoming increasingly disturbed by the mounting divisions over the teaching of Arius and those like him.

While the dispute over the Trinity and the status of the *Logos* in the Trinity in particular was increasing and deepening, Emperor Constantine was taking a firmer grip on the empire. In 324, he finally defeated his eastern rival, and co-emperor, Licinius, and immediately selected Byzantium as the site for a "New Rome", modestly calling it Constantinople. Following his victory, Constantine determined to go on a tour of his newly acquired eastern territories and cities to promulgate his rule, as well as to visit the churches and their leaders. The tour probably began in November 324 after the founding of Constantinople. Arabians, Indians, Ethiopians, Medes and Persians all did homage to Constantinople.[4] This tour was, however, cut short at Antioch and Constantine returned to Nicomedia. Indeed, his presence in Antioch was attested on 25 February of that year. This may have been because his defeated rival Licinius was assassinated in Thessalonica around then, and there were rumours this had been at Constantine's command, despite his oath to preserve his brother-in-law's life.[5]

Ossius continued the original tour, going to Alexandria and then Antioch, where he presided over two synods beset with contentious issues: in Alexandria the issue was principally the incipient Arian controversy, and in Antioch it was to do with the appointment of Eustathius as successor to Philogonius, who had died on 30 December 324. In addition, at Antioch there was the initial formulation of an intricately phrased creed in response to the burgeoning controversy over the Trinity. There was not, however, unanimity about this: Theodotus of Laodicea, Narcissus of Neronias and Eusebius of Caesarea, the Church historian and theologian, refused to sign it and were excommunicated. Ossius then returned to Nicomedia. A council called for Ancyra was cancelled and instead Constantine personally invited the bishops to Nicaea.

Constantine, as we have seen, had been involved in the debate in Alexandria for some months. He had written to the warring parties. He took the view that speculating on the nature of Godhead would lead to confusion and believed such things should not be publicly aired.[6] Furthermore, Constantine went on to say in a letter to the churches:

> Let us still more thoughtfully and with closer attention examine what I have said, and see whether it be right that, on the grounds of such trifling and foolish verbal difference between ourselves, brethren should assume towards each other the attitude of enemies, and the august meeting of the synod be rent by profane disunion, because you wrangle together on points so trivial and altogether unessential. This is vulgar, and rather characteristic of childish ignorance, than consistent with the wisdom of priests and men of sense. Let us withdraw ourselves with a good will from the temptations of the devil. Our great God and common Saviour of all has granted the same light to us all. Permit me, who am his servant, to bring my task to a successful issue, under direction of his Providence, that I may be enabled, through my exhortations, and diligence, and earnest admonition to recall

> his people to communion and fellowship. (And) As far then as regards the Divine Providence, let there be one faith, and one understanding among you, one united judgement in reference to God. But as to your subtle disputations on questions of little or no significance, though you may be unable to harmonize in sentiment, such differences should be consigned to the secret custody of your own minds and thoughts.[7]

The trouble was that the dispute was not about "trifling and foolish verbal differences", as even Christian rulers like Constantine thought, but about the fundamental understanding of the nature of the Godhead. Nor would the differences be overcome by sweeping them under the carpet or hoping for "secret custody" of these thoughts, consigning them to some form of mental dungeon. Therefore, Constantine, with his ecclesiastical advisers, came to realize that a great council of the Church was needed to thrash out these speculations about God once and for all, although even that proved far harder than he expected. Nevertheless, the newly confirmed emperor of the entire Roman empire invited the Church's leaders to his summer palace at Nicaea, having jettisoned an earlier idea of meeting in Ancyra.[8] A personal imperial order to attend went to bishops in both the western and eastern parts of the empire, and to facilitate this, Constantine allowed free use of the *cursus publicus* (the imperial transport system) with horses and carriages to convey them. Nearly 300 bishops attended, with a few from the west, including Gaul and Germany. The Bishop of Rome did not come, pleading age as an excuse, but sent two priests as representatives.[9] Athanasius came as Bishop Alexander's secretary.

The council assembled in June 325 and was formally opened by the emperor himself. Eusebius relates the scene:

> All rising at the signal which indicated the emperor's entrance, at last he himself proceeded through the midst of the assembly, like some heavenly messenger of God, clothed in raiment which glittered as it were with rays of light, reflecting the glowing radiance of a purple robe, and adorned with the brilliant splendour of gold and precious stones. Such was the external appearance of his person; and with regard to his mind, it was

> evident that he was distinguished by piety and godly fear. This was indicated by his down cast eyes, the blush on his countenance, and his gait. For the rest of his personal excellence, he surpassed all present in height of stature and beauty of form, as well as in majestic dignity of mien, and invincible strength and vigour.[10]

His biographer, Eusebius of Caesarea, was not at a loss for words. Constantine took his seat on a low but gilded and jewel-encrusted stool. Eusebius of Nicomedia gave an opening panegyric to the emperor. Constantine opened the council with a short address outlining his desire to see "you all united in one judgement". "Delay not", he continued, "begin from this moment to discard the causes of that disunion which has existed among you, and remove the perplexities of controversy by embracing the principles of peace."[11]

The course of the council and the Nicene Creed

We cannot be sure of the course of the council, as no record of the proceedings was either made or kept. It is quite possible that the two leading proponents of what would be Nicene orthodoxy, Ossius of Cordoba and Alexander of Alexandria, conferred immediately before the council, but no preliminary meeting occurred of which we know. They were closely supported by Eustathius, the newly appointed Bishop of Antioch, and Marcellus of Ancyra. One hostile but credible report from Philostorgius, another Church historian and Arian advocate, maintains that Alexander and Ossius had resolved to insert the *homoousias* into the creed from the outset. Basil of Caesarea, the Cappadocian Father, writing nearly 50 years after the council, maintained that a Cappadocian priest called Hermogenes substantially wrote the Nicene Creed before the council met.[12]

Whatever the preceding conversations between participants determined to influence the outcome, two camps became quickly discernible. The leaders of the Arian position—although they hardly regarded Arius as their leader, since he was only a priest whereas they were bishops, and in the fourth century hierarchy was almost everything—came to state their position. They were the two Eusebii: Eusebius of Nicomedia and Eusebius of Caesarea. It was most probably Eusebius of Caesarea who addressed the council, but from a position of some weakness despite his great learning, because of his recent excommunication by the Council of Antioch. His address was probably substantially the same as the letter he sent to his diocese shortly after the council. He presented a creed to the council which went as follows:

> We believe in one God, Father, Almighty, maker of all things seen and unseen:
>
> And in one Lord Jesus Christ the Word of God, God from God, Light from light, Life from Life, only-begotten Son, first born of all creation, begotten from the Father before all ages, through whom all things have come into being, who was incarnate for our salvation; and spent his life among men, and suffered and rose the third day and went up to the Father and will come again in glory to judge the living and the dead;
>
> And we believe in the Holy Spirit.[13]

Furthermore, we are told that in his letter following the council the emperor declared that this creed by Eusebius was entirely orthodox,[14] although it was later violently condemned by Eustathius of Antioch and Athanasius as being heterodox, and apparently publicly torn up at the council.[15] It seems, however, that memories of the council vary, and revisions of what went on took hold, depending on the party one supported. Quite possibly Constantine did not himself appreciate the fine distinctions in the creeds; or he may not have approved Eusebius's version. Yet at some point, the one which we know as the Nicene Creed was brought forward amongst other business of the council, which we will come to later.

This so-called Nicene Creed was confirmed at the later Council of Constantinople in 381 after intervening years of controversy. The council itself did not effectively promulgate the Creed; they left it to individual bishops to tell their dioceses what had been decided. One bishop, with a vested interest in handing on the Nicene Creed to his diocese, and explaining what he thought it meant, was Eusebius of Caesarea: he had been deposed as bishop, excommunicated at the preceding Council of Antioch, and had submitted his own creed to the council. At the same time, he had agreed to and signed up to the Nicene Creed. At first sight this seems a confusing set of circumstances, for on the one hand he had been deposed, while on the other he had accepted the Creed sponsored by Constantine, which was largely the result of the work of Ossius, Alexander of Alexandria, and possibly the priest whom Basil mentions, Hermogenes. Eusebius's actions were thus among the most glaring contradictions of the council.

In Eusebius's letter to his diocese immediately following Nicaea, he gives a record of what became known as the Nicene Creed, which they had agreed almost to a man. His account of the Creed as recorded by the Church historians Socrates[16] and Theodoret[17] is as follows:

> We believe in One God, the Father Almighty, Maker of all things visible and invisible:
>
> And in one Lord Jesus Christ, the Son of God, begotten of the Father, Only-Begotten, that is, *from the essence of the Father*: God from God, Light from Light, Very God from Very God, begotten not made, *one in essence with the Father*, by Whom all things were made, both things in heaven, and things on earth; Who for us men and for our salvation came down and was made flesh, was made man, suffered, and rose again the third day, ascended into heaven, and cometh to judge the quick and the dead.
>
> And in the Holy Ghost
>
> And those who say "Once he was not" and "Before His generation He was not" and "He came to be from nothing" or those who pretend that the Son of God is "of other subsistence or essence", or "created" or "alterable" or "mutable", the Catholic Church (meaning the universal Church) anathematizes.

The creed was clearly intent on excluding all Arian claims that there was a time when the Son was not. Yet Eusebius of Caesarea, and for that matter Eusebius of Nicomedia, two of the leading bishops and theological opponents of Alexander of Alexandria, signed the creed. Why was that?

Because of the gloss they put on what they were signing. Eusebius of Caesarea explains how he understood those parts of the creed designed to exclude Arians from the Church.

There are two phrases in the Nicene Creed (in italics above) which were designed both to exclude Arianism and to uphold the full divinity of the Son with the Father, by maintaining that there never was a time that the Son did not exist as consubstantial with the Father, nor was there a time when the Father was not a Father with an eternal Son. And so the Son was without a beginning, and hence eternal.

Eusebius went on to explain to his diocese how it was that he could sign up to the Nicene Creed and its anathemas, given that he had been excommunicated and exiled from his see by the Council of Antioch just a few months before Nicaea. To do so, he reinterpreted the term *homoousios*. After all, Arius, with whom Eusebius was linked, had specifically rejected the term and the idea that the Son could be consubstantial with the Father (share the same substance or being). Indeed, in his *Thalia*, Arius had specifically rejected the term, and had attacked it in his letter to Eusebius of Nicomedia.[18] Now Eusebius of Caesarea glosses what the council intended by the use of *homoousios*, by saying that "they [the council] professed, that the phrase 'of the essence' was indicative of the Son's essence as being from the Father, yet 'without being as if a part of him'".[19] Eusebius continues, "And with this understanding we thought good to assent to the sense of such religious doctrine, teaching, as it did, that the Son was from the Father, but not however a part of his essence."[20] Thus Eusebius thought the Son was from the Father, but not part of his essence. This explanation seems to stretch the face value meaning of the term *homoousios*, by making it what one might wish it to mean, rather than what it implicitly says. For surely if Nicaea meant that the Son was from the Father, but not part of his substance, then the orthodox party led by Alexander and Ossius would have conceded their central point, for which they would fight in the coming years, namely that the Father and Son were of the same substance.

It is more likely that Eusebius misunderstood the explanation of the word given by those he consulted; or that he consulted those who gave him the answer he wanted to hear; or that he constructed a meaning that reconciled signing the Creed in the presence of the emperor, whilst retaining his doubts about the Son being of the same essence as the Father. What we can be sure of is that Eusebius gave the phrase a meaning not intended by Ossius or Alexander, and this reinterpretation would create space for future debate about what was agreed at Nicaea. At root, although he signed up to the Creed in the presence of the emperor, as almost all the bishops did except two, Eusebius objected to the term *homoousios*, which had had a chequered history, and which he regarded as lacking biblical provenance. It was, however, to become the benchmark of Nicaea and was the term that encapsulated all the theology of Alexander, Ossius and others, such as Eustathius of Antioch, who had condemned and anathematized the teaching of Arius and his supporters. It was quite clear in two places in the Creed that the Son shared in the substance of the Father and that the Son was "out of the Father's substance or essence".

The other great controversial issue, and which the Creed pronounced on, was that the Son was begotten not made. The Creed itself says the Son is "begotten of the Father" and is the "only-begotten". Furthermore, the anathema attached to the Creed was especially designed to condemn any who taught that the Son was created by the Father, thus implying the Son is not eternal. So, the anathema says: "For those who say, there was when he was not, and before being born he was not, and that he came into existence out of nothing, or who assert that the Son of God is a different hypostasis or substance (or is created—omitted in some ancient sources), or is subject to alteration or change—these the Catholic Church anathematizes". This is entirely of a piece theologically with the earlier statement that the Son is of the same substance as the Father: it is because he is of the same substance that he cannot be made.

The anathema had a single target in mind: the Arians who maintained that the Son has a beginning.[21] Arius sought to sustain monotheism by denying the eternal existence of the Word, but in so doing destroyed the reality of the Trinity. For the Arians, the Son was a creature. He was created as "the first of his acts" (Proverbs 8:22). He was subsequently made Lord and Christ by the Father (Acts 2:36). He was the first-born of all creation (Colossians 1:15). These were some of the Arian prooftexts, as were other Scriptures that seemed to suggest inferiority of the Son to the Father—for instance Jesus's own admission that "the Father is greater than I" (John 14:28) and "this is eternal life, that they may know you, the only true God, and Jesus Christ whom you have sent" (John 17:3). The anathema (whose authenticity is rejected by some scholars, such as Maurice Wiles (see *Studia Patristica 26* (1991), pp. 428–33) clearly denied that the Son was created; that he came from nothing; that he was of different substance or hypostasis from the Father; or was himself subject to change. Anyone who subscribed to those views would be anathema to the Church. Yet although the anathema, and Nicene theology, struck one target very clearly, it left unanswered the other side of the Trinitarian equation: in what way was the Son distinct from the Father, and simply not an emanation of the Father as Sabellius had claimed? And how could the Nicene position guard against either incipient Sabellianism or a Christ who, though sharing the substance of the Father as an uncreated being, was also fully human and able to suffer? These were questions to be worked up in the coming century and a half, and that would lead to further division.

The council in general, and Alexander of Alexandria and Ossius in particular, made abundantly clear what they were against. They also made it clear that the Son was begotten not made and of one substance with the Father (though eternally begotten was not stated). The reasons for these statements were not self-evident. Alexander maintained, and likewise his secretary Athanasius, that Scripture attested to the divinity and immutability of the Word. Furthermore, to say that Jesus was not fully God was to fly in the face of the liturgy, and especially baptism, as candidates were baptized in the names of Father, Son and Holy Spirit—all of whom were coequal—and of prayers which were offered to the Son as God. But most importantly of all for Alexander, and as we shall see for Athanasius also, the Son must be fully divine to be a true mediator reconciling humanity to the Godhead. Athanasius would come to make this abundantly plain in *De Incarnatione*. All this was part of Nicene orthodoxy and would be tested almost to breaking point in the coming years.

A term used in the anathema alongside substance or *ousia* was *hypostasis*. The Creed asserted that "those who say the Son of God is from a different *hypostasis* or substance, the Catholic Church anathematizes". Here *ousia* and *hypostasis* are being used as synonyms or interchangeably. However, later in the fourth century a distinction was drawn between *ousia* and *hypostasis*: *ousia* retained the meaning of shared substance in the Godhead, but *hypostasis* came to mean the individuated person within the Trinity.[22] Indeed, there is some evidence that Alexander himself was beginning to use the term in this way in a letter to Alexander of Thessalonica.[23]

The Nicene Creed had a clear but limited effect. Negatively, it certainly fulfilled its aim of condemning the views of Arius. But it did not describe the unity of the three persons of the Godhead, as well as their distinctiveness. It also had little to say about the status, substance and distinctiveness of the Holy Spirit. In describing a mystery like the Trinity, it inevitably left some things out. There were unanswered questions that would fuel further speculation. In the future there would be some, such as Marcellus of Ancyra, who would overemphasize the unity of the Father and Son to the point of undermining the distinctiveness of the Word within the Godhead. Likewise, much later, Apollonaris of Laodicea (*c.*320–81) would emphasize the divinity of Christ while compromising his humanity, stating that the incarnate Jesus had a divine mind in a human body. The issue of how Jesus was both divine and human would come to dominate and divide the Church in the fifth century.

Nicaea had gone as far as it could in describing the Trinity, but more especially in outlawing Arius and his associates, but it was not successful in laying to rest all the issues related to describing the Trinity. This would take at least a further 60 years. What the Nicene Creed had given was a further theological benchmark for using the term *homoousios*, which critically summarized the relationship of Father and Son as being of the same substance. But it was also a word that caused controversy as soon as the council ended. Indeed, after two years the Arians, far from being on the back foot, were in the ascendancy. We will come to the reasons for this in the next chapter.

Other matters

The Council of Nicaea continued for another month after the agreement of the Creed. Many other canons were issued: on the date of Easter; on ordering of Church life; on morality, particularly sexual matters; and others to do with Church discipline of bishops, presbyters and deacons. Of these canons the most important concerned the date for the celebration of Easter.

In his *Life of Constantine*, the same Eusebius of Caesarea who found fault with the Nicene Creed recorded Constantine's desire to establish an agreed date for the annual Easter festival. In fact, such an agreement has eluded the Church to this day, and all attempts to align Christians in a celebration of Easter have failed. Eusebius set out the hope of the emperor as follows: "What can be more becoming or honourable to us than this feast from which we date our hopes of immortality, should be observed unfailingly by all alike, according to one ascertained order and arrangement".[24] He began at once to criticize the Jews and their method of establishing the lunar feast of the Passover in a manner typical of the period, saying, "let us then have nothing in common with the detestable Jewish crowd, for we have received from our Saviour a different way".[25] However, since no astronomical method was prescribed for agreeing the date of Easter (unlike the computations to be found in the 1662 *Book of Common Prayer*, which gives pages of tables about this calculation, based on the Golden Number), it was left to the bishops of Rome and Alexandria to cooperate and jointly fix the date annually. Indeed, Athanasius's Festal Letters issued in almost all the years of his episcopate were primarily written to inform his diocese of the date for Easter that year and the dates of the Lenten fast that preceded it. But in time, the bishops of Rome and Alexandria would differ on the date of Easter. Indeed, "in some years after 325, the churches of Rome and Alexandria celebrated Easter on different days".[26] And in Syria, the Protopaschites or Audiani who celebrated Easter on the eve of the Jewish Passover of 14 Nisan, continued to follow their ways. Once again, in matters defining the date for the celebration of Easter, Christians proved far less biddable to the emperor than his soldiers.

Some canons agreed at Nicaea demonstrated further attempts by Constantine and the bishops to unify the Church. Attempts were made to accommodate the secessionist groups of the Melitians in Egypt and the Novatianists in Rome (both of whom took a strict view on reincorporating the lapsed into the Church), but this proved difficult, and relations proved intractable. Canon 8 provided that clergy ordained in Rome by Novatian should have their ordinations universally recognized. Canons 11–14 dealt with the terms of penance for the inclusion of the lapsed. However, the Donatists in North Africa, in Carthage and beyond, proved obdurate and irreconcilable, as Constantine had found out earlier at the council at Arles in 314. Canon 6 affirmed the pre-eminence of the sees of Alexandria and Antioch in the east and downgraded Constantinople. Canon 7 provided a special status for the see of Jerusalem. Canon 19 required that any followers of Paul of Samosata should be rebaptized into the universal catholic Church.

Other canons ordered Church life. Canon 1 excluded eunuchs from the ranks of the clergy unless they had been castrated by barbarians or by doctors in an involuntary way. Canon 15 prevented the translation of a bishop from one diocese to another. Canon 20 forbade kneeling in prayer during worship or on feast days, requiring people to stand and pray. And in an apparent tightening against sexual offences, prevalent in Constantine's legislation,[27] and which may have resulted from an affair between his wife Fausta and Crispus, his son by an earlier wife (both of whom were executed), Canon 3 was introduced stating that no woman other than a family member should reside in a presbyter's house.

Nicaea ended on or around 25 July 325, and the bishops were once again sent home at Constantine's expense, although not before celebrating the start of the emperor's *vicennalia* year in nearby Nicomedia, which was the early celebration of 20 years of his rule since his accession in York in 306. If the bishops were suitably impressed by the splendour of his rule, and among them the young Athanasius, it did not mean that complete unity and harmony had been achieved. Too soon after the Council of Nicaea, division over defining God and expressing the Trinity broke out. For all Constantine's encouragement to the bishops at the end of the council "to act charitably to each other" and "to administer to each that which may tend to the health of the soul, to the end that the saving doctrine may be fully honoured by all",[28] discord very soon returned, and indeed would reach new levels. If the "saving doctrine" referred to was that the Son was *homoousios* with the Father, as Athanasius would strongly argue in his *De Incarnatione*, it would only be through many years of bitter controversy that a settled agreement about the status of the Son and the Spirit would be achieved. Indeed, as soon as the bishops reached home, further controversy erupted.

Notes

1 Rowan Williams, *Arius* (London: SCM Press, 2001), p. 48.

2 Williams, *Arius*, p. 49, and Athanasius, *De Decretis* 3, *Nicene and Post-Nicene Fathers: Second Series, Vol. IV Athanasius: Select Works and Letters*, ed. Philip Schaff (Edinburgh: T&T Clark, 1987), p. 152.

3 Williams, *Arius*, p. 51.

4 Timothy D. Barnes, *Constantine and Eusebius* (Cambridge, MA: Harvard University Press, 1981), p. 212.

5 Barnes, *Constantine and Eusebius*, pp. 214ff.

6 Eusebius, *Vita Constantini* II, op. cit., p. 103.

7 Eusebius, *Vita Constantini* II, op. cit., pp. 104–5.

8 R. P. C. Hanson, *The Search for the Christian Doctrine of God: The Arian Controversy 318–381* (Edinburgh: T&T Clark, 1988), p. 153.

9 Barnes, *Constantine and Eusebius*, p. 214.

10 Eusebius, *Vita Constantini* III, pp. 116–17.

11 Eusebius, *Vita Constantini* III, op. cit., p. 118.

12 Barnes, *Constantine and Eusebius*, p. 216.

13 Hanson, *The Search for the Christian Doctrine of God*, p. 159.

14 "Letter of Eusebius", in *Nicene and Post-Nicene Fathers: Second Series, Vol. I: Eusebius: Church History, Life of Constantine the Great, Oration in Praise of Constantine*, ed. Philip Schaff (New York: Cosimo, 2007), pp. 74–5.

15 Hanson, *The Search for the Christian Doctrine of God*, p. 160.

16 Hanson, *The Search for the Christian Doctrine of God*, p. 163.

17 Hanson, *The Search for the Christian Doctrine of God*, pp. 164–7.

18 Hanson, *The Search for the Christian Doctrine of God*, p. 167.

[19] Eusebius, "Letter to the Diocese", *The Nicene and Post Nicene Fathers: Second Series, Vol. I*, ed. Philip Schaff (Edinburgh: T&T Clark, 1987), p. 75.

[20] Eusebius, "Letter to the Diocese", op. cit., p. 75.

[21] J. N. D. Kelly, *Early Christian Doctrines* (London: A. & C. Black, 1960), p. 228, citing Arius's letter to Eusebius of Nicomedia in Epiphanius's *Panarion/ Adversus haereses*, 69.6.

[22] Lewis Ayres, *Nicaea and its Legacy: An Approach to Fourth Century Trinitarian Theology* (Oxford: Oxford University Press, 2006), pp. 99–100.

[23] Hanson, *The Search for the Christian Doctrine of God*, p. 168.

[24] Eusebius, *Vita Constantini* III, op. cit., p. 122.

[25] Eusebius, *Vita Constantini* III, op. cit., p. 122.

[26] Barnes, *Constantine and Eusebius*, p. 217.

[27] Barnes, *Constantine and Eusebius*, p. 219.

[28] Eusebius, *Vita Constantini* III, op. cit., p. 126.

CHAPTER 5

Athanasius and the reaction to Nicaea (325–37)

The emperor would live for a further 12 years after the end of the Council of Nicaea. As always, they would be active times for Constantine. He would formally dedicate the new city of Constantinople on 11 May 330, which in time would compete with Rome itself for supremacy in the Christian world, becoming the focus of the eastern Church by the fifth century, and even more so after the Arab invasions of North Africa and the Middle East in the seventh. Constantine's mother Helena, who took on the role of consort after the execution of Constantine's wife Fausta in 326, became a focus for Christian piety, going on frequent pilgrimages to the Holy Land. She visited the sacred sites of Christ's life in 326 and set in motion the building of basilicas in Bethlehem (the Church of the Nativity) and in Jerusalem (the Church of the Holy Sepulchre). Both survive today, although greatly added to. Constantine resumed military activities against the Goths in 332, and against the Sarmatians in 334, and was planning an invasion of Persia, where he saw himself as the protector of Christians, when he died on Whitsunday 337, being baptized shortly before his death.[1]

If the Council of Nicaea was intended as the means of bringing unity to the Church, Constantine was to be greatly disappointed. He continued to appeal to the leaders of the Church for unity and prompt disciplinary action was taken against those who did not sign up to the Nicene Creed, or who quickly disowned it. Constantine continued to lecture and admonish the Church in a style that did not greatly vary over the years: "What we possess of his writing . . . reveals that a predilection for leonine bombast, true hyperbole and arduous circumlocution was native to him, and did not overtake him suddenly after his seizure of the eastern capital in 324."[2] Despite the almost unanimous agreement with the Nicene Creed of nearly 300 bishops, within two years the tables had been turned and the Arian party appeared to be in the ascendancy.

Although two Libyan bishops refused to sign up to the Creed and were promptly exiled, the rest did, according to Church historian Philostorgius, some making the words mean what they wanted them to mean, rather than what they said. In that respect, they were like Humpty Dumpty in *Alice Through the Looking Glass* who famously said, "When *I* use a word it means just what I choose it to mean—neither more nor less."[3] Chief among such bishops was Eusebius of Caesarea, ironically the main contemporary historian and admiring biographer of Constantine. As we have seen, Eusebius signed up to the inclusion of the word *homoousios* and wrote a letter to his diocese of Palestinian Caesarea explaining what he meant by signing up to its use. For Eusebius, *homoousios* meant that the Son's being (*ousia*) came from the Father, but that the Son was not a part of the Father.[4] Eusebius thus signed up to the Creed whilst disregarding its implications. Furthermore, Eusebius of Nicomedia and Theognis of Nicaea subscribed to the Creed, but refused the anathemas appended to it. It looked like the Eusebians and Theognis had got away with dissembling and disingenuity, but when they showed their true feelings by entertaining some Arian sympathizers from Alexandria, Constantine, hearing of it, exiled all three of them. Constantine's letter "breathes an air of impatient annoyance and recites a long list of previously forgotten crimes".[5] At the same, a debate was ignited about the status of the word *homoousios* in the history of the Church. Eusebius of Caesarea regarded it as having no biblical standing and accused Eustathius of Antioch of Sabellianism.

Over the next two years or so, the position of the main protagonists changed substantially, whilst a number of new protagonists emerged. They were Arius himself, the Eusebians, Eustathius of Antioch and Marcellus of Ancyra; and last, but by no means least, Athanasius, who became Bishop of Alexandria in 328.

Arius and the Eusebians

Following the Council of Nicaea, Arius was sent into exile, but he was not to remain there for long. The course of events immediately after Nicaea remains cloudy, with scholars divided over whether a subsequent, much smaller, second session of the Council of Nicaea took place after its formal ending in July 325. The reason for supposing this second session of the council is that one Church historian, Theodoret, mentions that Bishop Alexander died five months after the council. Since we know from Athanasius's Festal Letter of that year that Alexander died on 27 April 328, this supposes a prolongation of the council of three years, which seems inconceivable. It is more likely that there may have been an after-meeting of some bishops at Constantine's court in Nicomedia after Alexander returned to Alexandria to consider the future of Arius and the Eusebians, all of whom had been exiled.

Arius wrote to the emperor from exile, petitioning for his return, and that of a fellow presbyter, Euzoius, and at the same time submitting a quite innocuous creed which touched on none of the points of controversy before and during Nicaea. Constantine wrote a reply "full of sweetness and light" summoning Arius to court so that he might be reconciled to the emperor and then return to his own country. The reason for this *volte face* is not known, but it could be that Eusebius of Nicomedia was already reasserting his influence at court, although previously exiled for some months in 325. It is thought that Arius attended the court of Constantine, agreed to the Nicene Creed, if not the anathemas, and was reconciled. This reconciliation was reported to a presumably sceptical Alexander in Alexandria.[6]

Whatever the precise narrative of events, which is hard to pin down with scant documentation and differing recollections and Church histories, by 327 a further council was held in Antioch at which the Arian party was much more in control. The Eusebians had written a humble letter or letters to the emperor, explaining their support for the Creed, but also their difficulty with the anathemas, and had returned to Constantine's court. At the same time, Constantine wrote to Alexander asking him to readmit Arius to fellowship and his former position. Alexander died before formulating a written reply, but he did send

Athanasius to the court to refuse to reinstate Arius. Athanasius was elected bishop in succession to Alexander and likewise gave no written answer.[7] The principle behind this response must have been: better not give a written contradiction of the emperor if you can go in person to his court.

After the Council of Antioch (to which we shall return in the context of Eustathius), the Arian party were clearly in the driving seat in Syria, Palestine and the east. On 27 November 327, Constantine summoned Arius to court and promised help in securing his return to Alexandria.[8] Arius submitted to Constantine a carefully worded description of his beliefs. He avoided the word *homoousios*, but declared his belief in Jesus Christ, the only begotten Son of God "begotten of god before all ages, divine Word, through whom everything was made". The Arians affirmed that they represented the teaching of the catholic Church and of Scripture, and begged for reconciliation. Constantine examined Arius and his colleague Euzoius and submitted their approval to a further council of bishops called to Nicomedia in December 327. Two hundred and fifty bishops assembled to consider how to end the Melitian schism in Egypt and hear the case of Arius. At the council, Eusebius of Nicomedia and Bishop Theognis of Nicaea submitted their desire to be readmitted to their sees. They maintained that they agreed with the term *homoousios*, but could not agree with the anathematizing of Arius, since his views had been misrepresented.[9] All three were readmitted. Alexander refused to comply with the decisions of the council, however, and Athanasius, as noted above, carried the reply of Alexander to the imperial court. It was a polite, respectful refusal to comply with the emperor's command to reappoint Arius. It was surely a moment that the young Athanasius, 33 years of age, would not forget. In a matter of months, he would be bishop of one of the most powerful sees in Christendom, confronting the same issue.

Arius had a habit of pushing his luck. Restored to fellowship by the emperor, although still not allowed back to his ministry in Alexandria by the now new bishop, Athanasius, Arius felt himself in limbo. He pressed the emperor to override Athanasius, and when it became apparent that Constantine would not, Arius threatened the emperor with starting a new church. Threatening the emperor was unwise. Constantine was not used to being threatened by a priest. In 333, two agents of the emperor, *agentes in rebus*, Syncletius and Gaudentius, arrived in Alexandria with the emperor's letters for the Egyptian Church in general, and Arius in particular. One was a brief letter to bishops and laity everywhere and the other a longer letter to Arius and the Arians. The former was read publicly in the governor's palace by the Roman prefect Patereius.[10] The letter to the Arians was excoriating in its condemnation: Arius was compared to Porphyry, the neo-Platonist who despised Christianity. Arius's writings must be burnt and anyone who kept copies of his works would be executed. The longer second letter was rambling, abusive and disparate, "the work of a man who feels angry and affronted".[11] In it, Arius is described as the mouthpiece of Satan. Furthermore, Constantine wrote that the Son was of the same substance as the Father and scolded Arius for sundering the Trinity. Arius is depicted as a dishonest fool, an impious ninny and an empty-headed chatterbox. Failure of Arians to rejoin the Church would incur heavy financial penalties and community service or "liturgies".

You would think that there would be no coming back from such ignominy, but it is not so. Arius is next seen travelling to Jerusalem in 335 where an important council was to be held at the same time as the consecration of the new church in Jerusalem. Begun by Constantine's mother Helena, and to be known as the Church of the Holy Sepulchre, it remains one of the oldest and most important churches in Christendom. The Council of Jerusalem was in fact part of an earlier and later council held at Tyre. Thus the bishops had begun a council at Tyre at the emperor's request to deal with issues between Athanasius and the Melitians of Alexandria and Egypt, but were summoned mid-point to a council in Jerusalem to coincide with the consecration of the Church of the Holy Sepulchre, before returning to Tyre to complete their work. While in Tyre they were charged with trying Athanasius (to which we will come), and while in Jerusalem they were to consider whether to readmit Arius to his office. Despite the imperial letters read in Alexandria in 333, two years later Arius and Euzoius were petitioning the emperor for readmittance. The emperor examined their plea and their attached statement of faith, and forwarded this request together with his opinion that they should be readmitted to the assembly of bishops in Jerusalem.

The final decision was left to the bishops, but the emperor's wish could not be easily ignored. Consequently, the council found Arius's doctrine sound and in accordance with the teachings of the apostles and the Church! Amazingly no such outcome was forthcoming for Athanasius at Tyre. The truth was that the Eusebians and their party had taken control of the councils and the emperor, who for reasons we shall see, was more inclined to follow them than Athanasius.

Arius would live for only one more year. He went to Constantinople where the emperor told the bishop, Alexander, to receive him. Arius had already shown signs of ill health. Indeed, the emperor had called attention to his poor health in his letters of 333, speaking of his wasting and emaciated flesh, his careworn countenance, his thinning hair and his half-dead appearance.[12] With some relish, the Church historian Socrates recalls Arius's final moments thus:

> As he approached the place called Constantine's Forum, where the column of porphyry is erected, a terror arising from the remorse of conscience seized Arius, and with the terror a violent relaxation of the bowels: he therefore enquired whether there was a convenient place near, and being directed to the back of Constantine's Forum, he hastened thither. Soon after a faintness came over him, and together with the evacuations his bowels protruded, followed by a copious haemorrhage, and the descent of the smaller intestines: moreover, portions of his spleen and liver were brought off in the effusion of blood, so that he almost immediately died. The scene of this catastrophe still is shown at Constantinople, as I have said, behind the shambles in the colonnade: and by persons going by pointing the finger at the place, there is a perpetual remembrance preserved of this extraordinary kind of death.[13]

There can be little doubt that the anti-Arians saw Arius's death as just desserts and divine punishment for pursuing the worst of heresies. But if they thought that the end of Arius was the end of the Arian controversy, they were gravely mistaken. It was just another staging post in the overall struggle and task of defining God the Holy Trinity. Indeed, there were a whole batch of heresies connected to defining God the Holy Trinity, of which Arius's was just one. If Arius failed to see that each member was coeternal and consubstantial, there were others who failed to see that each member of the Trinity, although *homoousios* (consubstantial), was also distinct and individuated. This was the other half of the mystery, and in this matter, two contemporary Church leaders, Eustathius and Marcellus, were in error.

Eustathius of Antioch and Marcellus of Ancyra

As we have seen, soon after Nicaea came the business of explaining what it all meant. The high-octane moment of the Creed being presented at the council in the presence of Constantine, and in which Bishops Ossius of Cordoba, Alexander of Alexandria and Alexander of Constantinople (New Rome) were in agreement, was followed by a relapse in which Eusebius of Caesarea and Eusebius of Nicomedia began to explain what they had signed up to, which was a very different thing. Indeed, Eusebius of Caesarea, who more or less disowned the word *homoousios*, arrived at a new definition of the relationship of Father and Son, which was *homoios kat' ousian*, meaning like in essence.

Eustathius of Antioch (*c*.292–*c*.360) was one of the main speakers at the Council of Nicaea and a leading bishop. He had recently been appointed to the see of Antioch, one of the principal sees in the eastern Church, shortly before the Council of Nicaea. At that time, the troubleshooting envoy of Constantine, Ossius of Cordoba, had intervened in December 324 after the death of the previous Bishop of Antioch, Philogonius, in order to seek a new bishop. The majority of the council of 50 bishops supported the appointment of Eustathius, although Eusebius of Caesarea objected.[14]

Eustathius was a firm supporter of Nicaea, but in his theology describing the relationship of the Father and the Son, he went further than Nicaea warranted. The problem was that in explaining that the Son was fully divine, Eustathius did so in a way that was too speculative about the relationship between the divine and human in Jesus. In order to hold to the idea of the immutable nature of Christ as divine (i.e., that Christ or the *Logos* did not suffer change through suffering, which was part of Arian theology), he maintained that there was a human soul or mind (*psyche*) in Jesus which experienced change, but that the divine *Logos* in Christ was immutable.[15] In many ways, this speculation anticipated the Christological controversy of the fifth century, which led to the Chalcedonian definition that had proven unacceptable to the Egyptian (Monophysite) Church.

In his anxiety to protect Jesus from imputation of change, Eustathius overstated the divine in Jesus at the expense of his humanity. If the Arians underrated the divine in Christ, Eustathius underrated the distinctiveness of the *Logos* taking on flesh, or the *Logos* becoming like us in all respects except sin (see John 1:14; Hebrews 2:11,14). It is because of this overstatement that Eustathius made himself vulnerable to theological attack by Eusebius, who believed that Eustathius was peddling a new form of Sabellianism, in which Jesus was not truly human and distinct whilst being of the same substance with the Father. By saying that the Son was *homoios kat' ousian*, Eusebius believed he rightly presented the humanity of Jesus within a divine substance that was like the Father. For their part, the Nicene party upheld the consubstantial nature of the Son, but unless carefully expressed, this diminished his unique humanity. Athanasius would attend to this in his theology, as we shall see. With this in mind, Sozomen in his *Histories* wrote, "Eustathius accused Eusebius of altering the doctrines ratified by the Council of Nicaea, while the latter declared that he approved all the Nicaean doctrines, and reproached Eustathius for cleaving to the heresy of Sabellius."[16]

Part of the dispute and animus between Eustathius and Eusebius of Caesarea resulted from their differing appreciations of Origen (*c.*185–254), whose influence ran like a fault line between theologians in the fourth and fifth centuries. Eusebius himself was the pupil of Origen's student Pamphilus (*c.*235–309) and the theological school and the library founded by Origen had been a deep influence. While Eusebius embraced Origen's teaching, Eustathius particularly disliked Origen's allegorical interpretation of Scripture, espousing the more literalistic and well-known Antiochene school of biblical interpretation. Eusebius was able to make the case that Eustathius was a Sabellian, and therefore in error. Eustathius was then deposed by a council chaired by Eusebius somewhere between 326 and 331,[17] or as Barnes says, in 327.[18] In any event, the deposition and exile of Eustathius showed the strength of the Arian party soon after Nicaea, and how an overstatement of the divinity of Christ at the expense of his individuated humanity pushed some of the pro-Nicene party into error. Not only that, but Eustathius laid himself open to other moral charges "of living in a disorderly fashion",[19] keeping a mistress and speaking disrespectfully of the emperor's mother, Helena. Although Athanasius defended him against these trumped-up charges, they showed that any vestige of moral failure or indiscipline could be used as an effective tool in prosecuting a doctrinal war.[20] However, the upshot in Antioch was a divided Church, with some clinging to Eustathius and forming a continuing Church devoted to his memory, and others heeding Eusebius. Divisions in Antioch would persist right up to the Council of Constantinople in 381. Despite promising beginnings (Acts 11:19–30), Antioch had become an unhappy place for the Church.

The other figure who quite possibly overcompensated for the Arian controversy and the teaching of the Arian party was Marcellus of Ancyra. Marcellus was one of the leading bishops of the east during the period of the Council of Nicaea. In 314, he had presided at a council held in Ancyra, which city was also proposed as the original site for the great council later held at Nicaea, since it was more convenient for the emperor. Marcellus took a leading role at Nicaea, but ten years later was deposed by a council held at Constantinople in *c.*336. He had become a well-known adversary of the Arian party, opposing them at Nicaea and writing a work against the teaching of the Arian philosopher, Asterius. Then, at the Council of Jerusalem, when Arius was all but reconciled to the emperor, Marcellus was required to withdraw his work against Asterius, since it seemed to favour the work of an earlier heresiarch, Paul of Samosata, who had been condemned in Antioch in 268/9. Once again, as with Eustathius, Marcellus's doctrine of the Son did not stress the unity of the *Logos* with the human Jesus sufficiently and sought instead to stress the complete identity of *Logos* with the Father.

Following his condemnation at Constantinople, Marcellus went into exile until, following the death of Constantine and the succession of Constantius, he was permitted to return to his see, as was the custom with the advent of a new emperor. He was exiled again in 338/9, however, and at that point travelled to Rome where he sought the support of the bishop there (not yet called pope). In 341, Julius summoned a council in Rome which proceeded to vindicate the teaching of Marcellus, who remained in Rome before travelling with the western bishops to the fruitless Council of Serdica, where there was a stand-off with the eastern bishops.[21] The controversy was now rapidly becoming regional or territorial as well as doctrinal. Once again it was Eusebius of Caesarea who was the main critic of Marcellus. In his work *Contra Marcellum*, Eusebius criticized the indistinguishability of the Son from the Father. The *Logos* was eternally present but seemingly inactive within the Godhead. Eusebius argued that just as the voice is present in the body though silent until speech is forthcoming, so too the *Logos* is present but inactive before the incarnation within the Godhead in Marcellus's description: "It was not a matter of one unbegotten and begotten God, the world and everything in it have been produced by one God-with-*Logos*."[22]

The issue was not whether the Son and the Father were of the same substance, which is clearly upheld by Marcellus and is thoroughly Nicene, but how the *Logos* is the Son before the incarnation, if the Father is eternally a Father. For Marcellus, the *Logos* is only called Son or Jesus after the incarnation. He seems to want to guarantee that the Father created directly, and not through any intermediary hypostasis. Yet what then are we to make of the Johannine statement that "All things came into being through him (the *Logos*), and without him not one thing came into being" (John 1:3)? Marcellus opposed the idea (later put forward by the Cappadocians) that there were three *hypostases*, as he took the Nicene position that *ousia* and *hypostasis* were one and the same. Not only that, but the existence of Jesus as the Son of God was for only 30 or so years. He was then subsumed within the Godhead as the *Logos* once more.[23] Marcellus appears to be saying that the individuated being of the Son resulted from an exercise of power and energy within the Godhead, which brought about the incarnation. Following his earthly life and resurrection, the Son was once again subsumed into the *Logos* within the Godhead. While this theory certainly maintained the sense of the *Logos* being of one substance with the Father, it failed to render the Son an eternal individuated being. In that way, it was deficient. Marcellus then speculated that it is the *Logos* in Jesus that plays the principal role in revealing the Father, undergoing the passion, and sending the Spirit. With the human part of Jesus relegated to a minor role, Marcellus's Jesus is a *Logos-with-a-human-body*.[24] In the same way, the proof text of Proverbs 8:22 is interpreted by Marcellus as Wisdom taking on a human body. Marcellus thus anticipates the Christological arguments of the fifth century over how the human and divine elements of Jesus are related, but for the present, he certainly identifies with the consubstantial nature of Father and Son as expressed at Nicaea. Nevertheless, the Jesus Marcellus depicts is unconvincing in representing the Christ of the New Testament.

There is a revealing anecdote about Athanasius and Marcellus recorded by Epiphanius of Salamis in Cyprus in his compendium of heresies called the *Panarion*. Epiphanius once asked Athanasius what he thought of Marcellus and recalls that Athanasius "neither embarked on a defence of him nor on the other hand did he bitterly attack him, but by the appearance of a smile on his face he intimated that Marcellus was not far from error, but that he was to be excused".[25]

The followers of both Eustathius and Marcellus would in time coalesce in Antioch under their own bishop, Paulinus, forming an ultra-Nicene Church that would further split the Church in the city. It would take Athanasius to chart a course which would do justice both to the Son being consubstantial with the Father, and also fully God and fully human, so that he might reconcile man to God. But the path would be far from easy, and sometimes made more difficult by Athanasius's own implacability and inflexibility. Nevertheless, those qualities, if difficult, were central to his determination to establish a biblical understanding of the Trinity and a Christology for the future.

Athanasius

We have seen Athanasius move from being secretary to the previous Bishop of Alexandria, Alexander, to becoming bishop himself in 328. By 335, he was in exile, proscribed by the very emperor who had been the instigator of the Nicene Creed which Athanasius supported. It was his character rather than his beliefs which brought this about. For a fuller evaluation of his character, we must wait until the close of his career, however.

Following Nicaea, Athanasius returned with Alexander to Alexandria having had the invaluable experience of being present at the council, seeing the bishops at work, knowing the personalities, hearing the arguments and observing the emperor at close quarters. No doubt he was awestruck by the splendour of the occasion. This all added to the education provided through Alexander: a superlative grounding in the Scriptures, less familiarity with classical and philosophical texts, but which had nevertheless taught him a clear and powerful writing style.[26] Between 325 and 328, we hear nothing of note about Athanasius, until his election as bishop at the young age of 33 (or 31, if you date his birth to 297). So, at 33 he became one of the most powerful bishops in the Church. He had no previous experience of being a presbyter in a local church, having worked solely in the office of Alexander.

One of the grievances against Athanasius, eventually leading to his first exile, was the manner of his election as Bishop of Alexandria. There can be no doubt that this was his predecessor Alexander's stated intention and a role for which Athanasius had been groomed. However, complaints were lodged by his enemies about the manner of his choice. Naturally there is controversy about this. The role of a bishop had been changing since the accession of Constantine as emperor. Bishops were now increasingly civic as well as ecclesiastical leaders. Alexandria had become a metropolitan see with wide powers in Egypt and Libya.[27] Bishops became judges and arbitrators. They were to be chosen by the local church but consecrated by a wider group of bishops from the province or neighbouring dioceses. In this way, both the local and the catholic were assured. How the election of Athanasius was organized in a city as large and influential as Alexandria we cannot be sure. The sources are confused.[28] His enemies accused him of being made a bishop underage, when not yet 31. He was consecrated swiftly before anyone could object, and only by six or seven bishops. A later statement by the bishops of Egypt in 338 maintained that Athanasius *had* been properly elected. Other rumours maintained that he was secretly consecrated. Whatever happened, a section of the Church, probably connected to the Melitians and the Arian party, objected to his appointment and were determined to depose him. Indeed, the Melitians would make a pact with the Eusebian party, led by Eusebius of Nicomedia, although there is little evidence of this before 332.[29] By 334, charges were being brought against Athanasius at Caesarea, at Tyre in 335 and much later at Serdica in 343. Much of the antipathy towards Athanasius resulted from his resolve to suppress the Melitians with a strong hand, and even violently.[30]

The charges against Athanasius escalated in gravity, with some becoming increasingly far-fetched. They do show the lengths to which people would go in defending their doctrinal positions, or just removing an opponent.[31] The Church was not immune to skulduggery. It is fair to say there were elements of truth in some of the accusations, but they were also elaborated in a world where ascertaining facts was difficult. This is even more difficult in retrospect (indeed thousands of years later) because the main record of the charges was provided by Athanasius himself in his *Defence Against the Arians*, written during his second exile from 340 onwards as a record of all that happened.

The first accusation made by the Melitians was obscure and had to do with the provision of linen garments for the worship of a church in Alexandria. The charge was rebutted by two presbyters who supported Athanasius at the court of the emperor. The second accusation, impugning Athanasius's loyalty to the emperor, was that he had given a bag of gold to an official, Philoumenos, who was himself suspected of disloyalty. It was necessary for Athanasius to leave Alexandria after Easter in 331 and answer the charge at an imperial palace near Nicomedia. While there, he fell ill and was not able to return to Alexandria until after Easter of 332. Worse was to follow when further charges were brought against him by the Melitians, in which, it was said, one of his representatives (called Macarius) had visited a church in the Mareotis region of Alexandria and had used violence against its presbyter, Ischyras, breaking in the process a bishop's chair and a chalice. More bizarrely, Athanasius was charged with murdering a bishop called Arsenius through sorcery involving the bishop's severed hand. Although Athanasius did not deny the violence against the presbyter Ischyras, he maintained that Ischyras was falsely ordained by Colluthus, a leader of a sect. Yet given the murdered bishop was seen alive and well some months later in Egypt and then in Tyre, the murder charge was all too apparently a fabrication.

Although some of these charges were clearly malicious and unfounded, others appeared to come from a tendency in the Egyptian Church to settle disputes with force. This would become much more marked in later years, when the Bishop of Alexandria or the Pope would rely on marauding monks to do their bidding. A nadir was reached in the episcopacy of Cyril, when monks murdered the pagan philosopher Hypatia in a gruesome manner in 415 for her philosophical views and her involvement in the political life of Alexandria.

By 333, the grievances of the Melitians became increasingly allied with the doctrinal dispute around the use of *homoousios* in the Nicene Creed and the campaign waged by the Eusebians to reverse this. The Eusebians and the Melitians were now allied through their animosity to Athanasius. In 334, a council of bishops was called to meet at Caesarea in Palestine to look into Athanasius's conduct. He was summoned to appear but refused to attend. The following year this council of some 60 bishops was transferred to Tyre, where it was overseen by the emperor's appointee, the consular Dionysius, and chaired by Bishop Flacillus of Antioch.[32] The Eusebian party was swollen by two new bishops: Valens of Mursa and Ursacius of Singidunum. Their opposition would continue for many years. Athanasius was forced to attend by the emperor, and he reluctantly did so. An almost interminable list of charges was brought against him, including acts of violence against Melitian bishops, sexual irregularities, the case of Ischyras, and the macabre charge, brought by John Arcaph, that Athanasius had used a withered hand (actually produced as evidence of sorcery) to obtain the death of Bishop Arsenius.[33] The charges were heard and a commission of enquiry set up to investigate them in the Mareotis part of Alexandria. The commission was comprised of many of Athanasius's enemies, such as Theognis of Nicaea, Maris of Chalcedon and the said Ursacius and Valens. The commission was given support by the prefect of Egypt and Count Dionysius. By September 335, the commission reported to the council, and on the basis of their findings, Athanasius, who had by now left for Constantinople, was condemned principally for failure to appear at the earlier Council of Caesarea. Other things counted against him, such as the affair of the broken chalice, and his general disrespect for the Council of Tyre. The charge of the murder of Arsenius was dropped, however.

Athanasius was now deposed and forced into exile. It was a crushing blow. Although few specific charges were upheld, he could not overthrow the impression of "the indefensible use of violence in his see".[34] Athanasius would later rebut the charges and uphold his innocence in his *Defence Against the Arians*.[35] Nevertheless, the tendency in North Africa to use violence against the Melitians and the Donatists, who were themselves intransigently opposed to receiving back those who had lapsed in the recent persecutions, was very real. The Eusebians and the Arians used Athanasius's treatment of schismatics as a pretext for condemning his theology as well, and thus to pick off one of the prime advocates of the *homoousios* theology of the Nicene Creed. For his part, Athanasius highlighted their opposition to his theology of the Trinity as the underlying reason for their condemnation of his style.

In October 335, Athanasius was in Constantinople, where he met the emperor in the street. Constantine's own account of this meeting can be found in a letter to the bishops assembled at Tyre. Constantine wrote, "I chanced at the time to be upon horseback, on a sudden the bishop Athanasius with certain others whom he had with him approached me in the middle of the road, so unexpectedly as to occasion me much amazement."[36] Athanasius no doubt put his case to the emperor later, and not in the street, and Constantine wrote to the bishops at Tyre making sure that Athanasius had been fairly treated. Indeed, Athanasius asked Constantine to recall the Council of Tyre which had now moved to Jerusalem for the opening of the new church dedicated to the Holy Sepulchre. Nevertheless, something occurred while Athanasius was in Constantinople to turn the emperor completely against him. It was quite possibly a threat, either falsely made by Athanasius's enemies (as Athanasius himself indicates in *Contra Arianos* 86),[37] or possibly some intemperate words of his own, that he would delay the sending of corn ships from Alexandria to the capitals of the empire.

However much Constantine might agree with Athanasius on the doctrine of the Nicene Creed, any threat to the emperor's rule or authority would be treated robustly. Furthermore, the bishops at Tyre had by then sent a delegation to Constantine in Constantinople, explaining their decision for deposing Athanasius and quite probably poisoning the emperor's mind against him further. Perhaps they even suggested this threat of delaying the corn ships upon which Rome and Constantinople were dependent.[38]

In consequence, Athanasius was banished to Trier, the capital of the northern part of the empire on the Moselle. He was sent by boat from Constantinople, most probably to Marseille, and then by river to Gaul. He would remain in Trier in the imperial residence of Constantine's older son, Constantine II, for nearly two years.[39] Unable to understand the local language and in an unfamiliar cold climate starkly different from that of North Africa and the Mediterranean, Athanasius needed occupation. It may have been there (although the dating is notoriously difficult) that he started to write, or at least sketch out, his seminal theological work *Contra Gentes* and *De Incarnatione*. He would have had every reason to do so and the time and resources to make a start. This dual work would be the benchmark of Athanasius's theological thought, and the foundation of all his indictment of Arianism.

Notes

1 Averil Cameron, "The Reign of Constantine", in Alan K. Bowman, Peter Garnsey and Averil Cameron (eds), *The Cambridge Ancient History, second edition, Vol. XII: The Crisis of Empire, A.D. 193–337* (Cambridge: Cambridge University Press, 2005), p. 105.

2 Mark J. Edwards, *Religions of the Constantinian Empire* (Oxford: Oxford University Press, 2015), p. 188.

3 Lewis Carroll, *Alice Through the Looking Glass* (Oxford: Oxford University Press, World's Classics, 2003), p. 15.

4 "Letter of Eusebius of Caesarea to the people of his Diocese", in *Nicene and Post-Nicene Fathers: Second Series, Vol. IV Athanasius: Selected Works and Letters*, ed. Philip Schaff (Edinburgh: T&T Clark, 1987), p. 74, para 5.

5 Timothy D. Barnes, *Constantine and Eusebius* (Cambridge, MA: Harvard University Press, 1984), p. 227, and Hans-Georg Opitz, *Urkunden*, p. 27.

6 R. P. C. Hanson, *The Search for the Christian Doctrine of God: The Arian Controversy 318–381* (Edinburgh: T&T Clark, 1988), p. 176; Opitz, *Urkunden* III No. 32.

7 Hanson, *The Search for the Christian Doctrine of God*, p. 178, citing Simonetti, *La Crisi Ariana nel IV Secolo* (Rome: Institutum Patristicum Augustinianum, 1975), pp. 120–4.

8 Barnes, *Constantine and Eusebius*, p. 229; Opitz, *Urkunden* 29.

9 Barnes, *Constantine and Eusebius*, p. 229.

10 Barnes, *Constantine and Eusebius*, p. 233; Opitz, *Urkunden* 33.

11 Barnes, *Constantine and Eusebius*, p. 233.

12 Barnes, *Constantine and Eusebius*, p. 233.

13 Socrates, *Church History* I.38, in *Nicene and Post-Nicene Fathers: Second Series, Vol. II: Socrates, Sozomenus: Church Histories*, ed. Philip Schaff (Grand Rapids, MI: Eerdmans, 1987), p. 34.

14 Barnes, *Constantine and Eusebius*, p. 213.

15 Hanson, *The Search for the Christian Doctrine of God*, p. 212.

16 Ayres, *Nicaea and its Legacy*, p. 101 (citing DGS 50, Sozomen, *Hist Ecc.* 2.8, NPNF, Vol. II.2).

17 Ayres, *Nicaea and its Legacy*, p. 101.

18 Barnes, *Constantine and Eusebius*, p. 228.

19 Barnes, *Constantine and Eusebius*, p. 228.

20 Athanasius, *Historia Arianorum* 4, in *Nicene and Post-Nicene Fathers: Second Series, Vol. IV Athanasius: Selected Works and Letters*, ed. Philip Schaff (Edinburgh: T&T Clark, 1987), p. 271.

21 Hanson, *The Search for the Christian Doctrine of God*, p. 218.

22 Hanson, *The Search for the Christian Doctrine of God*, p. 224, citing *Contra Marcellum* I.i.4.

23 Hanson, *The Search for the Christian Doctrine of God*, pp. 226–7.

24 Hanson, *The Search for the Christian Doctrine of God*, p. 229.

25 Epiphanius, *Panarion* 72.4.4.

26 David M. Gwynn, *Athanasius of Alexandria: Bishop, Theologian, Ascetic, Father* (Oxford: Oxford University Press, 2012), p. 5.

27 Henry Chadwick, Edward C. Hobbs and Wilhelm Wuellner (eds), *The Role of The Christian Bishop in Ancient Society protocol of the thirty-fifth colloquy, 25 February 1979* (Berkeley, CA: Center for Hermeneutical Studies, 1980), p. 4.

28 Hanson, *The Search for the Christian Doctrine of God*, p. 247.

29 Athanasius, *Apology against the Arians*, Section 8, in *Nicene and Post-Nicene Fathers: Second Series, Vol. IV Athanasius: Selected Works and Letters*, ed. Philip Schaff (Edinburgh: T&T Clark, 1987), p. 104.

30 Hanson, *The Search for the Christian Doctrine of God*, p. 255.

31 Hanson, *The Search for the Christian Doctrine of God*, p. 256.

32 Hanson, *The Search for the Christian Doctrine of God*, p. 259.

33 Hanson, *The Search for the Christian Doctrine of God*, p. 260.

34 Hanson, *The Search for the Christian Doctrine of God*, p. 262.

35 See Athanasius, *Contra Arianos*, in *Nicene and Post-Nicene Fathers: Second Series, Vol. IV Athanasius: Selected Works and Letters*, ed. Philip Schaff (Edinburgh: T&T Clark, 1987), Part II, paras 59ff., pp. 131–47.

36 Constantine, "Letter to the Bishops Assembled at Tyre", in *Apologia contra Arianos* 86, in *Nicene and Post-Nicene Fathers: Second Series, Vol. IV Athanasius: Selected Works and Letters*, ed. Philip Schaff (Edinburgh: T&T Clark, 1987), Part II, pp. 145–6.

37 Constantine, "Letter to the Bishops Assembled at Tyre", p. 146.

38 Constantine, "Letter to the Bishops Assembled at Tyre", p. 146.

39 Gwynn, *Athanasius of Alexandria*, p. 30.

CHAPTER 6

Laying theological foundations: *De Incarnatione*

It is hard to be precise about the development of Athanasius's theological thought, but we can be sure that although the foundations were laid early on, application to the Arian controversy developed considerably over time. In fact, the period from the laying of those foundations in *Contra Gentes: De Incarnatione* (to give this seminal work its full title) until the later work, *De Decretis* (*c.*355)—the period that includes his narrative work about the Arian controversy, *Apologia contra Arianos* (*c.*340 onwards)—covers a full 25 years. This very fact demonstrates the longevity of this controversy, with its many twists and turns, but also the development of Athanasius's own thought about it, and his views on how best to combat its influence.

Far from making the Nicene Creed the bulwark of his defence, it is worth noting that the term *homoousios* only occurs once in his *Orationes contra Arianos* (339–46),[1] the Council of Nicaea is barely mentioned at all, and there is no mention of Arianism until 335,[2] ten years after the council. In other words, it was a controversy with a long theological fuse, which took time to fully combust. But however long the framing of this controversy, Athanasius's theological foundations were all but set from early on, especially if we date his great work of *Contra Gentes: De Incarnatione* early in his ministry, and possibly from the time of his first exile in Trier.

Although the dating of this foundational work, for which Athanasius is generally best known, is notoriously difficult, recent scholarship prefers an earlier date of around 328–35.[3] If this is the case, it is not far-fetched to suppose that Athanasius may have written or completed it during his first exile in Trier (335–7), which was the northern capital of the empire, and well known to Constantine and his father, Constantius Chlorus. Detained at the discretion of Constantine, provided with the imperial support of board and lodging and quite probably with writing materials also, and removed from the day-to-day responsibility of running a large diocese, Athanasius certainly would have had the occasion, leisure and facilities to pen an important theological work. Also, the scope of the work is not limited to the controversy over the Nicene Creed, but in fact ranges over the wider ground of the corruption and errors of paganism and the nature of the incarnation.

It is therefore a twofold work or treatise: the first part, *Contra Gentes*, is negative and highlights the emptiness and deception of idolatry, while *De Incarnatione* is a sustained exposition of the significance of Christ's incarnation. C. S. Lewis, in his preface to an English translation published in 1944, wrote that "Athanasius stood for the Trinitarian Doctrine 'whole and undefiled' when it looked as if all the civilized world was slipping back from Christianity into the religion of Arius".[4] It is a work that has stood the test of time and repays close study.

Contra gentes

Contra gentes is the first part of a twofold work. It is the necessary backdrop to the second part *On the Incarnation* (*De Incarnatione*). It supplies the reason for the incarnation or the Word taking on flesh. It is the black cushion on which the jewel of Christ's coming is laid. In many ways, it approximates the first three chapters of the epistle to the Romans, in which Paul sets out a bleak diagnosis of the human condition, and quotes Psalm 14:3, "They have all gone astray, they are all alike perverse; there is no one who does good, no, not one". And in a world which had only recently, through the Edict of Milan (313) and the conquest of the east by Constantine (324), admitted Christianity as a religion which might be lawfully followed, Athanasius was giving a rational apology and defence of the Christian faith as well as an indictment of paganism.

Contra gentes was written to an individual, either historical or metaphorical, as indeed was the entire work, much in the same way Luke addressed his two-volume work of Gospel and Acts of the Apostles to Theophilus (see Luke 1:3 and Acts 1:1). In Athanasius's case, this person is called "lover of Christ", "lover of discipleship", "friend" or "blessed one" throughout, giving a sense it could be written for everyone, or that Athanasius may have had one friend in mind. In the opening section, Athanasius goes on to explain to this person that knowledge of the truth may come from Holy Scripture, the words of blessed teachers, and through contemplation of God's actions.[5] By contrast, pagans resort to mocking Christianity because they cannot understand the Cross:

> For if they had really applied their minds to his divinity, they would not have mocked at so great a thing, but rather would have recognized that he was the Saviour of the universe and that the cross was not the ruin but the salvation of creation. For if, now that the cross has been set up, all idolatry has been overthrown, and by this sign all demonic activity is put to flight, and only Christ is worshipped, and through him the Father is known . . . should one not rather confess that he who ascended the cross is the Word of God and the Saviour of the universe?[6]

Having begun so boldly, Athanasius contrasts the reality of Christianity with the unreality of paganism. Paganism is characterized by the deception that idols are real. In contrast, through contemplation, filtered through purity of belief and understanding, a Christian is able to attain blessedness. Athanasius summarizes this in a sweeping analysis:

> For God, the creator of the universe and king of all, who is beyond all being and human thought, since he is good and bountiful, has made mankind in his own image through his own Word, our Saviour Jesus Christ; and he also made man perceptive and understanding of reality through his similarity to him, giving him also a conception and knowledge of his own eternity, so that as long as he kept this likeness he might never abandon his concept of God or leave the company of the saints, but retaining the grace of him (Christ) bestowed it on him, and also the special power

> given him by the Father's Word, he might rejoice and converse with God, living an idyllic and truly blessed and immortal life.[7]

With other devotional writers of the fourth century, such as the Cappadocian Fathers, Athanasius goes on immediately to say that such a person "becomes superior to sensual things and all bodily impressions, and by the power of his mind clings to the divine and intelligible realities of heaven".[8] And furthermore, such a person "rejoices in contemplating [Christ] and is renewed by his desire for him, just as the holy scriptures say that the first man to be created, who was called Adam in Hebrew, had his mind fixed on God in *unembarrassed frankness*, and lived with the saints in the contemplation of intelligible reality, which he enjoyed in that place which the holy Moses figuratively called Paradise".[9] Here is more than an anticipation of Gregory of Nyssa's *Life of Moses* and of the tradition that "contemplation of intelligible reality" is the gateway to blessedness.

Having set this expectation before the reader, Athanasius now exposes the down-drag on humanity of the evil leading to idolatry, which in turn leads to deviant behaviour. Athanasius is uncompromising in following this progression. He says simply, "[Humanity] fell into selfish desires and preferred their own good to the contemplation of the divine."[10] And "they realized that they were not so much stripped of clothing as stripped of the contemplation of divine things, and they had turned their minds in the opposite direction".[11] "They exchanged contemplation of divine things to contemplation of the body." What a modern ring this has to it, given the almost obsessive regard for the body and its image in contemporary western society. For Athanasius this bodily obsession is the "unreality" born of evil, which results from false priorities. It is this evil that then leads to idolatry: "the prime cause of idolatry is evil. For since men learned to imagine evil *which had no reality*, similarly they also invented for themselves non-existent gods".[12] Athanasius then gives a lengthy description of forms of idolatry ranging from the worship of sun, moon and stars to the worship of various Egyptian and Greek pagan deities: Osiris and Horus to Zeus, Hermes or Dionysius. He makes the point that some gods, as in the case of emperors, are made by decree of the Roman Senate, which must be absurd: for how, he ironically asks, can a legislative body make a god? Quoting Wisdom 14:12–21, he says that "the idea of making idols was the beginning of fornication, and the invention of them was the corruption of life".[13] Just as Augustine would do in *City of God* written a hundred years later, Athanasius describes the pagan gods as debauched in their lifestyle. Thus, although Greeks and Romans do not have intercourse with their sisters, they nonetheless worship those (gods) who do often commit incest.[14] Scripture, whether Psalm 115:12–16 or Isaiah 44:10–20, shows the futility of idols and also demonstrates how suppression of the truth, or what Athanasius calls "reality", leads to deviant behaviour and sexual distortion.

Having set out the downward path of humanity that results from forsaking contemplation of the divine and true reality for concentration on the body and the creation of idols with its consequences for behaviour (especially sexuality), the latter part of *Contra gentes* moves to God's solution.[15] Athanasius stresses the immortality of the soul, present in a mortal body.[16] The soul has the capability of "meeting saints and angels no longer in their earthly bodies".[17] Furthermore, the soul may reach out and know the immortal God whose "attributes have been perceived and understood through his works" (here Athanasius cites Romans 1:20).[18] Indeed, the very order of creation, its symmetry and "concordant harmony" and its combinations of space and earth, of water and heat, of light and darkness, all display God's grandeur.[19] But then Athanasius poses the question: who is the Creator?[20] At this point he introduces the Word of the Father. "Who then is he, if not the all-holy Father of Christ, beyond all created being, who is supreme steersman, through his own wisdom and his own Word, our Lord and Saviour Christ, guides and orders the universe for our salvation and acts as seems best to him?"[21] The Word is further described as "the express image of the Father", not composite but one.[22] Having stated who the Word is, Athanasius describes with real tenderness the motives for God's mission and coming to created beings. In a piece teeming with theological ideas, he renders the purpose of the Word in redemption thus:

> He (the Word) is also kind. For a good being would be envious of no one, so he envies nobody existence but rather wishes everyone to exist (for exist we might understand flourish), in

> order to exercise his kindness. So, seeing that all created nature according to its definition is in a state of flux and dissolution, therefore to prevent this happening and the universe dissolving back into nothing, after making everything by his own eternal Word and bringing creation into existence, he did not abandon it to be carried away and suffer through his own nature, let it run the risk of returning to nothing. But being good, he governs and establishes the whole world through his Word who is himself God, in order that creation, illuminated by the leadership, providence, and ordering of the Word, may be able to remain firm, since it shares in the Word who is truly from the Father and is aided by him to exist, and lest it suffer what would happen, I mean a relapse into non-existence, if it were not protected by the Word.[23]

In other words, the Word is the one who brings hope and salvation out of the non-existence of humanity. The Word gives "life and protection".[24] And by obedience to this Word of God, "things on earth receive life and things in heaven subsist".[25] The Word is like a conductor of an orchestra, a choirmaster or a governor of a city, creating harmony where there was none.[26] The Word, "by a single mere act of will through his own power moves and supports both the visible world and the invisible powers, giving each their individual function, so that the divine powers have a more divine motion, and visible things are as we see them".[27] The Word is the messenger and interpreter of his Father.[28] Indeed, he is the window into the Father's being, as John said. "Whoever has seen me has seen the Father" (John 14:9). The Word is the one whom God created, speaking to him at the time of creation (Genesis 1:3–27). The Jews do not understand the nature of the Triune God: they grasp his unity but not his triune existence.[29] Only the Word can give knowledge of the Father.[30] But despite all this, people "exchanged the truth about God for a lie and worshipped and served the creature rather than the Creator" (Romans 1:25).[31]

This then is Athanasius's analysis of the human condition and the role of the Word. It is the first part of his great work, and he is now ready to move onto his second, for which he is best known, namely *De Incarnatione.*

De Incarnatione

De Incarnatione is the second half of Athanasius's major treatise, and as with the first part, *Contra Gentes*, so too with *De Incarnatione*: the starting point is that creation itself was created good, but humanity turned away from God through free will and so fell into evil. From the effects of this evil, humanity needed to be redeemed and for this purpose God in the person of the *Logos* took on human flesh. The result of this fall into evil was that "we were the cause of his incarnation, and for our salvation he had compassion to the extent of being born and revealed in a body".[32]

De Incarnatione pivots on a number of key theological arguments: the causes of the incarnation, the relationship of the *Logos* to human flesh and the consequences of the incarnation for humanity. As we can see, this work was not simply an answer to a set of problems which the Nicene party faced in view of the challenge of Arius. It is rather a wider statement, both of the status of the *Logos* in the Godhead, and the causes and consequences of the incarnation. Indeed, Athanasius's argument will be that if the *Logos* or the incarnate Christ was not fully God, not made from nothing, and without beginning but eternal, he could not have achieved the redemption of humanity for which purpose he came.

The cause of the incarnation was human corruption, and the subservience of the human race to death.[33] Because of the moral economy instituted by God himself in his creation, in which death followed the breaking of the law, the whole of humanity was subject to this interdict. "And it was impossible to flee the law, since this had been established by God because of the transgression."[34] This was the dilemma that confronted God as a result of human corruption. It was not that this was unanticipated in the wisdom and foreknowledge of God (see Ephesians 1:4; 1 Peter 1:20), but that the costs of remedying this headlong fall into corruption became inescapable. This is the first divine dilemma—how to rescue humanity from its wholesale consignment to the power of death whilst upholding the moral order first established for God's creation. As God could not repeal the law he had established, another way must be found (presumably known since before creation, see 1 Peter 1:20). This was the incarnation. At this point, Athanasius argues strongly God intervenes to reverse the sway of death and the dominance of corruption, saying, "by [humanity's] neglect the weakness (meaning vulnerability) of God rather than his goodness would be made known".[35] "For this reason, the incorporeal and incorruptible and immaterial Word of God came to our realm."[36]

Athanasius then begins to explain how the incarnation came about and the relationship of the *Logos*, the eternal second member of the Trinity, to the human body. "He took our body, and not simply that, but from a pure unspotted virgin ignorant of a man, a body pure and truly unalloyed by intercourse with men. For he, although powerful and the creator of the universe, fashioned for himself in the virgin a body as a temple, and appropriated it for his own instrument (*organon*) in which to be known and dwell."[37] This body, as we know, was subject to the normal corporeal restrictions (e.g., hunger, thirst, weariness, and time-place restrictions).[38] It was in this body that God acted as both man and God. Thus in the healing of Simon Peter's mother-in-law, it was a man, Jesus, who stretched out his hand, but the divine *Logos* who healed.

This relationship between the divine *Logos* and the human Jesus was a mystery which would continue to challenge the Church thereafter. How the divine *Logos* and the human Jesus were related was the subject of the Christological debates of the fifth century. The question would lead both to the definition of Chalcedon in 451 and the secession of the Egyptian Church, on the grounds that Chalcedon insufficiently stated the primacy of the divine *Logos*. For some, Athanasius's description of the incarnation can be compared to an astronaut putting on a space suit to exist in an atmosphere of weightlessness and vacuum. Thus, the Word or divine *Logos* put on a human suit to live and move in the mortal realm of humans.[39]

The second issue that Athanasius describes in *De Incarnatione* (after demonstrating that the only way of bringing about freedom from death for humanity was by God himself taking on human flesh) was how humanity might come to a true knowledge of God. Ever since the corruption of the human race following the disobedience in Adam, humanity's knowledge of God had been defiled by the worship of idols, which had replaced any true understanding. The question that Athanasius posed in this regard was, "what advantage would there be for those who had been made (human), if they did not *know* their own Maker?"[40] Although God had given the Law and the prophets to make known his ways, this proved insufficient.[41] Such knowledge could only come through God becoming like them: himself taking on human life. Indeed, Athanasius asks, "how could this be done, unless the very image of God were to come, our Saviour Jesus Christ?"[42] "So the Word of God came in his own person, in order that, as he is *the* image of his Father, he might be able to restore man who is in the image."[43] The purpose of the coming of the Son was "to lift [humanity] up and teach them his [their] true Father".[44] And Jesus gave many proofs through his miracles that he was "the Lord of the providence of the universe".[45]

Having shown how the incarnation deals with these two human predicaments of slavery to death and ignorance of true knowledge of God, Athanasius then shows how the death and resurrection of Jesus brings liberation from the bondage of death, without which the human race would be fatally enslaved. He maintains that Jesus's death was "justified because in no other way except through the cross did the salvation of all have to take place".[46] For Athanasius, the Cross, followed by the Resurrection, means "the dissolution of death".[47] The consequence of that dissolution means that "all believers in Christ tread on it [death] as something non-existent, and would rather die than deny their faith in Christ".[48] Athanasius then proceeds to indict the Jews for failing to believe that Jesus fulfilled their own Scriptures, and then indicts the Greeks who mock at God's wisdom as shown in the Cross.[49] Nor should the Greeks decry the incarnation, since Plato himself suggests that should the world "be in danger of sinking into a region of dissimilitude" he who begat the world would sit at its helm, help it and correct all its faults.[50] Again, in this part of *De Incarnatione*, Athanasius reverts to the idea that the *Logos* took on the body as a human instrument to achieve redemption. "Therefore, he became a man and used the body as a human instrument". Thus, if through a body death had come to all, now through a body life would overcome corruption.[51] (In many ways this echoes Paul's teaching of Romans 5:12–21).

In the final paragraphs of *De Incarnatione*, Athanasius comes to something of a peroration of his great work. In sentences of rhetorical power, he asks:

> When in short did the wisdom of the Greeks become folly, except when the true Wisdom of God revealed himself on earth? For formerly the whole world and every place were deceived by the worship of idols, and men thought nothing other than idols to be gods. But now throughout the whole world men are abandoning the superstitious worship of idols and are taking refuge in Christ and worshipping him as God: and through him they also recognize the Father, of whom they had been ignorant.[52]

And then, nearing the end of his great work, he famously writes:

> For he [Christ] became man that we might become divine; and he revealed himself through a body that we might receive an idea of the invisible Father; and he endured insults from men that we might inherit incorruption. He himself was harmed in no respect, as he is impassible and incorruptible and the very Word and God, but he cared for and saved suffering men, from whom he endured these things, by his impassibility. And, in short, the achievements of the Saviour effected through his incarnation are of such a kind and so great, that if anyone wished to expound them, he would be like those who gaze at the vast expanse of sea and wish to count the number of waves.[53]

Athanasius concludes this work by commending its teaching to "the lover of Christ" to whom he is writing. Furthermore, he recommends to this "lover of Christ" the reading of Scripture: "If you take the opportunity to and read the words of the Scriptures and really apply your mind to them, you will learn from them more completely and more clearly the accuracy of what has been said."[54]

Undoubtedly, this two-book treatise forms the bedrock of Athanasius's understanding of the incarnation and although it was not especially focussed on the specifics of the Arian controversy, it undeniably shows his understanding of how the *Logos*, who was without beginning and truly God, not made, took on a human body as an "instrument" of salvation. It would be Gregory of Nazianzus in his letter to Cledonius (*c.*382) who some years later would give us the dictum that "the unassumed (by the Son) is not healed" and then further extrapolate and develop the teaching of Athanasius, as we shall see.[55] *De Incarnatione's* understanding is principally derived from Scripture, and its propositions undergird the future framework of the Arian debate which we will come to. What *Contra Gentes* and *De Incarnatione* deal with in broad outline, Athanasius, in his later work of the *Orationes contra Arianos*, spells out with greater reference to the issues of the Arian controversy and the biblical texts from which the Arians wrongly derive their views.

Orationes contra Arianos

If Athanasius wrote his double treatise of *Contra Gentes* and *De Incarnatione* in or around his first exile in Trier in *c*.335–7, almost certainly his second more specifically anti-Arian work, *Orationes contra Arianos*, was written in Rome during his second exile (339–46). This exile resulted from the increasing power of the Arian party and the succession of Constantius after the death of Constantine the Great in 337. Constantius was to prove an implacable adversary of Athanasius, as indeed Athanasius was of him.

The *Orationes contra Arianos*, as it sounds, were a series of discourses against Arianism, probably assembled in the years between Athanasius's restoration after his first exile until and during his second exile in Rome as the guest of Pope Julius, who was himself organizing opposition to Arianism. While in Rome, Athanasius made the acquaintance of Marcellus of Ancyra, also a fierce opponent of Arianism, but widely thought, as noted, to be Sabellian—including by the eastern bishops. Sabellius virtually made the Father and the Son indistinguishable. There are four Orations, with the fourth being of doubtful provenance. They are mostly concerned with the misuse of particular Scriptures by the Arians in their attempts to present the Son as inferior to the Father.

The dating of the *Orations* is uncertain, but quite possibly between 339 and 345,[56] by which time, as we shall see, the controversy had moved onto another stage after the deaths of Constantine (337) and Arius (336), but with the voice of Asterius (d. 341) taking up the Arian cause. Of the three orations that can be attributed to Athanasius, the first clearly lays the foundations of the indictment of Arianism. Here Athanasius makes broad theological points. In the first, he demonstrates the theological genealogy of Arianism. As Ayres writes, "In the Orations Athanasius both constructs a genealogy of Arianism for ecclesio-political reasons and enters into an existing theological debate with some force."[57]

The *First Oration* begins with a general attack on the Arians, who had been seduced, Athanasius says, by the Devil. Athanasius goes on to show the error of Arius's teaching in the *Thalia*: in maintaining that God was not always a Father, and that there was a time when the Son was not.[58] Indeed, according to Arius, God was alone before the creation of the Son from nothing, *ex nihilo*. Arians, Athanasius says, come to their conclusions through a distortion of Scripture which Athanasius will have to refute.[59] By contrast, Athanasius demonstrates from scriptural texts the eternal nature of the Son,[60] especially John's statement in the Prologue of his Gospel that, "In the beginning was the Word, and the Word was with God, and the Word was God. He was in the beginning with God" (John 1:1,2). This is a foundational text proving the eternal nature of the Son from Scripture. Athanasius goes on to assert that there is One Godhead who is also a Triad.[61] It is the Greeks (or their philosophy) who introduced the idea of an originated Triad (i.e., one that was brought into being), "but the faith of Christians acknowledges the blessed Triad as unalterable and perfect and ever what it was, neither adding to it what is more, nor imputing to it any loss".[62] In order to emphasize the closeness of the Father to the Son, Athanasius interestingly does not use the disputed word *homoousios* from the Nicene Creed—it is only used once in the *Orations*—but instead uses the word *ídios*, meaning proper. So, Athanasius says, "this Wisdom is not a passion nor a part, but an Offspring proper to the Father".[63] "Thus, the nature of the Son was proper to human nature and also proper to the Godhead."[64] Once again this is an indication of a vocabulary being formed in the midst of a controversy to project orthodoxy. Furthermore, as the Son is the image of the Father, and the Father is impassible, so likewise is the Son in himself impassible.

Having set out a few home truths about the eternal nature of the Trinity and attacked the Arians in the main points of their misapprehension, Athanasius goes on to reinterpret their misleading use of Scripture. There are many Scriptures the Arians twist to their own ends, and whose false interpretation Athanasius refutes. Among them we will consider three.

In Chapter XI §37 of the *First Oration*, Athanasius responds to the false treatment by the Arians of the famous Christological passage in Philippians 2. The line of reasoning the Arians use in relation to Philippians 2:5–11, is that Jesus *became* the Son of God as a reward for his obedience to the Father. In other words, they read into the words "Therefore God has highly exalted him and gave him the name that is above every name, that at the name of Jesus every knee should bow in heaven and under the earth and every tongue confess that Jesus is Lord" that he *became* the exalted Son of God, and was given the name above every name as a reward. This is the Arian interpretation of one of the classic passages about the incarnation in the New Testament. In refuting this interpretation Athanasius writes, "He was not man, and then became God, but he was God, and then became man, and that to deify us . . . .He was not from a lower state promoted, but rather existing as God, he took the form of a servant, and in taking it, was not promoted but humbled himself."[65] In any event, the Arians gloss over the earlier affirmation by Paul in the passage that "though he was in the form of God . . . [he] emptied himself" (Philippians 2:6–7).

The most famous text stirring continual debate between the Arians and the Orthodox Nicene party was Proverbs 8:22, "The Lord created me at the beginning of his work, the first of his acts of long ago". The Arians used this as a proof text of the creation of the Word, which was synonymous with Wisdom, to demonstrate that Wisdom or the Word was the first of God's creations. Thus, the Word or the Son is seen as a created being and does not exist eternally. In Khaled Anatolios's text taken from the *Second Oration* against the Arians, Athanasius's reply runs to 64 pages.[66] The scope of this reply, or rebuttal, is both textual and broadly theological. It brims with vigour and argument. Athanasius is not slow to call the Arians heretics and is quick to deploy some of his well-worn lines of argument against them.

His theological rebuttal of the idea that Christ as Wisdom is the first of the Father's creation owes much to the writings of St John in his Gospel and to Paul. In other words, Athanasius interprets Scripture with Scripture and only agrees with an interpretation that sits well with all.

Referring to John 1:3, he thus says, "through him all things were made: without him nothing was made that has been made", and that "the Word would not be maker of all things if he himself was one of the things created".[67] Furthermore, the Son is described as proper to the Father (*idios*—an important term for Athanasius).[68] The Father expresses this likeness in saying, "This is my Son, the Beloved, with whom I am well pleased" (Matthew 3:17). The Father works providence and salvation through the Son.[69] Later in his rebuttal, Athanasius uses an *ousia* word, which is rare in his writings at this stage. So, he argues "if he (the Word) is not a beginning nor a creature, then clearly as far as his being and nature, he stands apart from creatures and is other than they are, being the likeness (*homoiosis*) and image of the only true God, and is himself unique and one".[70] It is worth pointing out that Athanasius uses the word *homoiosis* (and later *homoios*),[71] meaning like in substance, rather than the Nicene word *homoousios*, meaning of the same substance. Finally, Athanasius makes the point that there would have been no salvation or, to use his adventurous word, no deification (or *theosis*) if the Word had been created. To quote him fully:

> But humanity would not have been deified if joined to a creature, or unless the Son was true God. And humanity would not have come into the presence of the Father unless the one who put on the body was his true Word by nature. Just as we would not have been freed from sin and the curse unless the flesh which the Word put on was human by nature—for there would be no communion for us with what is other than human—so also humanity would not have been deified unless the Word who became flesh was by nature from the Father and true and proper (*idios*) to him. Therefore, the conjoining that came about was such as to join what is human by nature to what is of the nature of divinity, so that humanity's salvation and deification might be secured.[72]

Here is the nub of Athanasius's theology, in which any interpretation of a single verse must find its place. It is the starting point for any evaluation of the Arians' interpretation of Proverbs 8:22, or for that matter of any Scripture. For Athanasius, this was the sum of Scripture on the incarnation.

In this theological light, Athanasius comes to the Arian interpretation of Proverbs 8:22. Theirs is the simple case that this verse says that Wisdom, meaning the Word, is created. Therefore, the Word is not eternal. There was a time when the Word was not, and when the Father was not a Father, having no Son. If Athanasius had already shown that such an interpretation violates Scripture, in his exegesis he makes the case that the Arians have misinterpreted the verse in its own terms. Athanasius firstly says that in the passage, Solomon is speaking proverbially and figuratively: as in a parable and not literally.[73] Furthermore, the true meaning is more that God begets or brings forth rather than creates Wisdom or the Word. In other words, the verses speak of begetting rather than creating, and that the Word or Wisdom is an offspring and not a creation. The mystery of that begetting is that the Son is proper to the Father or of the same or like substance.

The third example of Athanasius's rebuttal of erroneous Arian teaching from a scriptural text comes in his *Third Oration* written around 345 and concerns the interpretation of John 14:10: "I am in the Father and the Father is in me". In his interpretation, the Arian teacher Asterius maintains that the Son follows the Father's desires and works in the Father's power, which is true, as John himself says in 5:19. Only Asterius goes on to say that this is because the Son lacks power and wisdom in himself. Athanasius responds to this by writing, "For the Son is in the Father, as it is allowed us to know, because the whole Being of the Son is proper to the Father's essence as radiance from light, and stream from fountain; so that whoso sees the Son, sees what is proper to the Father, and knows that the Son's being, because from the Father, is therefore in the Father."[74]

Athanasius once again falls back on the word "proper" (*idios*) rather than vocabulary indicating being of the same substance. Yet his point here is that although they are one, they are also distinct, and the Father is not the Son, and the Son is not the Father, in the sense that each has a separate role and function. Thus, the Son is the one who wipes away sin, and he is the Light of the world.[75] In this section, Athanasius is at pains to emphasize the unity of the Godhead, but also the distinctiveness of the activity of Father and Son.[76]

In these texts, including *Contra Gentes* and *De Incarnatione*, we see Athanasius laying the groundwork of his theology, and then, in the *Orations*, applying this theology to misinterpretations of the Scriptures by the Arians, and calling them theologically to account. It is a theology from which Athanasius will not swerve, but the controversy had many twists and turns ahead. Indeed, for the next 30 years, from the time of the *Third Oration* (*c*.345), and for the remainder of his life, he would have to recalibrate the theological terms in which he fought this fight and eventually revert to the terminology of the Nicene Creed, which was conspicuous by its absence in these early years of the controversy after Nicaea. And the controversy would ebb and flow in relation to the deployment of imperial power. With the death of Constantine the Great in 337, and although recalled to his see from his exile in Trier, Athanasius soon found that he had a far greater opponent in Constantius, the heir who took control of the eastern empire following his father's death. There were years of continuous struggle ahead, until others took up the baton of orthodoxy.

Notes

1 David M. Gwynn, *Athanasius of Alexandria: Bishop, Theologian, Ascetic, Father* (Oxford: Oxford University Press, 2012), p. 86.

2 Gwynn, *Athanasius of Alexandria*, p. 77.

3 Gwynn, *Athanasius of Alexandria*, p. 55.

4 *St. Athanasius on the Incarnation: The Treatise* De Incarnatione Verbi Dei, tr. and ed. A Religious of C.S.M.V., with an introduction by C. S. Lewis (London: Centenary Press, 1944), p. 9.

5 Athanasius, *Contra gentes* 1, tr. Robert W. Thompson, Oxford Early Christian Texts (Oxford: Oxford University Press, 1971), p. 3.

6 Athanasius, *Contra gentes* §2, op. cit., p. 5.

7 Athanasius, *Contra gentes* §2, op. cit., p. 7.

8 Athanasius, *Contra gentes* §2, op. cit., p. 7.

9 Athanasius, *Contra gentes* §2, op. cit., pp. 7–8.

10 Athanasius, *Contra gentes* §2, op. cit., p. 7.

11 Athanasius, *Contra gentes* §3, op. cit., p. 9.

12 Athanasius, *Contra gentes*, §8, op. cit., p. 21.

13 Athanasius, *Contra gentes* §11, op. cit., p. 31.

14 Athanasius, *Contra gentes* §13, op. cit., pp. 36–7.

15 Athanasius, *Contra gentes* §26, op. cit., p. 69.

16 Athanasius, *Contra gentes* §33, op. cit., p. 91.

17 Athanasius, *Contra gentes* §33, op. cit., p. 91.

18 Athanasius, *Contra gentes* §35, op. cit., p. 97.

19 Athanasius, *Contra gentes* §38, op. cit., p. 105.

20 Athanasius, *Contra gentes* §39, op. cit., p. 109.

21 Athanasius, *Contra gentes* §40, op. cit., p. 111.

22 Athanasius, *Contra gentes* §41, op. cit., p. 113.

23 Athanasius, *Contra gentes* §41, op. cit., p. 115.

24 Athanasius, *Contra gentes* §42, op. cit., p. 115.

25 Athanasius, *Contra gentes* §42, op. cit., p. 117.

26 Athanasius, *Contra gentes* §43, op. cit., pp. 120–1.

27 Athanasius, *Contra gentes* §44, op. cit., p. 123.

28 Athanasius, *Contra gentes* §45, op. cit., p. 123.

29 Athanasius, *Contra gentes* §46, op. cit., p. 129.

30 Athanasius, *Contra gentes* §47, op. cit., p. 131.

31 Athanasius, *Contra gentes* §47, op. cit., p. 133.

32 Athanasius, *De Incarnatione* §3, op. cit., p. 143.

33 Athanasius, *De Incarnatione* §5, op. cit., p. 145.

34 Athanasius, *De Incarnatione* §6, op. cit., p. 147.

35 Athanasius, *De Incarnatione* §6, op. cit., p. 149.

36 Athanasius, *De Incarnatione* §8, op. cit., p. 151.

37 Athanasius, *De Incarnatione* §8, op. cit., p. 153.

38 Hanson, *The Search for the Christian Doctrine of God*, p. 448.

39 Hanson, *The Search for the Christian Doctrine of God*, p. 448.

40 Athanasius, *De Incarnatione* §11, op. cit., p. 159.

41 Athanasius, *De Incarnatione* §13, op. cit., p. 165.

42 Athanasius, *De Incarnatione* §13, op. cit., p. 165.

43 Athanasius, *De Incarnatione* §13, op. cit., p. 167.

44 Athanasius, *De Incarnatione* §15, op. cit., pp. 171–3.

45 Athanasius, *De Incarnatione* §19, op. cit., p. 181.

46 Athanasius, *De Incarnatione* §26, op. cit., p. 197.

47 Athanasius, *De Incarnatione* §27, op. cit., p. 199.

48 Athanasius, *De Incarnatione* §27, op. cit., p. 99.

49 Athanasius, *De Incarnatione* §33ff., op. cit., pp. 215–35.

50 Athanasius, *De Incarnatione* §43, op. cit., p. 243.

51 Athanasius, *De Incarnatione* §44ff., op. cit., pp. 245–9.

52 Athanasius, *De Incarnatione* §46, op. cit., p. 251.

53 Athanasius, *De Incarnatione* §55, op. cit., p. 271.

54 Athanasius, *De Incarnatione* §56, op. cit., p. 273.

55 St Gregory of Nazianzus, *On God and Christ* (Yonkers, NY: St Vladimir's Press, 2002), p. 158.

56 Hanson, *The Search for the Christian Doctrine of God*, p. 419.

57 Ayres, *Nicaea and its Legacy*, p. 110.

58 Athanasius, *Orationes* I §2, in *Nicene and Post-Nicene Fathers: Second Series, Vol. IV Athanasius: Selected Works and Letters*, ed. Philip Schaff (Edinburgh: T&T Clark, 1987), p. 308.

59 Athanasius, *Orationes* I §3, op. cit., p. 310ff.

60 Athanasius, *Orationes* I §4, op. cit., pp. 312–14.

61 Athanasius, *Orationes* I §6, op. cit., p. 316.

62 Athanasius, *Orationes* I §6, op. cit., p. 317.

63 Athanasius, *Orationes contra Arianos* I §28, op. cit., p. 323.

64 Ayres, *Nicaea and its Legacy*, p. 114.

65 Athanasius, *Orationes contra Arianos* I §39, op. cit., p. 329.

66 Khaled Anatolios, *Athanasius* (London: Routledge, 2004), pp. 111–75.

67 Athanasius, *Orationes contra Arianos* II §26, op. cit., p. 116.

68 Athanasius, *Orationes contra Arianos* II §26, op. cit., p. 118.

69 Athanasius, *Orationes contra Arianos* II §26, op. cit., p. 119.

70 Athanasius, *Orationes contra Arianos* II §49, op. cit., p. 142.

71 Athanasius, *Orationes contra Arianos* II §61, op. cit., p. 155.

72 Athanasius, *Orationes contra Arianos* II §70, op. cit., p. 163.

73 Athanasius, *Orationes contra Arianos* II §44, 45, op. cit., pp. 138–9.

74 Athanasius, *Orationes contra Arianos* III §3, op. cit., p. 395.

75 Athanasius, *Orationes contra Arianos* III §4, op. cit., p. 395.

76 Athanasius, *Orationes contra Arianos* III §5, 6, op. cit., pp. 396ff.

CHAPTER 7

Humans seeking the divine (337–57)

Constantine the Great died on 22 May 337 at the Feast of Pentecost. He had felt ill soon after Easter that year. Although he took hot baths in Constantinople to relieve his symptoms and yet more in Helenopolis, the city dedicated to his mother, his condition deteriorated.[1] He summoned a group of bishops led by Eusebius of Nicomedia and requested baptism. For "he felt the time had come at which he should seek purification from sins of his past career, firmly believing that whatever errors he had committed as a mortal man, his soul would be purified from them through the efficacy of the mystical words and the salutary waters of baptism".[2] He was baptized in Nicomedia. Eusebius continued: "Thus was Constantine the first of all sovereigns who was regenerated and perfected in a Church dedicated to the martyrs of Christ; thus gifted with the Divine seal of baptism, he rejoiced in his spirit, was renewed, and filled with heavenly light".[3] He set aside his clothes of imperial purple and from then on wore only the purest white.

Historians and church people have debated the sincerity of the emperor's faith ever since. Eusebius's panegyric of Constantine is often doubted, since he was never close to the emperor.[4] He pretended to know Constantine's mind on the succession, for instance, when in reality he was ignorant of it. Undoubtedly Constantine was a complex person, given to strong passions, conservative in outlook, valuing the virtues of efficiency, hard work and moral restraint. Nonetheless, he publicly espoused the cause of Christ, both on the battlefield and at his court, and was more than content to lecture the court and his bishops on Christian faith. For this reason, he supported the building of churches in Palestine in Jerusalem, Bethlehem and Mamre.[5] He ended persecution and supported toleration. But to a figure so important in the history of the empire and the Church, other accretions soon attached themselves. A legend grew that Pope Sylvester (*r.*314–35) prayed effectively for Constantine's healing from leprosy, and the papacy gained as a result powers of supremacy and authority in the western empire, even over secular kings and rulers. This came to be known as the "Donation of Constantine" and was probably a ninth-century invention, quite possibly emanating from the Abbey of Dennis near Paris.[6] The authenticity of this document was later exposed by the Italian humanist, Lorenzo Valla, in 1440.

Power plays almost always followed the death of an emperor, and Constantine's death was no exception. Although Eusebius was confident that the empire was to be divided up on the death of Constantine, others were less so. Great public mourning greeted his death: "The soldiery came in respectful order to mourn as a flock the removal of their good shepherd. The people meanwhile ran wildly throughout the city [Constantinople], some expressing the inward sorrow of their hearts by loud cries, others appeared confounded with grief."[7] His body was taken to rest in an imperial mausoleum in a porphyry sarcophagus, along with the expectation that the other apostles would eventually come to be buried in tombs prepared around him in a newly built Church of the Apostles. This of course never happened. Only the bones of Timothy and Luke were located and buried nearby.[8] A later bishop of Constantinople removed Constantine's remains to another church, only to have them moved back to the Church of the Apostles by his successor Constantius. All these arrangements were ultimately destroyed in the sack of Constantinople by the Turks in 1453, when the mausoleum, the Church of the Apostles and the bones of Constantine were lost through the vagaries of history.

Even as the obsequies were underway, so was a process of seizing power. In September 337, there was a *coup d'état* in which several of the progeny of Constantine's father by his later marriage to Theodora were murdered. In what Gibbon called a "promiscuous massacre", nine members of this family were murdered with few survivors.[9] Julian, six years old in 337, survived and would become the apostate emperor on the death of Constantius II in 361. It was quite probable that Constantine wanted the empire shared between his sons and the descendants of his father by Theodora, but it is typical of Roman acquisition of power that such hopes would not be realized. With the very dubious blessing of Eusebius, the historian, Constantine's three sons divided the empire.

After the massacre of most of their cousins in September, the three sons of Constantine met at Pannonia in the autumn of 337 to effectively carve up the vast empire of Constantine. The eldest, Constantine II, retained Gaul, Spain and Britain where he had been appointed Caesar by his father, but where he wanted greater territory and control. Constantius II, who had masterminded the funeral arrangements and mourning for his father in Constantinople, retained the eastern empire and was based at Antioch. The youngest, Constans, who was Caesar of the rest of the western empire, controlled eastern Gaul, Italy and North Africa and was based at Trier and Rome. Each son now became *augustus* or emperor but inevitably their sibling rivalry, differing views and dissimilar challenges led to conflicting priorities in their government. Constantius II faced a resurgent Persia under Sapor I and a divided Church in the east following Nicaea. Constans faced incursions of barbarians from across the Rhine, and a rival claimant and usurper in Magnentius at Autun in eastern Gaul from 340. Constantine II, the eldest son, wanted to restore the east-west divide of the empire and so proceeded, fatally, against his younger brother Constans. In an ambush close to Aquileia, Constantine II was killed and his body thrown into the River Alsa (Ausa).[10] By 340, the empire was again ruled by two *augustii*: Constantius II in Antioch and Constantinople, and Constans in Trier and Milan. Rome's significance as a strategic and military centre was now passing. It was in this political melee of two emperors, two courts and two centres of power that the affairs of the Church were played out. Ecclesiastical politics had become affairs of state since the days of Constantine, and in fact this would remain the case in western Europe until the late nineteenth century.

Antioch

Following the division of the empire among the three sons of Constantine in Pannonia in 337, Constantius returned to his base at Antioch, where he had been *caesar* until his elevation to *augustus* in that year. It quickly became evident where his sympathies in the Arian controversy lay.

He secured the transfer of Eusebius from Nicomedia to the disputed bishopric of Constantinople in 338, where Eusebius remained until his death in 341. Known as a supreme political tactician and fixer, Eusebius had managed to effect the deposition of members of the Nicene party, including Eustathius of Antioch in 330, Athanasius in 335, and Marcellus of Ancyra in 336. Eusebius was to dominate ecclesiastical politics in the early years of Constantius's reign.[11] Although he was too late to reverse the decision taken by Constantine II to restore Athanasius to his see in 337, the following year in 338, at a council in Antioch, Eusebius managed to engineer the deposition of Athanasius, and consequently his second exile which lasted until 346. In fact, a new bishop called Gregory of Cappadocia was appointed to Alexandria and installed by the prefect of Egypt on Constantius's orders in March 339. In 341, the dedication of the Golden Church in Antioch, begun by Constantine, provided the opportunity to call a further Council of Antioch and revisit the theology and creed of Nicaea. It would be the first of many councils and many creeds in the coming years in the search to create a new creed.

—

The Council of Antioch met between May and September of 341 under the chairmanship of Flacillus. The main instigators were Eusebius, now Bishop of Constantinople, Akakius of Caesarea, and Gregory of Alexandria. The Arian theologian Asterius, loathed by Athanasius, was also in attendance. The background to the council was a desire by the Arian party to reverse the Nicene Creed, but also to coordinate a response to Pope Julius, who had intervened powerfully on Athanasius's behalf and had criticized the conveners of the Council of Antioch. Julius had himself held a council in Rome the previous year in late 340 to re-examine Athanasius's case.[12] The council had declared Athanasius innocent of all charges, and in particular of those brought against him at the Council of Tyre (335), in which he had been charged with using violence, breaking a communion chalice and murdering a bishop, Arsenius, who had since been seen alive! The council in Rome had further kindled the ire of Antioch for warmly receiving Marcellus, the exiled Bishop of Ancyra. Julius had written to the conveners of the Council of

Antioch but, according to Athanasius's journal of the Arian controversy, received a testy and impolite reply. Julius wrote, "I have read your letter which was brought to me by my presbyters Elpidius and Philoxenus, and I am surprised to find that, whereas I wrote to you in charity and with conscious sincerity, you have replied to me in an unbecoming and contentious temper; for the pride and arrogance of the writers is plainly exhibited in that letter."[13]

Beyond the ecclesiastical ping pong between Antioch and Rome, between Julius and Eusebius, and indeed between the rival *augustii*, Constantius and Constans, the Council of Antioch did set about the serious business of creed-making, and if possible, of replacing the Nicene Creed. Four credal formulae were produced, one after the end of the council.[14] Of these creeds the most important was the Dedication Creed or the Second Creed of the Council. This creed does seem a genuine attempt at compromise between the language of Nicaea and the aspirations of a more moderate Arian party. Of the Son it says:

> We believe in one Lord Jesus Christ. He is only begotten Son, God, through whom are all things, who was begotten from the Father before the ages, God from God, whole from whole, sole from sole, perfect from perfect, King from King, Lord from Lord, living wisdom, true Light, Way, Truth, unchanging and unaltering, exact image of the Godhead, and the substance and will and power and glory of the Father, first-born of all creation who was in the beginning with God.

At first glance, this creed appears to have turned its back on some of the tenets of Arianism. The Son is begotten of the Father and not created. It emphasizes the distinctiveness of the Son and is anti-Sabellian in tone.[15] "The Son was the exact image of the Godhead and the *ousia* and will and power and glory of the Father". Although the creed uses *ousia* language, it does so in imitation of the Arian teacher Asterius, who was present at the council.[16] And behind Asterius was the figure of Lucian of Antioch, the probable teacher of Arius himself.[17] Hence there was the suspicion among Athanasius and other Nicene bishops that in its many words, its use of *ousia* language—albeit less clear-cut than the *homoousios* language of Nicaea—the creed hid a trojan horse of Arianism. Further suspicion of this came from there being no mention that the kingdom of the Son would endure for ever.

More positively, it could be seen as an attempt to meet Nicene theology halfway. It used the X from X language (e.g., God from God, Light from Light etc., which was present in the Nicene Creed), indicating the unique relationship of the Son with the Father and underlining the Son's similar divinity. And the phrase "exact image", one that Athanasius himself used, was employed to describe the Son's relationship with the Father.[18] So convincing was the creed to the western Trinitarian theologian and bishop, Hilary of Poitiers (315–68) that he saw it as principally constructed against the Sabellianism of Marcellus of Ancyra, in which there is insufficient distinction between the Father and the Son, rather than being anti-Nicene. Such were the complexities of the times, people wondered which heresy any creed was designed to combat. Hilary, for his part, saw it as a creed he could incorporate in explaining his own Trinitarian theology.[19] Despite its nuances, the Dedication Creed did not gain sufficient traction in the churches of east and west to be more than a staging post in this extended period of creed-making. Indeed, we know that the Fourth Creed of Antioch was taken by a party of eastern bishops to Constans in Trier, to convince him of the orthodoxy of Antioch, and, on the strength of it, to summon with Constantius a further council of eastern and western bishops. What we do know is that by 343, just two years later, the emperors Constans and Constantius had called for a further council, this time at Serdica, present-day Sofia in Bulgaria.

The debacle of Serdica

Occasionally a council is a complete fiasco, as the Second Council of Ephesus would be a century later. Serdica was one such council. Motivated by a desire for reconciliation between east and west, it never came near its goal. Although Constans was first persuaded to call the council, both he and his brother Constantius were initially engaged in military campaigns: Constantius in Persia and Constans in Britain. But by the autumn of 343, Constans was ready to host the council, accompanied by Athanasius and several other deposed eastern bishops. A small group of western bishops, including Maximinus of Trier, Protasius of Milan, Ossius of Cordoba (now an old man in his late eighties), Fortunatianus of Aquileia, and Vincent of Capua attended.[20] Constantius was represented by some of his military commanders, who paved the way for the eastern bishops and helped with their travelling arrangements. In all, there were 178 bishops: 98 from the west and 80 from the east, small by comparison with Nicaea.

Soon the ecclesial-political axis was all too obvious. Constans supported his western bishops, Athanasius and Pope Julius, who, in keeping with the tradition of the popes, did not personally attend but sent presbyters to represent him. The reluctant eastern bishops were housed separately in a part of the imperial palace. They refused to meet with the western bishops until those eastern bishops, previously condemned by a council (eastern), were separated out from the western bishops.[21] As this was not going to happen, the council never met. As Hanson put it: "The Easterners had no intention of allowing the Westerners to review decisions which they were competent to make; the Westerners had no intention of behaving as if the decision of a Council of Rome could be regarded as ineffective. The Easterners had a perfectly good case, and this fact till recently has not been sufficiently realized. Western bishops had no right to review the verdicts of Eastern Councils."[22]

It was a complete breakdown of trust. Both sides issued their own documents and anathemas. The easterners wanted to reopen the case of Athanasius's behaviour in his diocese and have a further commission of enquiry sent to Alexandria, and in particular to the Mareotis region. Furthermore, the fact that Marcellus of Ancyra had been given unqualified support in the west increased their distrust of the western bishops and their seemingly Sabellian tendency, which was further reinforced by some of their published theology. For their part, the western bishops excommunicated ten eastern bishops, including the bogeymen Valens and Ursacius who had accused Athanasius. And while the eastern bishops issued the Fourth Creed from the recent Council at Antioch as a summary of their Trinitarian theology, the western bishops published eight documents, five of which were addressed to the Egyptian Church, on issues relating to Athanasius and his treatment.[23]

When it came to the theology of the Trinity, both east and west showed that they were on a journey of expression. The eastern bishops had sent to Constans the Fourth Creed of Antioch as their theological summary and benchmark of their creeds. Although it was orthodox in so far as it went, it pointedly did not include any of the *ousia* language which had been in the Dedication Creed of Antioch and which was a yardstick for the west. Equally, the western bishops issued a long profession of faith at Serdica. In this profession, they were at pains to outlaw any notion that Christ was not true God and not of the same substance as the Father; to outlaw any sense that the *Logos* suffered and died (i.e., was not impassable); and finally to outlaw any notion that the *hypostases* of the Father, Son and Spirit were distinct.[24] If you were "marking the homework" of east and west impartially, you would maintain that the eastern bishops were very weak in demonstrating that the Father and Son were of the same substance, and therefore both fully God. You would also say that the western bishops had yet adequately to express the distinctiveness of Father, Son and Spirit as individuated *hypostases*, and that they needed to show how the human and divine in Jesus suffered and died. But it is right to say that the misunderstandings between east and west related to differing use of the terms *ousia* and *hypostasis*: with the west looking for *ousia* to express unity between Father and Son, and the east using *hypostasis* to express the distinctiveness of Father, Son and Spirit in terms of their activities and roles. Further confusion was added by the west using *hypostasis* interchangeably with *ousia*, while the east followed a tradition of Origen which allowed for each person of the Trinity to be a distinct *hypostasis* in the Godhead.

What we do know is that by the end, far from it being a reconciling or healing event, Serdica left both sides further apart than they had been at the beginning. The rift had only deepened, and Serdica demonstrated how little either side knew of the theology of the other, or indeed wanted to know. Although the Council did not help forward any reconciliation between East and West, Serdica did mark a significant milestone in the influence of papal power. After such a shock it was incumbent on true members of the body of Christ to look for ways of reconciliation. Put at its simplest, one side was guilty of Arianism, and the other of Sabellianism: a way forward needed to be found.

Attempts at rapprochement

Both emperors had a role to play in bringing about reconciliation, just as their father had attempted at Nicaea, but each was occupied with other political and military matters. Constantius had been bequeathed a war by Constantine in the east and, while the Council of Serdica took place, he was in Persia engaging in the Battle of Singara. Later he would relieve the important city of Nisbis from Sapor II's siege. Much of this campaign was fought around holding or losing fortresses in Mesopotamia, and Constantius was soon bogged down—as his successor Emperor Julian quickly pointed out. Meanwhile, by 350 Constans faced a usurper in the west in Magnentius, a popular general in Gaul and Britain who raised a rebellion.

Constans fled in the face of this rebellion and was killed by Magnentius's followers, accused of corruption and vice. On hearing of this, Constantius left off his campaign in the east and marched to engage Magnentius at Mursa in present-day eastern Croatia, where Magnentius was defeated. A final battle took place between Constantius and Magnentius at Mons Seleucus in south-eastern France close to the Alps, after which Magnentius died by suicide.

It is worth remembering that the emperors whose religious attitudes had become integral to the peace of the Church were at the same time administering vast areas of empire, dealing with almost incessant rebellions and incursions, and were often threatened by the people closest to them in their courts. However, despite so many distractions, it had become the policy of Constantine's family to take the lead in Church affairs according to their own lights. Following the failure of Serdica, Constans, a man of mixed reputation, took up the cause of Athanasius and, according to Socrates's *Ecclesiastical History,* threatened his brother Constantius with war unless he reinstated Athanasius to the see of Alexandria.[25] Whether Constans's embassy to his older brother contained such a threat (which seems unlikely), Constantius wrote to Athanasius asking him to come to his court, then in Edessa, before returning to Alexandria.[26] In fact, three letters were written by Constantius to Athanasius and the people of Alexandria. In the second, the emperor wrote, "We have thought good to send back to you your Bishop Athanasius, a man known to all men for the uprightness that is in him, and for the good disposition of his personal character."[27] Athanasius proceeded slowly and circumspectly to his diocese via Trier, Aquileia and Jerusalem, where a synod was held by Bishop Maximus, and where Athanasius's communion with other regional bishops in Syria and Palestine was restored. He probably met Constantius in Antioch in 346, and at some point, at the end of this year, was restored to his see. He would remain there relatively untroubled for ten years (346–56) in what became known as "the Golden Decade".

East-west relations in the Church moved slowly and haltingly towards a fragile and temporary reconciliation. Immediately after Serdica, a delegation to restore relations between east and west had gone from Pope Julius to Antioch, consisting of Bishop Euphrates of Cologne and Bishop Vincentius of Apua. Stephen, Bishop of Antioch, hardly helped matters by placing a prostitute in the bedroom of Bishop Euphrates and accusing him of fornication. It sounds more like an old KGB honeytrap than fraternal relations between churches! The plot miscarried and the instigator was exposed. Stephen was deposed, another bishop of Antioch was appointed, and a further Council of Antioch was called in 345, which produced yet another creed.

This creed became known as the Macrostitch Creed because of the way it was written in a long line form. The first part is almost identical with the Fourth Antiochene Creed of 341 which had previously been sent to Constans. A few new anathemas were added: against those who say there are three gods or that Christ is not God; that neither Christ nor the Son of God existed before all ages; that the Father, Son and Holy Spirit are the same; that the Son is unbegotten; or that the Father did not beget the Son either by his counsel or will.[28] A further lengthy explanation was added to this, but traces of Origenist subordination of the Son to the Father can be found, although there is no mention of three *hypostases*. Thus, the explanation goes on:

> The sole self-sufficient and unbegotten and invisible God is one only, the Father of the Only-begotten, who alone has being and graciously gives being to other things. This is not to deny that Christ is God, and we reject the doctrine of Paul of Samosata that he became God after the Incarnation and was till then a

> mere man. Even though he is subordinated to the Father, still he is God "according to his perfect and true nature".[29]

The creed goes on to condemn Sabellians, Patripassians (those who hold that the Father suffered in the Son), Marcellus of Ancyra, and Photinus, Bishop of Sirmium. Although there is no mention of separate *hypostases* and the divinity of the Son is affirmed, it also refuses to use *ousia* language and in particular *homoousios*. It maintains the subordination of the Son to the Father, and that the Son was not eternally generated, leaving open the suggestion that there was a time when he was not begotten, but in the substance of the Father. You might say the authors had moved away from crude Arianism, were firm in their condemnation of Sabellianism in all its forms, but were not ready to subscribe to the idea of the Son being of the same substance as the Father. The new Bishop of Antioch, Leontius, wanted to take steps towards the west, but subscribing to Nicaea was still a step too far.

The Macrostitch Creed was brought to Milan in 345 as the latest credal offering of the east along with a lengthy theological explanation. The council in Milan agreed to the excommunication of Photinus. The bishops Valens and Ursacius, who had earlier accused Athanasius at Tyre and Serdica, now disowned Arius, so the mood music for reconciliation was hopeful. In 347 or 348, a further council was held in Sirmium, present-day Sremska Mitrovica on the Sava, west of Belgrade, when Constantius II was passing through. The decision of Milan was noted, but nothing substantive changed. If Constantius at this moment was all sweetness and reason, three years hence his attitude would change from cooperation to coercion. By then politics would have put him in the driving seat across the empire.

In 351, Constantius, as we have seen, defeated the usurper, the popular general Magnentius, who had rebelled against Constans's rule and who in turn had been accused of corruption, cruelty and homosexuality. We are told by the chronicler, Sulpicius Severus, that during the battle Constantius was at prayer in a nearby church when news of the outcome was brought to him by Bishop Valens of Mursa, the early accuser of Athanasius. The civil war continued until August 353 when Magnentius was finally defeated. At this point, Constantius ruled over the whole of the empire from Milan. His success was limited, however.

Ancient historians tend to take anything but objective positions in their biographies. For instance, Constantine the Great was lionized by Eusebius of Caesarea, while Zosimus, a very inaccurate pagan historian, regarded Constantine the Great as vicious and profligate. Thus, he wrote, "Constantine, having done this [founded Constantinople] not only continued to waste the revenue of the empire in useless expenses, and in presents to mean and worthless persons, but oppressed those who paid tributes, and enriched those that were useless to the state, for he mistook prodigality to munificence."[30] Likewise, when it came to assessing Constantius, there were contrasting views. Ammianus Marcellinus regarded him as an inconstant and vacillating emperor, generally persuaded by the last person who spoke to him. Church historians, including Athanasius in his *History of Arianism* (*c*.340), regarded him as a full-blooded Arian and persecutor of the true Church.[31] Later historians, such as Edward Gibbon, regarded him as weak and degenerate, while von Harnack saw him as an oriental despot. Still others testified to a mildness of manner in his actions. His successor, Julian the Apostate (who was no fool), in his panegyric extolled him as "tolerant, even at times merciful".[32] Perhaps the truth lay somewhere between the extreme accusations of Lucifer of Calaris, whom Constantius hardly upbraided for his outspoken attacks, and the description of a meek emperor who prayed during battles. In fact, he may have had the same desire as his father to bring peace to the Church, been closer to the Greek Fathers' description of the Trinity and espoused the *homoian* cause to which we shall come, and then used force to impose this "solution" and sought to silence Athanasius once and for all.

By 351, the movement towards reconciliation which had followed the disaster of Serdica had begun to swing into reverse, although it would not reach a new pitch until 356. A further Council of Antioch set about deposing Athanasius again and replacing him with George of Cappadocia (Gregory having died before Athanasius's return in 346). George was a learned individual with strong anti-pagan opinions, but firmly in the eastern camp when it came to the Trinity. He had to bide his time replacing Athanasius, whose pomp in Alexandria, after his triumphal return to the city in 346, was compared by Gregory of Nazianzus to Christ's arrival in Jerusalem on Palm Sunday. A further creed was produced at Antioch. It began with 27 anathemas and was firmly anti-Nicene. In its sixth anathema, it condemned any who said that "the Son is *ousia* of God extended, or the extension of his *ousia*". Once again, the term *ousia* was front and centre in the debate.

Constantius was now beginning to exert greater control over the Church in the west and through his officers in the east and Alexandria as well. A series of councils were called in the west, namely at Milan and Arles. In 353, a council met at Arles at which pressure was exerted on western bishops to disown Athanasius and what he stood for, and to support the appointment of George of Cappadocia to Alexandria. By this point, a new Bishop of Rome (or pope), Liberius, and Dionysius, Bishop of Milan, were willing to abandon Athanasius.[33] A further council met in Milan in 355, at which further Arian-izing doctrines were put forward, but we have few details. Other bishops who had been faithful to Nicaea, in particular Ossius of Cordoba, were now put under greater pressure and there was a definite movement towards rehabilitating Arian teaching.

Athanasius was becoming more and more isolated as Constantius wrested control of the Church's teaching and intimidated bishops into obeying him or face exile. Athanasius issued a long defence of his actions to Constantius in his *Apologia ad Constantium*. He denied supporting Constans against his brother, categorically stating, "I never saw your brother by myself, nor did he ever converse with me in private."[34] He rejected the charge of wrongly using a church that had not yet been dedicated for an Easter communion, citing occasions where this had happened before.[35] But by the late summer of 355, Constantius's officers, including General Syrianus, were circling in Alexandria ready to arrest Athanasius.[36] On the night of 8/9 February 356, soldiers surrounded the Church of Theonas where Athanasius was at prayer and attempted to arrest him. There were few more dramatic moments in Athanasius's career as a bishop, but he managed to elude capture and escape into hiding.

The next few years would see Athanasius hiding in the Egyptian desert. At the same time, they would see the appearance of a new brand of Arianism, variously designated *homoian* or *homoiousion* or *anomoios*, whose niceties we will explain, led by Aetius and Eunomius. These years also saw the fightback by Athanasius in his most pugnacious rendering of the Arian controversy, his *Defence against Arianism*. Furthermore, Athanasius, who had initially been slow to use the *ousia* terms of Nicaea and the benchmark term of *homoousios* in his earlier writings, now solidly pitched his tent on defending the language of the Nicene Creed in his *Defence of Nicaea* or *De Decretis Nicaenae Synodi*. And later we will see him excoriate the Arian creeds of Sirmium and Seluchia.

Constantius had only five years to live until 361, but in many ways the years from 356 saw the fulcrum of the controversy before new protagonists in succession to Athanasius took up the cause. Whilst Athanasius was hiding in the desert, out of reach of Constantius, and producing a steady stream of writings, time proved to be on his side.

Notes

1 Eusebius, *Vita Constantini* IV, op. cit., p. 206.

2 Eusebius, *Vita Constantini* IV, op. cit., p. 206.

3 Eusebius, *Vita Constantini* IV, op. cit., p. 207.

4 Timothy D. Barnes, *Constantine and Eusebius* (Cambridge, MA: Harvard University Press, 1981), p. 266.

5 Barnes, *Constantine and Eusebius*, p. 267.

6 David Potter, *Constantine the Emperor* (Oxford: Oxford University Press, 2013), p. 295.

7 Eusebius, *Vita Constantini* IV, op. cit., p. 209.

8 Potter, *Constantine the Emperor*, p. 292.

9 David Hunt, "The Successors of Constantine", in Averil Cameron and Peter Garnsey (eds), *The Cambridge Ancient History, Vol. XIII, The Late Empire,* AD *337–425* (Cambridge: Cambridge University Press, 1997), p. 3.

10 Hunt, "The Successors of Constantine", p. 5.

11 Hunt, "The Successors of Constantine", p. 11.

12 David M. Gwynn, *Athanasius of Alexandria: Bishop, Theologian, Ascetic, Father* (Oxford: Oxford University Press, 2012), p. 34.

13 Athanasius, *Apologia contra Arianos* 2, in *Nicene and Post-Nicene Fathers: Second Series, Vol. IV Athanasius: Selected Works and Letters*, ed. Philip Schaff (Edinburgh: T&T Clark, 1987), p. 111.

14 R. P. C. Hanson, *The Search for the Christian Doctrine of God: The Arian Controversy 318–381* (Edinburgh: T&T Clark, 1988), p. 285.

15 J. N. D. Kelly, *Early Christian Doctrines* (London: Adam and Charles Black, 1960), p. 247.

16 Lewis Ayres, *Nicaea and its Legacy* (Oxford: Oxford University Press, 2006), p. 119.

17 Hanson, *The Search for the Christian Doctrine of God*, p. 289.

18 Ayres, *Nicaea and its Legacy*, p. 120.

19 Ayres, *Nicaea and its Legacy*, p. 121.

20 Hanson, *The Search for the Christian Doctrine of God*, p. 294.

21 Hanson, *The Search for the Christian Doctrine of God*, p. 295.

22 Hanson, *The Search for the Christian Doctrine of God*, p. 295.

23 Hanson, *The Search for the Christian Doctrine of God*, p. 299.

24 Ayres, *Nicaea and its Legacy*, p. 125.

25 Socrates, *The Ecclesiastical History* (Amazon Publication, 2021), Chapter XXII, p. 87.

26 Hanson, *The Search for the Christian Doctrine of God*, p. 307.

27 Athanasius, *Apologia contra Arianos* §55, op. cit., p. 129.

28 Hanson, *The Search for the Christian Doctrine of God*, p. 309.

29 Hanson, *The Search for the Christian Doctrine of God*, p. 310.

30 Zosimus, *The New History, Book II*, Odins Library Classics (Amazon Printing, 2021).

31 Hanson, *The Search for the Christian Doctrine of God*, p. 318.

32 Hanson, *The Search for the Christian Doctrine of God*, p. 321.

33 Hanson, *The Search for the Christian Doctrine of God*, p. 330.

34 Athanasius, *Apologia ad Constantium* §3, in *Nicene and Post-Nicene Fathers: Second Series, Vol. IV Athanasius: Selected Works and Letters*, ed. Philip Schaff (Edinburgh: T&T Clark, 1987), p. 239.

35 Athanasius, *Apologia ad Constantium* §14, op. cit., p. 243.

36 Athanasius, *Apologia ad Constantium* §22, op. cit., p. 246.

CHAPTER 8

The teeth of the storm

Arianism was never the work of a single man: in all of its stages of development it had many advocates giving it various nuances of meaning. It was also a mixture of theology, Greek philosophy and the exercise of imperial power. If imperial power had ended the persecution of the Church with the Edict of Milan, it had also sought to establish peace in the Church at the Council of Nicaea. Later, in the person of Constantius, imperial power espoused a form of Arianism which it thought reasonable, but which was not biblical. By 356, Constantius was ready to move against Athanasius, whom he saw as his main opponent in reaching a settlement over the Arian issue.

In a way reminiscent of the much later attack by King Henry II's knights on Thomas Becket, Constantius sent soldiers on the night of 8/9 February into the great Alexandrian church of Theonas to arrest Athanasius and remove him from office. In his *Defence before Constantius*, Athanasius maintains that soldiers led by the imperial general Syrianus came looking for him:

> When I saw the assault begin, I first exhorted the people to retire, and then withdrew myself after them, God hiding and guiding me, as those who were with me at the time witness. Since then, I have remained by myself, though I have all confidence to answer for my conduct, in the first place before God, and also before your Piety, for that I did not flee and desert my people, but can point to the attack of the General upon us, as a proof of persecution.[1]

From then on, Athanasius went into hiding and began his long third exile which would last until the end of the emperor's reign in 361.

During his exile, Athanasius was replaced by George of Cappadocia, who was made Bishop of Alexandria in his stead. But far from being an unproductive time for Athanasius, he produced some of his most creative and important works whilst in hiding. In the meantime, further nuances of Arianism were arising at the same time as Athanasius was strengthening his commitment to the language of Nicaea.

The catalyst of Sirmium (357)

In 357, there was a relatively minor meeting of bishops at Sirmium (Mitrovica, Serbia) that signalled a hardening of thought with reference to the *ousia* language used to define the relationship of the Father and Son in the Trinity.[2] The agitators behind this move were the old opponents of Athanasius, Bishops Ursacius and Valens, who managed to pressurize the now almost centenarian bishop, Ossius of Cordoba, into agreeing with them. Other bishops, such as Potamius of Lisbon and Germinius of Sirmium, were also present, but it was a small gathering. The document or creed produced by this meeting was based on the Fourth Antiochene Creed of 341 which had become a kind of benchmark for the Arian position. It was marked by a complete absence of any *ousia* terminology and went as far as saying that "to speak more explicitly *homoousion* or *homoiousion*, there should be no mention of it whatever, nor should anyone preach it".[3] Indeed, some more moderately Arian bishops like Akakius of Caesarea and Eudoxius of Antioch saw *homoian* as a way forward, in terms of a compromise with the Nicene party. It was a way of describing the Son as like the Father, without using *ousia* terminology. However, *homoian* as a statement of how Father and Son related was quite insufficient for Athanasius.

This Latin Creed of Sirmium of 357 went on to say unambiguously that the Father is greater than the Son. Thus, it proclaimed:

> Nobody is unaware that this is catholic doctrine, that there are two Persons (personas) of the Father and the Son, and that the Father is greater, and the Son is subjected in common with all things which the Father subjected to him; that the Father has no

> beginning, is invisible, immortal and impassable; but the Son is born from the Father, God from God, Light from Light, whose generation as Son, as has been said already, no one knows except the Father.[4]

It was on the one hand unambiguously Arian in its subordination of the Son to the Father, but on the other, it had little to say about the relation of the Word to the Son, the manner of the Son's generation or the suffering of the Word in Christ's human body received through Mary and the Spirit.

The reaction to this creed was not slow in coming. It was called "The Blasphemy of Sirmium" by its opponents. Hilary called it "Ossius' Lunacy", and it provoked a reworking of the Nicene position both by Hilary in the west and in Egypt by Athanasius. It also precipitated a harder Arian response in the writings of Aetius and Eunomius, to whom we will come.

Athanasius, *De Decretis* and *De Synodis*

We have already seen how Athanasius was gradually building up his polemic against the Arians. The bedrock of his thinking may be found in *Contra Gentes* and *De Incarnatione* and then in his slightly later *Orations against the Arians.* Furthermore, he built up a history of the Arian controversy in his *Apologia contra Arianos* from around 345. But having eschewed the *ousia* language in most of his writings, preferring to answer the Arians in their own terms point by point, he then returns to the great phrases and words of Nicaea to rebut the resurgent Arianism of Sirmium 357 and before. Athanasius had probably begun this process or reappraisal of his defence before his third exile and the meeting of bishops at Sirmium in 357. But the outcome of Sirmium, when he came to learn about it, must have only strengthened his decision to revisit the declaration of Nicaea and its language.

There were two works from around this period which demonstrate Athanasius's thinking. They were *De Decretis* and *De Synodis*, on the

Councils of Ariminum and Seleucia. Scholars tend to date *De Decretis* from 353–6 and *De Synodis* from 359–61.[5]

The principal aim of *De Decretis* was to uphold the language of *homoousios* as the best defence against all the assaults of Arianism. Athanasius begins by cataloguing the problems Arians had with the Council of Nicaea. He compares the Arians to the Jews who could not elevate the Word to being part of the Godhead.[6] The Arian party led by Eusebius of Nicomedia was treated with courtesy. Although they had signed their agreement to the Nicene Creed, it soon became evident that they believed something else. They maintained that the Son was created out of nothing, that there was a time when he did not exist,[7] and only when the Son was brought into existence was God known as Father. Athanasius's main concern against the teaching of Eusebius and Asterius the Sophist, the other leading Arian of the mid fourth century, was to maintain the ontological unity of the Father and the Son.[8] Having stated the errors of the Arians, Athanasius now moved to an explanation of the Nicene Creed, its method and the language it chose to defend the ontological unity of Father and Son. This section of *De Decretis* is the kernel of its teaching:

> The Council, wishing to do away with the irreligious phrases of the Arians, and to use instead the acknowledged words of the Scriptures, that the Son is not from nothing but "from God", and is "Word" and "Wisdom", and not creature or work, but a proper offspring from the Father. But the Eusebians, compelled by their inveterate heterodoxy, understood the phrase being "from God" as belonging to us. . . . But the [Church] Fathers, perceiving their craft and the cunning of their irreligion, were forced to express more distinctly the sense of the words "from God", in order that "from God" might not be considered common and equal in the Son and in things originate, but that all others might be acknowledged as creatures, and the Word alone as from the Father (*ek tēs ousias*).[9]

Later on, when the bishops still saw the Arians "winking with their eyes and making out that words like 'always' and 'power' and 'in him' were as before common to us and the Son, they sought to clarify yet further, and in an unmistakeable way, that the Son was 'of the essence' and 'one in essence'" thus placing all 'catchwords of irreligion' out of reach".[10] The watchword was that the Father was *homoousios* with the Son.

Athanasius had given new breath and power to the Creed. Whereas neither he nor the Church had hitherto used it in their defence of the Trinity, from now on it would become centre stage in the expression of orthodoxy. Barely known in the western Church, Athanasius made the Nicene Creed the touchstone of Trinitarian orthodoxy. There was no better single word like *homoousios* that succinctly defended the ontological reality of the Father, Son and Spirit.[11] The treatment of the Spirit in Nicaea and beyond was an important benchmark, to whose significance we shall come.

However, Athanasius was not yet done with theological writing. Much else poured out from him whilst he was in this long exile from 356–61, but one final salvo was written by Athanasius against the emperor's attempt to engineer a compromise in the long-running Arian controversy. This compromise took the form of a separate agreement by the western and eastern bishops to a new creed, the so-called Dated Creed, in 359.

Constantius's plan was to have two almost concurrent councils drawn from the west and the east and to get a separate agreement to a preordained creed, which had elements of compromise in it from the differing theological parties. The two sites selected for these concurrent councils were Seleucia in Cilicia for the eastern empire and Ariminum in Italy for the western. Although the plan seemed neat enough, it would prove inadequate for the task of reconciling deeply held differences across the Arian divide. At the very least, the two councils showed there was little traction for neo-Arianism of a more extreme kind, and as proposed by Eunomius, to whom we will come. The issue would remain the extent to which Father and Son were of the same substance.

The prearranged creed for the councils to agree to was the Dated Creed (itself a term of mockery for the Nicene party: for how could a creed which expressed eternal verities be dated?) Following a council in Ancyra in 358, Basil of Ancyra had the emperor's ear and for a while had been his chief theological adviser. Basil represented the *homoiousios* faction, in which the Son and the Spirit were *like in substance to the Father*. The Dated Creed was a joint effort created by Mark of Arethusa, George of Alexandria, Basil and the duo Valens and Ursacius.[12] The terminology of the creed sought to gain the support of the *like in substance* lobby and the *like in will* lobby (*homoian*), but this was not to be achieved easily. The creed was accompanied by a letter from George of Laodicea in which further theology about the Trinity was set out. In particular, George stated the individual *hypostasis* of each member of the Trinity using the term which had been used to suggest the individuated entity of each member. He maintained that "the person (*hypostasis*) of the Son is like the Person (*hypostasis*) of the Father"; but he fought shy of the Nicene conviction that although each member is their own *hypostasis*, they share a common substance.[13] His letter and the creed were therefore still subordinationist; it was just a question of how that was expressed.

With preparation done, the councils had only to agree, but once again the bishops were shown to be unruly officers of the empire. In the east at Seleucia, 160 bishops came together, although some prominent leaders, like Basil of Ancyra, Cyril of Jerusalem and Eustathius of Sebaste, could not attend because there were suits or cases against them in the Church courts. The main body of bishops fell into two parties, the *homoiousians*, and the *homoians* led by Akakius of Caesarea, Basil of Ancyra's main rival. Akakius was to take the initiative and maintain the Son was only *like the Father in will but not in substance*. Akakius would now have the ear of the emperor. At Ariminum (Rimini), 400 western bishops gathered and were not in conciliatory mood towards the emperor. They objected to the Dated Creed and declared loyalty to the Nicene. They appointed a delegation of ten bishops to come to his court at Adrianople, but Constantius refused to see them and began to pressure them to agree, intimating they might be exiled. A series of anathemas were agreed which broadly condemned Athanasius. On the basis of this and a subsequent meeting of some bishops at Nice in Thrace, the Dated Creed was agreed, with one amendment: all mention of *ousia* and *hypostasis* was erased. It was a clear victory for the *homoian* party, but from the deserts of Egypt and in exile Athanasius would have a further, if not the final, word.

It is an indication of Athanasius's finger on the pulse of the developments at Seleucia and Ariminum that he began writing *De Synodis* about these two councils even before they finished. Not only that, but he appears to have had faithful and reliable informers from the councils who told him of the proceedings and furnished him with texts of creeds being considered (see §26, 27), and of the correspondence that ensued with the emperor, such as in an open letter to Constantius from Ariminum.[14] Although an exile and fugitive in the deserts of Egypt, Athanasius still very much had his heart set on the continuing struggle with the advocates of Arianism.

Athanasius began to compose his *De Synodis Arimini et Seleuciae* even before the Council of Seleuciae had broken up on 1 October, and the emperor had forced a new creed on the delegation from Ariminum on the tenth of that month.[15] It was a typical piece of Athanasian writing: thorough and clear, with extensive use of texts and a brief narrative of the Arian controversy. Athanasius was increasingly willing to distinguish between the differences in the debate and how to respond to them. If, on the one hand, the more clearly Arian bishops, such as Ursacius, Valens, George of Cappadocia (§37), Germinius, Auxentius and Germainicus at Sirminium, were condemned for their Arian tendencies, on the other Athanasius showed that he was prepared to reach out to the *homoiousians* and in particular Basil of Ancyra, and show himself more willing to engage with them, instead of simply classifying them as enemies.

In Section 41, Athanasius makes an important distinction between an intention behind the use or choice of words and the expression of that intention. He makes the assertion that those who accept Nicaea but have difficulty with the idea of Father and Son being of the same essence "should not be regarded as enemies":

> For, confessing that the Son is from the essence of the Father, and not from other subsistence, and that he is not a creature nor a work, but his genuine and natural offspring, and that he is eternally with the Father and being his word and wisdom, they are not far from accepting the phrase "coessential" (or *homoousios*). Now such is Basil who wrote from Ancyra concerning the faith.[16]

If Athanasius recognized that overtures might be made to Basil of Ancyra and those represented by him in order to widen support for the Nicene position of *homoousios*, in reality such a move was hard to achieve. By the end of the Council of Arminum, Constantius had committed himself to the less Nicene *homoian* position, which was now advocated by Akakius who had become Constantius's chief ecclesiastical adviser. Even that position was short-lived. In 360, Constantius was having to move east again and confront a resurgent King Sapor of Persia whilst at the same time being threatened by his cousin Julian in Gaul and Pannonia.[17] Julian would succeed him, and become known as Julian the Apostate, as he would revert to paganism. Having dedicated Hagia Sophia, new great church in Constantinople—an earlier version of Justinian's great church—on 15 February 360, Constantius moved via Cappadocia to Edessa. In fact, Sapor did not give battle and Constantius returned to Antioch ready to take on Julian, but he fell ill and died near Tarsus.

The death of Constantius and accession of Julian was the occasion for Athanasius's restoration to his episcopacy in 362. The unpopular George, who had replaced Athanasius as Bishop of Alexandria during his years of exile, was first imprisoned and later lynched on 21 December 361, quite probably by the supporters of Athanasius, once again illustrating the swift descent into violence that could occur in Alexandria.[18] Athanasius then called a council in Alexandria and sought to bring reconciliation to the fissiparous Church in Antioch where two groups of Nicene Christians supported rival bishops, Paulinus and Melitius. Paulinus led a kind of extreme Nicene congregation, and division in the city between these various groups would rumble on for a further 20 years until the advent of the emperor Theodosius.

If it seemed that with the death of Constantius one of the chief barriers to a settlement over Arianism had been removed and the possibility of an orthodox Nicene settlement advanced, such optimism was soon dashed. The nature of Arianism was that it was not located solely in imperial power, nor in particular individuals like Arius himself, or Eusebius of Nicomedia, or even in some tiresome bishops who opposed Athanasius because they disliked his strength. No, the reason for Arianism was more fundamental: it represented a Greek philosophical position evident in neo-Platonism and elsewhere, which was continually regenerated by individuals who sought a synthesis between biblical Christianity and Greek philosophy, which in the case of Plotinus elevated the One to complete transcendent supremacy from which other emanations of divinity came. If this was the model of reality with which various advocates of Arianism were working, while seeking to squeeze biblical Christianity into its mould—either consciously or unconsciously—no wonder a gap soon opened up between their synthesis and the concept of a Triune God. Moreover, many saw the presence of the Jewish view: that Jesus could not be part of the Godhead. Because of this, as soon as one threat to Nicene orthodoxy was removed, as in the person of Constantius, another presented itself in the teaching of the neo-Arians in the second half of the fourth century. In many ways, this was the final intellectual and ecclesial challenge of Arianism to Nicene orthodoxy in the fourth century.

The Neo-Arians

The neo-Arians for the most part were led by two individuals: Aetius (300–67) and Eunomius (335–93). Aetius came from Antioch and after an early career as a vine dresser and goldsmith, took up medicine, becoming particularly able in medical disputations. Turning from medicine to philosophy and theology, he was patronized by a number of bishops, including Paulinus of Antioch, Athanasius of Anazarbus in Cilicia, and eventually the Arian bishop, Gregory of Alexandria (bishop during Athanasius's second exile). He was ordained deacon by Bishop Leontius of Antioch in *c.*346.[19] A dispute in Antioch, which was unsurprising, led him to Alexandria, where he met Eunomius, who would become his most able and faithful disciple. After finding Athanasius in Alexandria enjoying his golden decade and in full command of the diocese, it is not surprising that Aetius did not stay long there but once again returned to Antioch, where he won the favour of Gallus, the half-brother of Julian and the *caesar* who would succeed Constantius as emperor. But Constantius was no supporter of Aetius, who by then had become committed to the teaching of Basil of Ancyra before the Councils of Seleucia and Ariminum. Constantius banished Aetius, sending him into exile in Phyrgia.

Aetius's views about the Trinity were expressed in his work titled the *Syntagmation* ("little book") which was published or circulated from 359. It contained 37 propositions drawn up as an answer to *De Decretis* of Athanasius, itself a defence of the Nicene Creed.[20] The *Syntagmation* was essentially a philosophical work with little or no mention of Jesus

Christ and little attempt to understand the Bible in its own terms. Says Hanson: "His sole concern is philosophical, to point out how illogical and impossible it is, in the light of the logic and philosophy of his day, to hold that the *ousia* of the Father and the Son can be either like each other or identical with each other."[21] As so often in this controversy, it is difficult to pin down exact meanings. Although called neo-Arians, there were areas in which they were quite distinct from Arius.[22] In this respect, they stressed both the likeness and the unlikeness of the Son to the Father. Although they were often accused of being *anomoians* (meaning they stressed that the Son was unlike the Father), they defended themselves against this attack, preferring the label *heterousian.* The inference being that Aetius and his followers regarded the Son as like the Father in some aspects, and unlike in others and in this sense, it was a further calibration of meaning compared to the definitions *like in substance* (*homoiousian*) and *like in will* (*homoian*) which had come to define other parties. However, in the key areas of substance and generation, Aetius held that the Son was unlike the Father, and in this sense the sobriquet neo-Arian is not far from the mark. Essentially Aetius was an Aristotelian philosopher rather than a theologian. He found it philosophically near impossible to hold that there could be two or more ingenerates, that is, beings who had no beginning but were coeternal.

Aetius's pupil and most influential successor was Eunomius, who probably came from Cappadocia. He was Aetius's secretary in Alexandria from about 355 and, having been ordained deacon and priest by Bishop Eudoxius of Antioch, was made Bishop of Cyzicus in 360. Eunomius's main works were his two *Apologies* (or Defences) and his *Confession of Faith.* Much of his work is preserved in the refutation of his opinions by Basil of Caesarea and Gregory of Nyssa, both of whom wrote extensively against Eunomius. Eunomius's main views were that Jesus Christ was wholly dependent on the Father. Indeed, the monarchy of the Father was complete and none could share his supremacy. Thus:

> He has no sharer of his Godhead, nor participator of his glory, nor joint possessor of his authority, nor consort of the throne of his kingdom, for he is one and sole Almighty: God of gods, King of kings, Lord of lords, highest over all the earth.[23]

Nor should the Father's substance be confused with his energy or activity. His substance makes him unique.

Distinct from this, the Son is "the first-born of all creation, the only begotten God, true Son, not ingenerate, truly generated before the ages, not uncreated, existing in the beginning".[24] In other words, Eunomius could not be more unequivocal in his subordination of the Son to the Father, and what was true of the Son was also true of the Spirit. Nor did Eunomius have any doctrine of the incarnation. Being a rationalist, he had little understanding of the reality of evil, and therefore of the necessity for redemption. It was a thoroughly deficient theology in light of the Bible. It bore a close resemblance to neo-Platonism and expressed a hierarchical view of reality consonant with Platonism. Although he was not an emanationist (the idea of the One emanating or producing a descending scale of godlike beings superior to creation), he was a total subordinationist. He thought the Nicene concept of the Father begetting the Son and the Spirit too material, as expressed in the phrase "Light from Light, true God from true God".[25] And Eunomius believed that when the *Logos* took on flesh, he had no human psyche, was immutable and impassible, and in these respects there was clear water between the *homoians* and the *heterousians* of whom Eunomius was a leader. In the modern world, Eunomius could be compared to a rationalist Unitarian with a Platonic perspective and employing Aristotelian logic. Sir Isaac Newton might have been found among his supporters, or he may have been a member of the Cambridge Platonists. But he was certainly not a Trinitarian Christian.

By 362, Athanasius was entering the final decade of his life. His attendance at Nicaea must have seemed an age away. He had borne many trials, written many works, come through many storms. His ministry had taken him far afield to Trier on the Moselle, Rome, Constantinople and its environs, and to Antioch as well as many other Roman cities. He came to be regarded as the weather-beaten rock of orthodoxy in the storms of doctrinal opinion; others were now running with the ball and at last the Nicene party was growing in influence, especially in the west, but in Cappadocia as well. Hallowed by the years, Athanasius took on the mantle of exile, ascetic and bishop. He led the ranks of monk-bishops, which was to be such an influential role in the fourth century.

Notes

1 Athanasius, *Apologia ad Constantium* §25, op. cit., p. 248.

2 Lewis Ayres, *Nicaea and its Legacy: An Approach to Fourth Century Trinitarian Theology* (Oxford: Oxford University Press, 2006), p. 137.

3 Ayres, *Nicaea and its Legacy*, p. 138.

4 R. P. C. Hanson, *The Search for the Christian Doctrine of God: The Arian Controversy 318–381* (Grand Rapids, MI: Baker Academic, 2005), p. 345.

5 Ayres, *Nicaea and its Legacy*, p. 140.

6 Athanasius, *De Decretis* §2, *The Nicene and Post-Nicene Fathers: Second Series, Vol. IV*, ed. Philip Schaff (Grand Rapids, MI: Eerdmans and Edinburgh: T&T Clark, 1987), p. 151.

7 Athanasius, *De Decretis* §6, p. 154.

8 David M. Gwynn, *Athanasius of Alexandria: Bishop, Theologian, Ascetic, Father* (Oxford: Oxford University Press, 2012), pp. 86–7.

9 Athanasius, *De Decretis* §19, op. cit., p. 162.

10 Athanasius, *De Decretis* §20, op. cit., p. 164.

11 Ayres, *Legacy of Nicaea*, pp. 144ff.

12 Hanson, *The Search for the Christian Doctrine of God*, p. 362.

13 Hanson, *The Search for the Christian Doctrine of God*, pp. 365–71.

14 Athanasius, *De Synodis* §10, in *Nicene and Post-Nicene Fathers: Second Series, Vol. IV Athanasius: Selected Works and Letters*, ed. Philip Schaff (Edinburgh: T&T Clark, 1987), pp. 454ff.

15 Gwynn, *Athanasius of Alexandria*, p. 95.

16 Athanasius, *De Synodis* §41, op. cit., p. 472.

17 John Drinkwater, "Maximinus to Diocletian and the 'crisis'", in Alan K. Bowman, Peter Garnsey and Averil Cameron (eds), *The Cambridge Ancient History, second edition, Vol. XII: The Crisis of Empire, A.D. 193–337* (Cambridge: Cambridge University Press, 2005), pp. 39–43.

18 Hanson, *The Search for the Christian Doctrine of God*, p. 639.

19 Hanson, *The Search for the Christian Doctrine of God*, p. 599.

20 Hanson, *The Search for the Christian Doctrine of God*, p. 607.

21 Hanson, *The Search for the Christian Doctrine of God*, p. 610.

22 Ayres, *Nicaea and its Legacy*, p. 145.

23 Taken from Gregory of Nyssa's *Refutatio Confessionis Eunomii*, cited Hanson, *The Search for the Christian Doctrine of God*, p. 619.

[24] Hanson, *The Search for the Christian Doctrine of God*, p. 620.

[25] Hanson, *The Search for the Christian Doctrine of God*, p. 633.

CHAPTER 9

Bishop, exile and ascetic

Much of the authority of Athanasius came from being a bishop. The role of a bishop had ever been critical in the life of the early Church. Anyone reading the Apostolic Fathers and in particular the letters of Ignatius, the Bishop of Antioch, who was taken in chains to Rome to be martyred there, will soon see that the health of the Church depended on a good relationship between the community and its bishop. Thus Ignatius, writing to the Ephesians, said, "I have received your entire congregation in the name of God through Onesimus, who abides in a love that defies description and serves as your bishop in the flesh—and I ask by Jesus Christ that you love him, and that all of you be like him. For blessed is the one who has graciously granted you, who are worthy, to obtain such a bishop."[1] Later Ignatius said to the Smyrneans, "Let the congregation be wherever the bishop is; just as wherever Jesus Christ is, there also is the universal Church."[2] Again to the Smyrneans, where the beloved Polycarp was bishop, Ignatius wrote: "The one who honours the bishop is honoured by God; the one who does anything behind the bishop's back serves the devil."[3] And the *Didache*, that handbook on Church practice, tells the churches, "Elect for yourselves bishops and deacons who are worthy of the Lord, gentlemen who are not fond of money, who are true and approved. For these also conduct the ministry of the prophets and teachers among you."[4] The position of a bishop was therefore highly honoured and accorded considerable authority.

The role increased greatly in the fourth century after Constantine published his Edict of Toleration in Milan in 313 and the Church became an established and accepted institution in the empire. Bishops were given new privileges and responsibilities whilst at the same time becoming more accountable to imperial power. The effect was almost immediately to extend their social remit. Bishops became responsible for travelling missionaries. They were to support the poor from church treasuries. Orphans were often made wards of the Church or of bishops. Bishops became involved in the administration of courts and justice—something Augustine of Hippo found very burdensome.[5] In brief, bishops became leading social and spiritual figures in the community and had access to the highest echelons of imperial administration. We see this clearly in the correspondence of Basil the Great in Cappadocia, where he was able to correspond on equal terms with the officials of the emperor in the late fourth century.

If the status of the bishop had increased greatly due to the patronage of Constantine from 313 onwards, in Alexandria there were additional reasons for the elevation of the authority of the bishop. The episcopal teaching office was enhanced in the third century by the drawn-out conflict with Gnosticism, which had had a powerful presence in Egypt as in Rome, as evidenced by the collection of Gnostic writings in the cache at Nag Hammadi on the Nile. By 189–231 and the episcopacy of Demetrius, it is clear that the see of Alexandria was becoming critical to the eventual triumph of biblical Christianity over against the speculations of Gnosticism. Not only that, but Demetrius sought to exercise greater control over the catechetical school of Alexandria made famous by Origen before he left for Caesarea in Palestine. The third century saw a number of important bishops continue to consolidate the authority of the role in Alexandria, namely Heraclas (231–47), Dionysius (247–64), Maximus (264–82) and Theonas (282–300).[6]

However, the greatest challenge came to the see with the beginning of the Great Persecution under Diocletian in 303. Bishop Peter of Alexandria went into hiding, and it was his absence that provided the opportunity for the Melitian schism to take root.[7] The Melitians, like the Donatists, wanted a stricter policy over the incorporation of lapsed Christians into the fellowship and ministry of the Church. Nevertheless, whatever authority Peter may have lost through hiding during the persecution, he managed to reclaim with his eventual martyrdom. Swift on the heels of the Great Persecution came the Arian controversy, and once again the Church needed a clear lead in both explaining the faith and containing the heterodoxy of Arius and his colleagues. In this doctrinal maelstrom, first Bishop Alexander and then Athanasius gave a lead.

Athanasius, as we have seen, had been groomed for the office of bishop from an early age, with little Church experience other than service on Bishop Alexander's staff. There Athanasius had witnessed Alexander's attempts to reassert his institutional authority as patriarch (and later pope) over the competing claims of local presbyters.[8] But Athanasius was not primarily motivated by control when his time came to be elected bishop in 328, although he undoubtedly became an imposing figure well aware of the authority granted him by members of his church. We know little of his daily routine as a bishop compared with what we know of Augustine of Hippo. And for almost all of his episcopacy, Athanasius was drawn into the politics and the theological melting pot of the Arian controversy. There is one place where we can look beyond the ecclesiastical politics of the age and see into Athanasius's pastoral and fatherly heart, however. This is in the Festal Letters which he wrote to the diocese to fix the date of Easter and to give the dates of the Lenten fast almost every year without fail. There are 45 of these letters, even if some are barely fragments. Among them are letters which are deeply revealing of Athanasius's pastoral theology, his love of the Scriptures and his yearning as a father for his diocese. So, in Letter I, issued in Easter 328, he commends the discipline of fasting: "Wherefore, my beloved, having our souls nourished with divine food, with the word, and according to the will of God, and fasting bodily in things external, let us keep this great and saving feast as becomes us."[9] Athanasius goes on in the same letter to encourage his readers to receive "the new wine even the Holy Spirit that we may properly keep the feast".[10]

By contrast, Letter IV of 332 was written from the emperor's court and taken to the diocese by a soldier. Plainly Athanasius is not in a comfortable place: he is ill, he has opponents much like Judith in the Apocrypha who killed Holophernes, and he has become like Esther who has to save her people.[11] Nevertheless, giving pastoral advice, Athanasius writes:

> We need in this (struggle) to put on our Lord Jesus Christ that we may celebrate the feast with him. Now we are clothed with him when we love virtue, and are enemies to wickedness, when we

> exercise ourselves in temperance and mortify lasciviousness . . .
> when we do not forget the poor but open our doors to all men,
> when we assist humble-mindedness, but hate pride.[12]

Here we see Athanasius fulfilling the ancient calling of a bishop: speaking boldly, calling out immoral turpitude, remembering the poor actively, caring for the vulnerable and defenceless and pointing to Christ.

Since we lack any evidence of Athanasius's preaching, the Festal Letters are about our only window into his liturgical emphases.[13] It seems that following his first exile to Trier (335–7), and a consequently greater understanding of the liturgical practices of the wider Church, he proposed that the Egyptian Church should follow the six-week Lenten fast kept throughout the Church, rather than the six-day fast before Holy Week it had hitherto practised.[14] In fact, Athanasius appears to have been thinking about extending the fast even before his exile, as he suggests this in his sixth Festal Letter of 334. In Section 13, he states, "We begin a fast of forty days on the first day of the month Phamenoth (25 February) and prolong it till the fifth of Pharmuthi (31 March) and then have the six-day fast before Easter ending on Holy Saturday". There was no fast on the Saturdays and Sundays during this period.[15] In this way, Athanasius brought the Egyptian Church into line with the Church in the east and the west and burnished his credentials as an ascetic bishop, to which we will return. In what purports to be his twelfth Festal Letter written from exile in Rome in 340, but is in fact a letter written to Serapion, Athanasius tells his episcopal friend to encourage the Church in Egypt to take up the 40-day fast. "But O my beloved," he addresses Serapion, the Bishop of Thmuis, "whether in this way or any other, persuade and teach them to fast the forty days. For it is a disgrace that when all the world does this, those alone who are in Egypt, instead of fasting, should find their pleasure."[16]

Athanasius was well aware of the practice of the wider catholic Church and wanted to align the Egyptian Church with this practice. He saw value in these 40-day fasts in galvanizing the whole Church in spiritual endeavour, and he wanted Egypt to be in step with the universal Church.

The Festal Letters were also a way for Athanasius to bare his soul as he faced increasing tension as a result of his championing of the Nicene position against Arius. In 338, in the window between his first and second exile, he wrote powerfully of his own sufferings drawing strength from the example of Jesus:

> For he [Christ] suffered to prepare freedom from suffering for those who suffer in him, he descended that he might raise us up, he took on him the trial of being born, that we might love him who is unbegotten, he went down to corruption, that corruption might put on immortality. He became weak for us, that we might rise with power, he descended to death that he might bestow on us immortality and give life to the dead. Finally, he became man that we who die as men might live again, and that death should no more reign over us; for the Apostolic word proclaims, "Death shall not have dominion over us".[17]

In this quotation, we have a distillation of Athanasius's theology, more fully described in *Contra Gentes: De Incarnatione*, but here pressed into service as the cause of his own suffering. It is for these truths that he is holding out. It is for this theology that he stands firm against Arianism, and armed with the knowledge of a Saviour who "prepared freedom from suffering", he appeals to his see to stand with him. Not until Gregory of Nazianzus's 29th *Oration of the Son of God* was there such an eloquent description of Christ's divinity and humanity.[18]

Athanasius used his Festal Letters to communicate a Christian lifestyle to his flock, as well as draw them into his confidence so that they might pray for him in his struggles. And in speaking about his own struggles, he is able to prepare them for their own, as well as teach them patience from the example of Christ. Furthermore, the letters were opportunities to give his flock important exegetical instruction. To this end Letter XXXIX, written in 367, gives the oldest extant list of New Testament books, as well as an almost complete list of the books of the Old Testament. The purpose of sharing this list was to demonstrate that God's wisdom and truth comes through the revelation of the Word, and by 367 a complete authoritative list of Scripture had been established. Indeed, this list of New Testament books is reflected in the great codices of the period: namely Codex Sinaiticus, Codex Alexandrinus and Codex Vaticanus.

By giving the Church a categorical list of books in the Old and New Testaments, Athanasius was affirming the Canon of Scripture and the extent of God's true revelation since, for Athanasius, "in these books alone the teaching of piety is proclaimed".[19] A further poignancy was added to these Festal Letters by the fact that they were frequently written whilst he was in exile, and often these exilic missives were only fragments of the originals (see Letters XXVIII from 356 and XXIX from 357) and in some years no letters survived.

Athanasius: The exile

Exile was a common Roman punishment. It was used repeatedly by the emperors against officials and members of their own families, as with Caesar Augustus and his wayward daughter Julia, who was exiled to the island of Pandateria in southern Italy on account of her debauched lifestyle. For very different reasons, many bishops were exiled in the fourth century for holding views contrary to the emperor; and perhaps most famously, John Chrysostom, the Bishop of Constantinople, who was exiled in 406 by the Empress Eudoxia, wife of the eastern Emperor Arcadius, for his strictures on her court life.

Exile for the Christian was endowed with a kind of holy opportunity. Since bishops were removed from most of their daily and sometimes burdensome tasks, they could instead use the time for study, reflection and prayer. For Athanasius, exile was an opportunity to hone and express his views, principally against the Arians. We have already seen that during his first exile in Trier (335–7) as a guest of the emperor he began, and possibly completed, his foundational work *Contra Gentes: De Incarnatione*. During his second exile (in 339–46), which was largely spent in the west, principally in Rome, Athanasius gathered support for the fight against Arianism. He also began to assemble his narrative work on the Arian controversy, *Apologia contra Arianos*, and started the important *Orationes contra Arianos*. His third exile (356–62), which followed the storming of the Theonas Church in Alexandria where Athanasius was conducting worship, lasted six years and was spent in hiding in the Egyptian desert. He was actively pursued by imperial troops, but his secret hiding place was never disclosed, and from there he continued to rule the Egyptian Church and to write a number of very important works, including his *Life of Antony*, his polemical *History of the Arians* and his letters to Serapion on the Holy Spirit. Although hidden away in the desert, he was still well informed, as his account of the recent synods at Arimini and Seleuciae shows.

In these writings, Athanasius showed the full extent of his interests, from his workmanlike accounts of the proceedings of synods, and exploratory thoughts on the person of the Holy Spirit, to the first biography and account of the life of an ascetic monk, Antony. Exile for Athanasius was put to good use. In fact, you could argue that they were creative times of theological writing indispensable in carrying forward the campaign against Arianism. And although Athanasius resented his treatment by Emperor Constantius, who he increasingly condemned, he nevertheless defended his actions in his *Defence of His Flight*, saying that he followed the example of Christ, who only gave himself up to his opponents when his hour had come.[20] In other words, there is a time for flight and exile, and there is a time for yielding and martyrdom, and it is for the individual to discern which is right. For Athanasius, following the example of Antony, it was a time for ascetic withdrawal.

Athanasius: The ascetic

An ascetic movement in the Church had begun in the late third century. In part, this was hastened by persecution. As early as the mid third century, during the reigns of Decius and Valerian, Christians escaped persecution by moving into the deserts of Africa and Syria. Paul of Thebes or Paul the Hermit (*c*.227–341) lived in the Thebaid south of Oxyrhyncthus on the Nile. And it was here, as legend has it, that as an old man of 113, Paul met and inspired the young Antony who was to be at the epicentre of Egyptian monasticism in the fourth century. If the movement into the desert did not occur till the third century, asceticism or the practice of *askesis* had been part of Christian and Jewish life from the earliest beginnings.

In Judaism, we can trace the practice of separation from the world in order to pursue a calling of prayer and study from the days of Samuel and the formation of prophetic bands. It seemed that these groups lived outside conventional human society, gave insightful and ecstatic utterances, and lived a life of renunciation (see 1 Samuel 10:5–7). A continuing tradition of asceticism linked to prophetic insight in Judaism could be found in the life of the *hasidim* and then the community of Qumran also. These communities were linked to the restoration of Israel and the fulfilment of Messianic expectation. In the Christian tradition, this practice would find its readiest focus in the life and ministry of John the Baptist. An ascetic individual if ever there was one, the Baptist spoke the Word of the Lord in preparation for the Messiah (see Luke 3:1–20; 7:18–35).

If a clear ascetic tradition was present in Judaism and Christianity, it was also present in a Platonic life that sought to subjugate the flesh and its weakness to the mind and spirit. Plotinus was a prime example of neo-Platonism. The ancient philosophers advocated the philosophical life, a life of renunciation, contemplation and reflection. And indeed, many of the Church leaders of the fourth century, such as Athanasius, Basil of Caesarea, and Gregory of Nazianzus, sought a similar opportunity to seek God through solitude, prayer and contemplation in far-off places. The Church and landscape of Egypt was to provide an especially fertile place for this particular pursuit of God.

In essence, there were two ways of seeking God in the deserts or wadis of Egypt: either singly, as an anchorite, or with others in a community. These two forms of monasticism were exemplified in Egypt by two men: Pachomius and Antony. Antony (*c*.251–356), to whom we will come (and who was patronized by Athanasius, who went on to write his biography), became the prototype of an anchorite movement made up of individuals known as the Desert Fathers or Mothers. They lived in extreme simplicity, deep humility, utter poverty and engaged in fierce struggle with the Devil and his temptations.

Pachomius was born at least 20 years after Antony and was conscripted into the Roman army at the age of 20. Whilst serving in the forces, he was impressed by the charity of the Christians who brought food and drink to the young recruits, and he prayed that if he were released from his military service, he would devote himself to God.[21] With the defeat of Maximinus Daia, in whose army he served, by the eastern emperor,

Licinius, Pachomius was free to follow his calling. He was baptized in the village of Chenoboscia and became linked to a local ascetic Christian called Palamon who helped him found his first monastery.[22] In *c.*320, Pachomius founded a community in a deserted village of Tabennesi and with an influx of many aspirants created a communal structure based on mutual support. "Over time regulations were developed to cover food, clothing, and sleeping patterns, and an organized monastery began to appear."[23] Later Pachomius wrote a rule which was circulated after his death. A further monastery was founded at Phbow, and the two monasteries held about a thousand monks. By the time of his death, the movement had spread throughout the Thebaid, following the course of the Nile from Panopolis in the north to Thebes in the south. It is estimated that by the end of the fourth century there were some 7,000 monks.

Nor was Pachomius's the only initiative in coenobitic (community) monasticism in Egypt. A well-to-do young man called Amoun persuaded his wife on her wedding night to live a life of chastity: two cells were subsequently built in the neighbourhood of Nitria for each of them, and from these beginnings others came to settle in the area of Scetis and in nearby Wadi-el-Natrun.[24] Macarius the Great settled in Scetis. He was the very paragon of humility, self-deprecation and abandonment. And to this day, the area still nurtures several of the great Coptic monasteries, with new ones like Anaphora begun. In the fourth century, roots were thus laid for an enduring spiritual tradition which has lasted till this day. If Pachomius was the great founder of coenobitic communities, Antony was the great example of a solitary or anchorite in Christian history. And it is to his story, written by Athanasius, that we must turn.

It seems that Antony was born around 251 in Herakleopolis Magna in Egypt as part of a Christian family. He was Egyptian, spoke Coptic, was well born and from an early age decided to live a life devoted to prayer and the knowledge of God.[25] His parents died when he was in his late teens or early twenties, and he became responsible for the care of the home and for his younger sister. One day, on hearing the Gospel reading, "If you would be perfect, go sell what you possess and give to the poor, and you will have treasure in heaven", Antony determined to sell all his possessions, give the money to the poor and put his sister in the charge of some well-respected virgins.[26] Having cleared himself of responsibilities to family and property, he took up the life of a solitary near to his own village, worked with his own hands to secure his bread, gave any surplus income away and prayed continuously. This was the basis of Antony's life.

By the time Athanasius was consecrated Bishop of Alexandria in 328, Antony, if born in 251 or thereabouts, was an old man in his seventies (even if his birth were somewhat later). Antony was a well-known figure. Athanasius's biography of Antony was written between 356 and 362 when he had narrowly escaped being martyred at the Church of Theonas, at a time when Antony was a hundred years old or thereabouts. Each had much to gain from the other. By the time Athanasius came to write Antony's biography, he was in his third exile, at his most unpopular with the imperial power, and literally in hiding for his life. But Athanasius was also supported by Antony in his struggle against Arianism. In 338, Antony had visited Alexandria to give public support to Athanasius, and in so doing gave him popular acclaim. Just as in the fifth century Simeon Stylites (390–459) became a legend in his lifetime, consulted by all, from paupers to princes born in the purple, so Antony had become in his long life a paragon of ascetic virtue. In writing a biography of Antony, Athanasius was to start a trend in ascetic biography which would last a thousand years: to include Bede's life of Cuthbert, Asser's life of Alfred the Great and Eadmer's life of Anselm. Nevertheless, few monks could have had such a prestigious chronicler as Athanasius of Alexandria, and few carried more influence across Christendom than Antony. If Antony's support of Athanasius gave him wide popular appeal, Athanasius's biography of Antony ensured Antony lasting visibility and enduring fame. In many ways, Athanasius's biography is the classic description of a solitary or anchorite. The synergy between the bishops of Alexandria and the increasing number of monks in the region was set to continue, although not always beneficially. In later years, during Bishop Cyril's tempestuous episcopacy (412–44), these monks were often more feral than contemplative, a kind of mob bishops could call on, and some were even involved in the shocking murder of the pagan philosopher, Hypatia.

In his *Life of Antony* (although his authorship is contested by some scholars), Athanasius gives us a time-honoured account of what it means to seek a solitary life of prayer, albeit in a very dramatic way. Antony's life was framed by his asceticism and struggles with the Devil. He appears to have left his village, befriended an older ascetic who acted as a guide and mentor, and lived in one of the tombs of a village cemetery for a time.[27] People would leave food for him there: "He charged one of his friends to supply him periodically with bread, and he entered one of the tombs and remained alone within, his friend having closed the door on him."[28] Athanasius goes on to say that here Antony was confronted by demonic attack motivated by the desire to prevent him spreading this discipline of prayer across the Egyptian desert. The attack was literally physical.[29] Antony was much weakened by his fasting and on occasions had to be carried to his resting place, so weak was he.

Antony continued in this ascetic life for nearly 20 years: combatting the demons who came either to seduce him through temptations to imagined fornication or to frighten him with "apparitions".[30] He gave himself to prayer day and night, instructing others who came to him for teaching from the Scriptures.[31] Not that Antony would have had a complete copy of the Bible, but he would have committed to memory large tracts of Scripture, especially the Psalms. Some believed that he had memorized the whole Bible from which he would instruct visitors.

After two decades in which his reputation grew and large numbers of people sought him out, Antony determined to look for greater isolation. At first, he thought of moving to the Upper Thebaid, in the region of Thebes and Luxor, but then the Lord commanded him to go into "the inner mountain".[32] Since he did not know the way, God brought some Saracens to guide him into this new area.[33] When Antony reached the new site for his solitary life, he was delighted. Athanasius writes: "After journeying three days and three nights in [the Saracens'] company, he came to a very high hill. Below the hill there was water—perfectly clear and sweet, and quite cold, and beyond there were plains, and a few untended date palms."[34] It was here that Antony was to continue his vocation into old age, and a monastery taking his name would be founded. He established a kitchen garden, and like Francis of Assisi, he spoke to the wild animals that threatened his vegetables. We are told by Athanasius, "From then on, as if being afraid of the command, they did not come near the place."[35]

While living and praying in this inner mountain, Antony received many visitors. On one occasion he saw the departing soul of Amoun, the monk of Nitria, ascending to heaven.[36] Later Antony saw in a vision two pilgrims who were on their way to him, but dying of thirst. Monks were despatched immediately with water, but already one had died on the road. On another occasion, a young man with an evil spirit came to him. Antony stayed up all night praying for him, and he was liberated.[37] For this reason, Antony was credited with spiritual power and prophetic insight.

Not only was his teaching condemning the Arians thoroughly orthodox, it was also proclaimed in unmistakeable terms. Antony asserted, "it is sacrilegious to say, 'There was (a time) when he was not', for the word coexisted with the Father always. Therefore, you are to have no fellowship with most ungodly Arians, for there is no fellowship of light with darkness."[38] On another occasion, Antony fell into a trance and a lament, having received a vision about the power of Arianism in the Church in which mules surrounded the altar of the Lord and kicked down its trappings.[39] Antony was extolled by Athanasius for his orthodoxy, his opposition to the Arians and the Melitians.

His ministry of healing the sick and liberating those oppressed by the Devil was all of a piece with his orthodox teaching, for in both he was following the example and teaching of the Lord. Indeed, Athanasius would often characterize Antony's entire life as a struggle with the Devil after the manner of Paul's teaching in Ephesians 6:12.[40] Central to victory in this struggle was the power of the Cross, "for where the sign of the cross occurs, magic is weakened and sorcery has no effect".[41] It was a life of unending prayer, teaching faithful to the full incarnation of the divine Christ, manifestation of the kingdom through healing and deliverance, wisdom in speech and plentiful reasons for believing.[42] In a telling sentence, Athanasius says of Antony, "for those in whom the action through faith is present, the demonstration through arguments is unnecessary, or perhaps even useless".[43] Or we might say actions speak louder than words.

Athanasius's life of Antony ends appropriately. Antony's ways and habits remained unchanging, we are told, to the very end.[44] He retired to the inner mountain to await death. He refused all fuss over his grave or burial, wanting to be buried in an unmarked and secret location. His few possessions, two sheepskin rugs and a cloak, he gave to Bishops Athanasius and Serapion. In fact, his testimony lay in this *Life*, which became his memorial and his legacy.

Athanasius's *Life of Antony* was not his only work on asceticism and its importance to the Egyptian Church. Other works on the subject were his *Letters to Virgins* (338 and *c*.346) and a less widely circulated work, *On Virginity*. In his *Letter to Virgins*, written for the already large communities of virgins in existence in Egypt, he extols the vocation of virginity as superior to marriage. "Virginity having surpassed human nature and imitating the angels, hastens and endeavours to cleave to the Lord."[45] But although the lifestyle of virginity was both demanding and sacrificial, there was no reason to downgrade marriage: they were different ways of following the same God. Athanasius goes on to describe the character of a virgin whose life would be modelled on Mary the mother of Jesus. Such a person would be modest, humble, not given to excess or to too much food. Instead, she would give herself to useful work like weaving or study or copying of the Scriptures. He did not encourage excessive or extreme ascetic practices as found with some hermits in the desert, but rather a practical, modest and useful life centred on worship and prayer.

In summary, the ascetic life which Athanasius advocated was one that found its inspiration in the incarnation, where we see Jesus both *giving up* the trappings of Godhead which could not be grasped (see Philippians 2:6,7) and taking on humble obedience which led to the Cross and exaltation. Likewise, for the virgin, hermit or monk there will be the giving up of independence, and in particular rights to property, sexual fulfilment and personal ambition. Instead, the ascetic life is to find its fulfilment in simplicity, in renunciation of sexual life, and in embracing a discipline of work and prayer.

Athanasius's own inclination to espouse this way of life—in so far as he was able to combine it with episcopacy—gave him a ready acceptance among the ascetics of Egypt. In fact, throughout his episcopacy there was an accord and synergy between the ascetics of Egypt and himself, which was both comforting and strengthening. Indeed, "the mutual bond between the ascetic movement and the hierarchical Church that

Athanasius forged in Egypt has lasted down to the present day and created a reservoir of strength upon which he and later Alexandrian bishops would draw".[46]

Athanasius had to work at forging bonds between himself and these ascetic communities. His *Letter to Amoun*, an ascetic residing in the Nitrian mountains, his *Letters to Virgins* and his two *Letters to the Monks* bear witness to this. Athanasius was at pains to prevent Arians finding a foothold in these communities, to give an account of his own misfortunes at the hands of the Arians and to give an explanation of true doctrine.[47] Athanasius's vision for bishop and ascetic was for a complementary ministry: bishops having the prayerful support of such communities as well as enjoying places of retreat; and monks not only giving that support but at times, like Dracontius, being willing to serve as bishops. Indeed, Dracontius, although a monk, was called to exercise a ministry as a bishop in the region of Hermopolis, which had jurisdiction over the ascetic Mountain of Nitria. He refused to do so, returning to his monastery, whereupon Athanasius wrote to him blaming him for his withdrawal from the episcopacy, explaining how monasticism and episcopacy were compatible, and that if he did not step up, the see would go to a Meletian opponent.[48]

The evidence of Athanasius's success in creating solidarity against the Arians with these ascetic communities, especially the virgins of Alexandria, was that they became the target of persecution by Constantius's officials, led by Duke Sebastian at the start of Athanasius's third exile in *c*.356. We are told that "many virgins who condemned [the officials'] impiety, and professed the truth, were brought out from their houses and insulted".[49] It was a form of persecution that was often repeated.

By 370, some thousand miles almost due north of Alexandria, a new monk bishop with a yet closer relationship with an ascetic community and also with episcopal oversight had taken root. The 40-year-old Basil of Caesarea, who had himself written a monastic rule with the intention of serving the poor, not only provided a historic example of a bishop monk, but also with his colleagues, the Cappadocian Fathers, provided fresh and creative impetus for understanding the nature of the Trinity. The groundwork laid down by Athanasius would now be creatively developed and defended by the Cappadocian Fathers.

Notes

1 Ignatius, in *The Apostolic Fathers I*, Loeb Classical Library, Vol. 24 (Cambridge, MA: Harvard University Press, 2003), p. 221.

2 Ignatius, op. cit., p. 305.

3 Ignatius, op. cit., p. 305.

4 The Didache, in *The Apostolic Fathers I*, Loeb Classical Library, Vol. 24 (Cambridge, MA: Harvard University Press, 2003), p. 441.

5 Henry Chadwick, Edward C. Hobbs and Wilhelm Wuellner (eds), *The Role of The Christian Bishop in Ancient Society protocol of the thirty-fifth colloquy, 25 February 1979* (Berkeley, CA: Center for Hermeneutical Studies, 1980), p. 6.

6 See David M. Gwynn, *Athanasius of Alexandria: Bishop, Theologian, Ascetic, Father* (Oxford: Oxford University Press, 2012), p. 21.

7 Stephen J. Davis, *The Early Coptic Papacy* (Cairo: American University Press, 2004), p. 37.

8 Davis, *The Early Coptic Papacy*, p. 52.

9 Athanasius, *Festal Letters* I:7, *The Nicene and Post-Nicene Fathers: Second Series, Vol. IV*, ed. Philip Schaff (Grand Rapids, MI: Eerdmans and Edinburgh: T&T Clark, 1987), p. 508.

10 Athanasius, *Letters* I, op. cit., p. 509.

11 Athanasius, *Letters* IV:2, op. cit., p. 516.

12 Athanasius, *Letters* IV:3, op. cit., p. 516.

13 Athanasius, *Letters* IV:3, op. cit., pp. 506ff.

14 Gwynn, *Athanasius of Alexandria*, p. 140.

15 Athanasius, *Letters* VI:13, op. cit., p. 523.

16 Athanasius, *Letters* XII, op. cit., p. 538.

17 Athanasius, *Letters* X:8, op. cit., p. 530.

18 Gregory of Nazianzus, *On God and Christ: Five Theological Orations* (Yonkers, NY: SVS Press, 2002), p. 69.

19 Athanasius, *Letters* XXXIX, op. cit., p. 551.

20 Athanasius, *Apologia de fuga* §13, in *Nicene and Post-Nicene Fathers: Second Series, Vol. IV: Athanasius: Selected Works and Letters*, ed. Philip Schaff (Edinburgh: T&T Clark, 1987), p. 259.

21 Gwynn, *Athanasius of Alexandria*, p. 109.

22 Derwas Chitty, *The Desert a City* (Yonkers, NY: SVS Press, 1999), p. 10.

23 Gwynn, *Athanasius of Alexandria*, p. 110.

24 Chitty, *The Desert a City*, pp. 12–13.

25 Athanasius, *Life of Antony*, tr. Scott Cairns (San Francisco: HarperOne, 1980), p. 5.

26 Athanasius, *Life of Antony*, op. cit., p. 6.

27 Athanasius, *Life of Antony* §8, op. cit., p. 198.

28 Athanasius, *Life of Antony* §13, op. cit., p. 199.

29 Athanasius, *Life of Antony* §9, op. cit., p. 198.

30 Athanasius, *Life of Antony* §14, op. cit., p. 200.

31 Athanasius, *Life of Antony* §14, op. cit., p. 200.

32 Athanasius, *Life of Antony* §49, op. cit., p. 209.

33 Athanasius, *Life of Antony* §49, op. cit., p. 209.

34 Athanasius, *Life of Antony* §51, op. cit., p. 210.

35 Athanasius, *Life of Antony* §50, op. cit., p. 210.

36 Athanasius, *Life of Antony* §51, op. cit., p. 210.

37 Athanasius, *Life of Antony* §64, op. cit., p. 213.

38 Athanasius, *Life of Antony* §69, op. cit., p. 214.

39 Athanasius, *Life of Antony* §82, op. cit., p. 218.

40 Athanasius, *Life of Antony* §74, op. cit., p. 215.

41 Athanasius, *Life of Antony* §78, op. cit., p. 216.

42 Athanasius, *Life of Antony* §72, op. cit., p. 215.

43 Athanasius, *Life of Antony* §77, op. cit., p. 216.

44 Athanasius, *Life of Antony* §88–94, op. cit., pp. 219–21.

45 Cited Gwynn, *Athanasius of Alexandria*, p. 112.

46 Gwynn, *Athanasius of Alexandria*, p. 121.

47 Athanasius, *First Letter to the Monks* (*c*.358–60) §3, in *Nicene and Post-Nicene Fathers: Second Series, Vol. IV: Athanasius: Selected Works and Letters*, ed. Philip Schaff (Edinburgh: T&T Clark, 1987), p. 563.

48 Athanasius, *Letter to Dracontius*, in *Nicene and Post-Nicene Fathers: Second Series, Vol. IV: Athanasius: Selected Works and Letters*, ed. Philip Schaff (Edinburgh: T&T Clark, 1987), p. 557.

49 Athanasius, *Historia Arianorum* §59, in *Nicene and Post-Nicene Fathers: Second Series, Vol. IV: Athanasius: Selected Works and Letters*, ed. Philip Schaff (Edinburgh: T&T Clark, 1987), p. 292.

CHAPTER 10

The Cappadocian Fathers

Following the death of Constantius II in November 361, events moved fast in the imperial household. Julian the Apostate, a nephew of Constantine the Great who had turned his back on Christianity and attempted to return the empire to its former paganism, succeeded Constantius. He had shown an early interest in the pagan philosophy of the Greeks and had been a fellow student with Basil at Athens University. But his reign was brief, lasting only until 26 June 363, when he was defeated by the Persians in Mesopotamia. His successor, Jovian, not a member of the imperial family, was acclaimed emperor by the imperial guard. His rule lasted only until February 364, whereupon the western emperor, Valentinian I, nominated his brother Valens as emperor of the east.

Valens would remain emperor until his historic defeat by the Goths at Adrianople in 378. For military, imperial and ecclesiastical reasons, the battle at Adrianople would mark a significant shift in the fortunes of the empire for both Church and state. Valens governed for 14 years and did so, like Constantius before him, with strong Arian leanings. It was in this period that the Cappadocian Fathers—consisting of Basil of Caesarea, his younger brother Gregory of Nyssa and his friend Gregory of Nazianzus—became leaders in forging a new definition of the Trinity which built upon the years of heroic resistance by Athanasius to the Arian tendencies of the eastern Church and its emperors. Without Athanasius, there might have been no Nicene position to defend and explain, and without the Cappadocians, there might have been no development of the doctrine of God with the beauty of expression and the growing sure-footedness they displayed.

Shortly before the death of Constantius, a further small council was held in Constantinople to ratify the decisions (such as they were) of Ariminum and Seleucia. As we have seen, Bishop Akakius had the emperor's ear by now and his *homoian* theology was the flavour of the time. Basil of Ancyra and his *homoiousian* theology had been moved to one side. Indeed, there was again a fundamental turning away from all *ousia* theology in the Creed of Niké, which was now used at the Council of Constantinople. Indeed, the council goes on to say:

> The word *ousia*, which was simplistically put down by the Fathers, being unknown to the people, has become a scandal, because the Scriptures do not contain it, we have decided should be removed and there should be absolutely no mention of it at all, since the Holy Scriptures never mention the *ousia* of the Father and the Son. For neither should *hypostasis* concerning the Father, the Son, and the Holy Spirit be used.[1]

Thirty-five years after Nicaea, the Church was hardly further forward in expressing the nature of the Trinity. The whole teaching of *ousia* or shared substance was questioned, and by some parties discarded; the Son was at most only said to be *like in will* to the Father, but not like in essence or substance (*ousia*). This remained the imperial doctrinal policy during this unsettled period and was taken on by Emperor Valens. During this time, the Cappadocian Fathers became the principal opposition to the Arian movement in and around Constantinople and in the imperial palaces close to Byzantium. Of the three Cappadocian Fathers, the first to take up theological cudgels with the Arianism espoused by Valens was Basil of Caesarea.

Basil of Caesarea

Basil came from a pious Cappadocian family with deep roots in the Church and a distinguished record of Christian presence and leadership in the region of Pontus. He was born in 330 when Emperor Constantine was still alive. He was educated initially in Caesarea, then Constantinople, and finally as a student for six years in Athens. Born into a prosperous and locally prominent family, it was expected that Basil would take his place in the elite leadership of the province. Christianity had been part of the family for some time. Basil's grandmother Macrina had herself been deeply influenced by Gregory the Wonderworker (Thaumaturgus), a pupil of Origen from the school at Caesarea Maritima in Palestine.[2] Basil's parents were deeply pious and, although wealthy, were committed to the greatest simplicity of life, care of the poor and prayerfulness. Basil was one of six children, several of whom were to become Christian leaders in their own right. His sister Macrina was an ascetic and contemplative and a deep influence on the other members of the family, while his younger brother Gregory of Nyssa would prove the most mystical of them all, as well as a worthy advocate of the Nicene cause.

Having returned from Athens in 356 after a lengthy classical education which marked Basil out in his breadth of interests as well as enabling him to hold his own with the elite of the day, he was quickly thrust into the Trinitarian controversy brewing in Constantinople. A young man of 26, with a glittering education, a passion for the contemplative or philosophical life, and a willingness to take part in theological debate was bound to be noticed. After a tour of ascetic communities in 356–7 in Syria, Egypt and Palestine, as well as exposure to the teaching of Origen along with his friend Eustathius of Sebaste (with whom he later disagreed), Basil formed his own community in Annesi on his father's estates, which included Gregory of Nazianzus. He was baptized, ordained deacon in 360, and priest in 362 by Dianius, Bishop of Caesarea.[3]

By 360, and the issuing of the Constantinopolitan or Niké Creed sponsored by Constantius and Akakius,[4] which refused all use of *ousia* language, it was clear that Basil must express himself on this subject. Initially he had a preference for the term *homoiousian*, since he stressed the difficulty of understanding *homoousios* appropriately. In a letter to Apollinarius (albeit thought by some to be a forgery), Basil maintained that "like without a difference" accorded better with him than "consubstantial".[5] The reason for this preference was that it militated against suggestions that there might be two gods, Father and Son. But in the end, Basil would get over these scruples. Indeed, Basil had yet to articulate "his mature distinction between unitary shared nature at one level, and the personal distinctions of Father, Son and Spirit at another".[6]

This distinction would introduce one of the main contributions of the Cappadocians to the Trinitarian debate of the fourth century.

If 360 provided an opportunity for Basil to put down a marker, albeit tentatively, about his Trinitarian convictions, the publication of Eunomius's *Apology*, somewhere between 361 and 365, called for a much more robust response. Eunomius, Bishop of Cyzicus, the pupil of Aetius, took the position that the Son being begotten signifies that his essence cannot share the Father's simplicity and in effect cannot share his substance. The Son is therefore at best *homoios* (like in will) to the Father, but not of like substance (*ousia*); and indeed, Eunomius will go so far as to say that Father and Son are *anomoios* or unlike. For Eunomius, no generated being can share the ingenerate nature of God, and this was his fundamental sticking point. It effectively sealed off the uniqueness of the Father and the subordination of the Son, and made them *homoians*, that is, the Son is like the Father. In the face of this seeming triumph of the *homoians* and the peddling of the more extreme ideas of the *anomoians* (the Son being unlike the Father), Basil struck back with his publication in 364 of *Contra Eunomium*. It was a response to an essentially philosophical work by Eunomius, which separated different forms of being in the Godhead, and graded them in scale of divinity. Basil's *Contra Eunomium* is written in three books, with the second and third concerned with the generation of the Son and the Spirit, and the first with human speech about God the Father.[7] Basil makes the distinction that we can never know God except by *epinoia*, which was the discipline of meditative reflection on the qualities of something. And it is by this reflective meditation "that we can know that there is a unity of *ousia* between Father and Son, although what that essence is remains unknown".[8] Basil was creating a new theological path here: what can be known through reflection on the biblical description of the activity of each person of the Godhead and ascertaining each's *idiomata* (properties) and what remains unknown and unknowable. Or to put it another way, Basil had begun to distinguish the unknowability of the divine essence and the knowability of the particular characteristics, the *idiomata*, of the Father and the Son. Thus, the substance of the Godhead in which each share fully (*homoousious*) cannot be fully known; rather that is part of the apophatic nature of God, Father, Son and Spirit; although each may be known through their individuated characteristics or *idiomata*. By the 370s, Basil had taken this theology one step further, arguing that the activities of God all come from the Father, are worked in the Son and are completed in the Spirit. Furthermore, Basil increasingly used the term *hypostasis* to describe the individuated character of each member of the Trinity.[9] For Basil, *hypostasis* meant the person of the Trinity as distinct from substance. *Hypostasis* was a way of bringing into focus that which could not be previously understood; it was "that which presents and circumscribes that which is general and uncircumscribed".[10]

What is clear is that in his response to Eunomius, Basil had found a rich and creative vocabulary to elaborate further the mystery of the Trinity. Not only that, but he had linked to a spiritual discipline of meditative enquiry (*epinoia*), which sought out the *idiomata* of each person of the Trinity and indeed their *energeia*. It was with this progressive understanding of the Trinity that he was able to teach through his letters his young mentee, Bishop Amphilochius of Iconium.[11] Not that any of this meant that Basil was rowing back from the seminal term *homoousios*, or from standing by it—very much the reverse. But he was finding new ways of understanding how in prayer and theology it might be better used and understood. In a letter to Athanasius in the 360s, Basil demonstrates even-handed condemnation of Arius on the one hand and Marcellus on the other for failing to distinguish the Word from the Father.[12]

Among his other responsibilities, including creating an order to care for the poor and dying in Caesarea (named the Basiliad), and forming a new party of bishops in east and west to stand for Nicaea against Emperor Valens and his ecclesiastical party, Basil found time to write the first full-length book on the Holy Spirit. We shall return to it soon, but in many ways, it completed his work against Eunomius, extending the third book of *Contra Eunomius*, which dealt with the divinity of the Spirit, to a full-length work. Basil did not labour alone in his struggle for orthodoxy. His brother Gregory of Nyssa and his college friend Gregory of Nazianzus, in particular, worked towards the same goals.

Gregory of Nazianzus (*c*.330–90)

Gregory was a very different character from Basil, and each was to be a challenge to the other, although they shared the same profound theological outlook on the Trinity. Basil was very much like the older brother: strategic in his thinking, resourceful in his approach, sometimes dominating in his expectation of others, hugely industrious as his voluminous correspondence shows, and very much a leader. By contrast, Gregory was sensitive, easily wounded, an exacting if not fussy stylist, and more at home alone than leading a group of opinionated and fractious bishops, as he would later have to do briefly in Constantinople. They met at the University of Athens and soon afterwards cemented their friendship by embarking on the contemplative or philosophical life together in Basil's hideout on his family estates at Annesi. Basil wrote to Gregory about the thinking behind this way of life as follows:

> Withdrawal from the world does not mean bodily removal from it, but the severance of the soul from sympathy with the body, and giving up city, home, personal possessions, love of friends, property, means of subsistence, business, social relations, and knowledge derived from human teaching; and it also means the readiness to receive in one's heart the impressions engendered there by divine instruction.[13]

The result of this abstinence and asceticism was prayer which "engenders in the soul a distinct conception of God. And the indwelling of God is this—to hold God ever in memory, his shrine established within us".[14] For his part, Gregory looked back, half in jest, on his time with Basil in Pontus in an early letter. He wrote, "for my part I will admire your Pontus and your Pontic darkness, and your dwelling place so worthy of exile". He then hopes it is an entrance to the Kingdom and not to Hades, as Gregory finds the environment harsh and demanding.[15]

But despite its remoteness, or indeed because of it, Pontus was to be the destiny of his flight from the ordination proposed by the other demanding man in his life, his father, the Bishop of Nazianzus. Perhaps more than any other of his early writings, the work entitled *In Defence of his Flight to Pontus*, or Oration 2, shows the inner workings of Gregory's mind after his ordination on Christmas Day 361. The truth was that he never saw himself as a priest: "I did not, nor do I now, think myself qualified to rule a flock or herd, or to have authority over the souls of men."[16] A little later, he made the seminal and classic statement about the labours of pastoral care: "For the guiding of man, the most variable and manifold of creatures, seems to me in very deed to be the art of arts."[17] Gregory of Nazianzus dwells on the complexity of leading others in their faith: "the varied need of the rich and poor, the sanguine and despondent, the sick and whole, rulers and ruled, the wise and ignorant, the cowardly and courageous, the wrathful and the meek, the successful and the failing".[18] Gregory would remain for some years in Nazianzus, learning to be that priest he so much feared becoming. He was subject to his father, and he implored his brilliant brother Caesarius to leave the court of Julian the Apostate where he was the imperial doctor. But tragically, in 369 Caesarius died of the plague, and to add to Gregory's sorrows, his ascetic and much-loved and holy sister died soon afterwards in *c.*372.

By now, Basil, Bishop of Caesarea, was trying to build a Nicene party and appointed Gregory to the newly created diocese of Sasima, which Gregory considered a flyblown crossroads in the middle of nowhere, an "utterly dreadful pokey little hole". He escaped from Sasima whenever possible to pray, contemplate, write and reflect. It was while on an extended retreat from 375 at a convent in Seleukia that he received a summons to Constantinople that was to change his life, and indeed everything prior could be seen as a preparation for this moment.[19] Much hung in the balance. It was a time of great change, soon after the premature death of Basil in 379, aged only 49, and Emperor Valens's crushing defeat by the Goths at Adrianople in 378. Theodosius, the emperor who succeeded in January 379, had not yet fully got into his stride, and Constantinople seemed to be in almost perpetual theological ferment, with questions about the Trinity uppermost in the population's mind, more so perhaps than the results of the chariot races in the Forum.

As Gregory of Nyssa famously said, "If you ask anyone for change, he will discuss with you whether the Son is begotten or unbegot. If you ask about the quality of bread, you will receive the answer that 'the Father is greater, the Son is less'. If you suggest that you require a bath, you will be told that, 'There was nothing created before the Son was created.'"[20]

It was in this febrile atmosphere of theological debate that some cousins of Gregory of Nazianzus from the minority Nicene party in the city conceived of the idea of a preaching mission to the city, to be conducted by Gregory himself at a private chapel called Anastasia. They invited him to come from his isolated retreat in Seleukia and conduct this mission, which was to prove so significant in the development of Trinitarian Christianity. The exact site of the chapel is uncertain, but it was probably part of a private house between the Mese and the Golden Horn.[21] The villa was a splendid dwelling belonging to his cousin Theodosia, and in it a room was designated as the Church of Anastasia.[22] (It was here for a few brief months of 380 that Gregory in words of "exquisite opacity" described the relations of the members of the Trinity. Not only that, but early in the year he was attacked by an Arian mob while teaching and deceived by an Egyptian philosopher called Maximus.[23] Out of this cauldron of conspiracy and opposition of various kinds, Gregory was able to craft, and later polish, his *Orations on the Trinity* and one in praise of Athanasius.)

Before delivering what became known as the *Five Theological Orations* in 380, Gregory had given a miscellany of orations at the same location. The first of these was in tribute to Athanasius himself.[24] The opening sentence reads: "In praising Athanasius, I shall be praising virtues." In itself, it was a classic piece of Gregory of Nazianzus's thought, conflating the Greek philosophical idea of virtue with the stance and example of Athanasius. What follows is a comparison between Athanasius and the patriarchs, prophets and apostles of the past, and then a very selective description of Athanasius's life in which his character is presented without fault: "He was sublime in action, lowly in mind, inaccessible in virtue, most accessible in intercourse; gentle, free from anger, sympathetic, sweet in words, sweeter in disposition, angelic in appearance, more angelic in mind, calm in rebuke, persuasive in praise without spoiling the good effect of either by excess, but rebuking with the tenderness of a father and praising with the dignity of a ruler."[25] Athanasius might not have recognized himself! Furthermore, in his ministry, Athanasius was able to unite and bring together the insights and manner of working of the ascetics, monks and solitaries and the town clergy.[26]

Gregory's knowledge of Athanasius, his life and teaching, was in fact very sketchy, and he had virtually no first-hand knowledge of him. What he saw in him was a man who heroically fought for the Nicene cause and who stood by the *homoousions*' definition of the Trinity. Later, fifth-century Church historians such as Socrates, Sozomen and Theodoret filled out the picture of Athanasius, while in contrast, the Arian historian Philostorgius claimed that Athanasius was typically high-handed in his actions, such as his election as bishop and the way he ruled his diocese.[27] Having nailed his colours to this Athanasian mast in Constantinople in 379, Gregory demonstrated the way he was going, and the next year he began his benchmark description of the Father, Son and Spirit in his famous *Five Theological Orations.*

In the initial oration of this group (No. 27), Gregory set about critiquing the methods and theology of Eunomius, suggesting that his love of logic and intellectual problems was like sham-wrestling for entertainment.[28] There follows a brief discussion on how theology should and should not be done.[29] The next oration (No. 28) is in essence a contemplation of the nature or the essence of God. Here in a typical Cappadocian distinction between the substance of God (*ousia*) and the differentiating activity of each member of the Trinity (*hypostasis*), Gregory begins his contemplation of the Godhead, and in doing so takes the popular Cappadocian trope or type of Moses's quest for God on Mount Sinai when receiving the Commandments (Exodus 20). What we have is a biblical exploration of the substance of God which goes beyond what Athanasius attempted. Indeed, "as for knowing God himself, that is his nature and essence, as opposed to discerning the traces of revelation he has left about himself in creation, then the task is impossible".[30] Nazianzus concludes that "faith rather than reason shall lead us, if that is, you have learned the feebleness of reason to deal with matters quite close at hand and have acquired enough knowledge of reason to recognize things which surpass reason".[31] Contemplation and faith gave the possibility of understanding in a way of which reason is incapable, but further revelation is at hand, as Gregory of Nazianzus will now explain in the next oration, No. 29: On the Son.

Oration 29 breaks new ground with regard to our understanding of the ingeneracy (i.e., existence without a beginning) of the Son, going beyond Athanasius's description while still building on his *Contra Arianos*,[32] and secondly, in stating beautifully the expression of Jesus's perfect manhood and divinity. From the outset Gregory is answering the claim of the Arians that there was a time when the Son was not, and that he was therefore generate rather than begotten of the Father. Gregory writes in 29:2,3,4 that the Trinity always existed as Trinity: "For this reason, a one eternally, changes to a two and stops at three—meaning the Father, the Son and the Holy Spirit. In a serene, non-temporal, incorporeal way, the Father is parent of the offspring and originator of the emanation".[33] Although Gregory thinks better of the Platonic term emanation and says, "we limit ourselves to Christian terms and speak of the Ingenerate (the Father), the Begotten (the Son) and what proceeds from the Father."[34] These three occupy the same *ousia*.

Having established the existence of each member of the Trinity as part of the Godhead from eternity, he answers the Arian claim that any expression of the Word's humanity is a reason to disbelieve his divinity. In fact, Gregory goes on to argue the reverse: that the very essence of his incarnation and the glory of Christianity is the perfect combination of humanity and divinity in Jesus.[35] Thus, in a famous passage he says that biblical words or phrases like "God", "Word", "He who is in the beginning", "the only begotten-Son, who is in the bosom of the Father, he has declared him"; He is the "way", "truth" and "light", all demonstrate his Godhead.[36] Then, showing the deep paradox of being both human and divine he draws on a number of vivid contrasts, saying that Jesus was thirsty and "yet he exclaimed: 'Whosoever thirsts let him come to me and drink (John 7:37)'. He was tired, yet he is the rest of the weary and the burdened."[37] In other words, in his humanity, he identified with the weaknesses of the human race (he was no superman exempt from human vulnerability—see Hebrews 2:10–11,17; 4:14–5:3), and then from his divine resources healed them.

A further oration on the Son, No. 30, follows swiftly on from No. 29. Indeed it is quite possible that originally they were delivered as a single entity and then divided in Gregory's careful later writing up of his orations.[38] And once again it is structured around a rebuttal of many

Arian proof texts which were now extremely familiar. For instance, like Athanasius, Gregory rebutted the Arian misinterpretation of Proverbs 8:22: "The Lord created me [Wisdom] at the beginning of his work." For Gregory, this verse refers to the incarnation, the birth in flesh of wisdom; it does not refer to "the pre-existent generation of Wisdom from the Father before all time".[39] In all, Gregory deals with ten Arian proof texts, including from St John's Gospel where the Father is described as "greater" than the Son (see John 14:28b; 20:17). Gregory's answer is that the role of Son and Father may be distinct, but the status of equality between Father and Son is shown elsewhere in Scripture and notably in Philippians 2:5ff.[40] And when dealing with Jesus's admission of ignorance of his Second Coming, Gregory reiterates that part of the Son's laying aside of aspects of divinity in becoming human (see Philippians 2:6,7) was laying aside specific knowledge of his return. In this way, Gregory shows that he takes seriously the idea of *kenosis* (self-emptying), in which the Son voluntarily lays aside aspects of his majesty in becoming human. This does not put in jeopardy the reality of his divine substance, however.[41]

One more Oration, No. 31, follows on the Holy Spirit, which we shall look at in the next chapter, along with other teaching on the Holy Spirit in the fourth century. The Five Orations of Gregory on the Godhead were to form a bulwark against Arianism. In fact, they came at a moment just before the turning of the tide against Arianism in the empire, with the victory of Theodosius against the Goths (after the catastrophic defeat of Valens in Adrianople in 379), and his establishment as emperor over the whole empire. He was firmly of the Nicene party and was prepared to suppress Arianism wherever he found it. Gregory of Nazianzus's contribution, up until his abortive attempt to become Bishop of Constantinople in 381, was one of using the new and the old in the struggle with Arianism. Like Athanasius, he robustly answered the false proof texts on which they built their case, but he went further in his understanding of the nature of the incarnation, and in particular the relationship of the human and divine in Jesus. The debate had moved on and was no longer simply about the shared *ousia* of Father, Son and Spirit. It was now about the expression of the roles of Father, Son and Spirit in the Godhead. The Cappadocians had opened the way to this exploration. Basil and Gregory of Nazianzus had made a prominent start. The third and youngest and most mystical of the Cappadocians, Gregory of Nyssa, was now to take the reassertion of Nicene orthodoxy made at the Council of Constantinople in 381, over which Gregory of Nazianzus had briefly presided, to the dioceses of the region.

Gregory of Nyssa (335–95)

In Gregory of Nyssa, we find the most speculative of the Cappadocians, the most mystical in approach and the most Platonic in outlook. He lacked the administrative and pastoral genius of Basil, and the yearning for influence of Gregory of Nazianzus, but like both, he too was deeply committed to Nicene orthodoxy, taking up the pen powerfully on behalf of his brother Basil against Eunomius, who had responded aggressively to Basil's own version of *Against Eunomius.* Eunomius was essentially a logician who worked from the premise that anyone who was begotten could not be God. God alone was *agennetos.* However, the Cappadocians maintained that the Son was both begotten of the Father, having the Father as his source, and also in a sense unbegotten, with no beginning and having been eternally in existence with the Father prior to all creation (John 1:1). Gregory of Nyssa continued the struggle against the neo-Arians as found in Eunomius, taking the Nicene and Athanasian position that the Son and Spirit are of the same substance (*ousia*) as the Father.

As previously remarked, the Cappadocians developed the understanding of the Trinity as a single *ousia* or substance and defined the Godhead and three *hypostases* as a particular way of being God.[42] The analogy commonly used to explain this was that just as three men like the Apostles Peter, James and John all shared a common humanity (i.e., that which made them human) each was individuated with their particular gifts or hypostases. Likewise, the Trinity had a common divine substance making them equally part of the Godhead, yet each with their own individuated life. Basil himself makes this clear in his letter to Gregory of Nyssa where he describes the difference between substance and person and where he too uses this illustration about the commonality and individuality of humans as an analogy of the Trinity.[43] It was a useful analogy. But it quickly laid Gregory and others open to the charge of Tritheism, so it was not long before Gregory of Nyssa was defending his explanation in his work *Ad Ablabius: Not Three Gods*, published in 375. Here Gregory emphasizes the indivisibility of the divine nature shared by each member of the Trinity.[44] Equally, the unknowability of the divine nature is balanced by the knowability of divine power, or each member of the Godhead as a *hypostasis* or expression of divine power.[45]

Indeed, the substance, nature or being of the Godhead is not divisible, and is also unknowable to normal human intellect. It is this point which is so central to the Cappadocian understanding of the experience of God. It derives from their grasp of the apophatic or negative aspect of God's life—negative in the sense of being beyond human reason or measurement. After all, God is invisible, eternal, inscrutable, immortal, incomprehensible, immeasurable and indescribable. The substance of the Godhead, including this side beyond knowing, may only be grasped by *epinoia*, a spiritual process of contemplative prayer involving *askesis*—the stretching out of our being in costly prayer in order to understand, and the laying aside of *the garment of skin* or mere human life. At the same time, knowledge of each member of the Trinity in their actions enables us to understand the whole, for each member of the Godhead may be found in the other.

In the work of Gregory of Nyssa, this process of *epinoia* may be found especially in his studies of the Beatitudes, in his teaching on the Song of Songs and the life of Moses. His aspiration to understand the Trinity through a path of contemplative prayer, in which God reveals his love for us as Father, Son and Spirit through Scripture, is a long way from the bald doctrinal statements of the Nicene Creed. The Creed was a necessary starting point, a rallying point that Father, Son and Spirit shared the same substance. Yet the Trinity had to be experienced to be understood, and without prayer and submission this could not be done.

As the century moved on, there was a twofold development: in understanding what this substance of the Godhead was by using the discipline of *epinoia*, but also in understanding the work, energy and power of each member of the Trinity. This inevitably meant a deeper understanding of the incarnation. Athanasius had with bold lines sketched out the broad terms of the incarnation: the redemption of humanity by the

Word made flesh through the Cross and the consequent defeat of death. But how God and man subsisted as one such that Jesus was both fully human and fully God needed further explanation. Gregory of Nazianzus in particular began this process. On the one hand, the Arians had to be seen off with the affirmation from Scripture that Christ was fully God and of the same substance as the Father, but on the other the affirmation was required that Christ fully shared our humanity. There could be no truck with the extreme anti-Arians such as Apollinaris of Laodicea, who upheld Christ's divinity at the expense of him being truly human. (Apollinaris maintained that Jesus's human mind was replaced by a divine one.) In Gregory of Nazianzus's famous dictum to the young priest Cledonius: "The unassumed is the unhealed, but what is united with God is also being saved".[46] In other words, Jesus must fully assume all our humanity in order to save us in our entirety. Our humanity must be his humanity, except without sin: nothing can be left out, nothing replaced on the grounds it is too inferior to be inhabited by the Word. It was only a matter of time before the full focus of the fourth-century Fathers would be concentrated on the Spirit. Since Origen's day, theological reflection on the Spirit had lagged behind both devotional practice and time spent defining the incarnation in relation to the Father. The Spirit was barely mentioned in the first Nicene Creed. As it was an anti-Arian creed in which the Spirit played second fiddle to the Word in the concerns of Arius, little ink was spilt on the Spirit. But as the doctrine of the Trinity was developed, so the person and status of the Spirit came into full view.

Notes

1 Lewis Ayres, *Nicaea and its Legacy: An Approach to Fourth Century Trinitarian Theology* (Oxford: Oxford University Press, 2006), p. 165, citing Athanasius, *De Synodi* §30, in *Nicene and Post-Nicene Fathers: Second Series, Vol. IV: Athanasius: Selected Works and Letters*, ed. Philip Schaff (Edinburgh: T&T Clark, 1987), p. 467.

2 Philip Rousseau, *Basil of Caesarea* (Berkeley, CA: University of California Press, 1998), p. 3.

3 Lewis Ayres, *Nicaea and its Legacy: An Approach to Fourth Century Trinitarian Theology* (Oxford: Oxford University Press, 2006), p. 188.

4 Ayres, *Nicaea and its Legacy*, p. 164.

5 Basil, Letter 361, in Basil, *Letters* IV, ed. Roy Deferrari, Loeb Classical Library, Vol. 270 (Cambridge, MA: Harvard University Press, 2005), p. 331.

6 Ayres, *Nicaea and its Legacy*, p. 190.

7 Ayres, *Nicaea and its Legacy*, p. 191.

8 Ayres, *Nicaea and its Legacy*, p. 194.

9 Ayres, *Nicaea and its Legacy*, p. 210.

10 R. P. C. Hanson, *The Search for the Christian Doctrine of God: The Arian Controversy 318–381* (Edinburgh: T&T Clark, 1988), p. 690.

11 Basil, Letter 234–6, in Basil, *Letters* III, ed. Roy Deferrari, Loeb Classical Library, Vol. 243 (Cambridge, MA: Harvard University Press, 1989), pp. 371ff.

12 Basil, Letter 69, in Basil, *Letters* II, ed. Roy Deferrari, Loeb Classical Library, Vol. 215 (Cambridge, MA: Harvard University Press, 1926), p. 45.

13 Basil, *Letters* II, Vol. I, Loeb Classical Library, Vol. 215 (Cambridge, MA: Harvard University Press, 1926), p. 7.

14 Basil, *Letters* II, op. cit., p. 17.

15 Gregory of Nazianzus, *Letters* IV, in *Nicene and Post-Nicene Fathers: Second Series, Vol. VII: Cyril of Jerusalem, Gregory of Nazianzen*, ed. Philip Schaff (New York: Cosimo, 2007), pp. 446–7.

16 Gregory of Nazianzus, *In Defence of his Flight to Pontus* §9, in *Nicene and Post-Nicene Fathers: Second Series, Vol. VII: Cyril of Jerusalem, Gregory Nazianzen*, ed. Philip Schaff (New York: Cosimo, 2007), p. 207.

17 Gregory of Nazianzus, *In Defence of his Flight to Pontus* §16, op. cit., p. 208.

18 Gregory of Nazianzus, *In Defence of his Flight to Pontus* §25, op. cit., p. 210.

19 John A. McGuckin, *St Gregory Nazianzus: An Intellectual Biography* (Yonkers, NY: St Vladimir's Seminary Press, 2001), p. 231.

20 Gregory of Nyssa, *De Deitate Filii et Spiritus Sancti*, cited in Patrick Whitworth, *Three Wise Men from the East: The Cappadocian Fathers and the Struggle for Orthodoxy* (Durham: Sacristy Press, 2015), p. xlvi.

21 McGuckin, *St Gregory of Nazianzus*, p. 242.

22 McGuckin, *St Gregory of Nazianzus*, p. 241.

23 McGuckin, *St Gregory of Nazianzus*, p. 257.

24 *Oratio* 21, see in *Nicene and Post-Nicene Fathers: Second Series, Vol. VII: Cyril of Jerusalem, Gregory Nazianzen*, ed. Philip Schaff (New York: Cosimo, 2007), p. 269.

25 Or. 21, pp. 271–2.

26 Or. 20, p. 275.

27 Gwynn, *Athanasius of Alexandria*, p. 165.

28 Gregory of Nazianzus, Or. 27.20, in *On God and Christ* (Yonkers, NY: SVS Press, 2002), p. 25; McGuckin, *St Gregory of Nazianzus*, p. 279.

29 Or. 27.7, *On God and Christ*, op. cit., p. 30.

30 McGuckin, *St Gregory of Nazianzus*, p. 287.

31 Or. 28.28, *On God and Christ*, op. cit., p. 60.

32 McGuckin, *St Gregory of Nazianzus*, p. 291.

33 Or. 29.2, *On God and Christ*, op. cit., p. 70.

34 John 15:26, my parentheses; Or. 29.2, *On God and Christ*, op. cit., p. 70.

35 Or. 29.17–22, *On God and Christ*, op. cit., p. 82.

36 Or. 29.18, *On God and Christ*, op. cit., p. 84.

37 Matthew 11:28; *On God and Christ*, op. cit., p. 87.

38 McGuckin, *St Gregory of Nazianzus*, p. 298.

39 McGuckin, *St Gregory of Nazianzus*, p. 298.

40 Or. 30.7, *On God and Christ*, op. cit., p. 98.

41 McGuckin, *St Gregory of Nazianzus*, p. 300.

42 Morwenna Ludlow, *The Early Church* (London: I. B. Tauris, 2009), p. 132.

43 Basil, Letter 58, in Basil, *Letters* I, ed. Roy Defferari, Loeb Classical Library, Vol. 190 (Cambridge, MA: Harvard University Press, 1926), pp. 197ff.

44 Lewis Ayres, "Not Three People: The Fundamental Themes of Gregory of Nyssa's Trinitarian Theology as Seen in To Ablabius: On Not Three Gods", in Sarah Coakley (ed.), *Rethinking Gregory of Nyssa* (Oxford: Blackwell, 2003), pp. 16ff.

45 Ayres, "Not Three People", p. 33.

46 Gregory of Nazianzus, *On God and Christ*, op. cit., p. 158.

CHAPTER 11

The Holy Spirit

The work, activity and person of the Holy Spirit is clearly described in Scripture: present in creation, brooding over the face of the waters (Genesis 1:2), inspiring the prophets in their prophetic ministry (Isaiah 61:1; Ezekiel 43:5ff.) and giving life to a spiritually moribund Israel (Ezekiel 37). The Spirit prepared the way for the coming of the Messiah by blessing Mary at the annunciation (Luke 1:35) and by descending on Jesus at his baptism like a dove (Luke 3:22). Jesus promised the Spirit to his disciples, to live in them after his ascension and to be with them for ever as another counsellor (John 14:16). And on the Day of Pentecost, the Spirit was given to the Church, to empower, to guide and to direct its mission (Acts 2), as the Acts of the Apostles bears witness to.

From earliest times, following Pentecost, the activity of the Spirit was clear to the early Church. This work is described by Luke in the Acts of the Apostles and by Paul in his correspondence with the churches, especially with the Corinthian church (see 1 Corinthians 12–14). What was clear was that the threefold name of God in whom new converts were to be baptized and instructed was a dominical command which the early Church obeyed (see Matthew 28:19; Acts 2:38). The pattern for reception had been outlined on the Day of Pentecost. For on the Day of Pentecost repentance and faith in Christ's death and resurrection were the basis for reception of the Spirit.

In the early second century, the sense of the Spirit being conferred in baptism was continued among the Apostolic Fathers. That "the Spirit is received in Baptism is made clearer by the writer of 2 Clement".[1] Indeed, Clement talks about living in the seal of our baptism (see 2 Clement 6:9; 7:6; 8:6), and baptism was the place in which this seal was conferred, as it had been in the baptism of Christ (see Matthew 3:13ff.). In the *Didache*, written around 100, the writer encourages the use of baptism, specifying how it is to be practised. Thus, he says if there is no cold running water available for baptism pour warm water on the head of the candidate three times, "in the name of the Father, the Son and the Spirit" (*Didache* 7:2–4).

What is clear is that from earliest times in the liturgical practice of the Church, the expectation was that the convert would be sealed with the Spirit at baptism. Furthermore, the Spirit would be active making God present in the Church's fellowship and mission, and in applying the holy Scriptures to the community. In other words, the activity of the Spirit was acknowledged in the believer and in the fellowship from the start. But what was in question from the third century onwards, and which came to a head in the fourth century with the Arian crisis, was the status of the Spirit.

As we have seen, the so-called Monarchian crisis over the status of the persons within the Trinity had been brewing in the late second and early third centuries. Sabellius had begun teaching in Rome that there was a single divinity that expressed itself in different modes. This teaching was in contradistinction to the teaching of Justin the Martyr, who had in turn been influenced by the Apostle John's *Logos* theology. Indeed, Justin went so far as to say that the *Logos* was another God.[2] In this theological atmosphere it is no wonder that the status of the Holy Spirit became a reason for disputation among theologians. Bishop Alexander of Alexandria (312–28) repeated the old affirmation that the Spirit inspired the prophets and the apostles, but gave little further explanation of status or activity.[3] Arius regarded the Spirit as a third power and "third from the Supreme Cause and that one of the creations of the *Logos*". Likewise, Aetius and Eunomius regarded the Spirit "merely as the noblest of creatures produced by the Son at the Father's bidding".[4] On the other hand, Cyril of Jerusalem, who gave his famous *Catechetical Lectures* in 348 in Jerusalem, held a more orthodox position in which he regarded the Spirit as part of the Trinity, "for we do not divide the Holy Triad as some do, nor do we work confusion in it as Sabellius does".[5]

All this serves to show the confusion there was as to the status, if not the activity, of the Spirit in the early fourth century. The exuberant or strategic record of the Spirit's work found in the Gospels, especially in Luke and John, the Acts of the Apostles and the Epistles, was thrown into question by many asking if the Spirit was of the same substance as the Father. By 359 and 360, Athanasius himself was to enter the fray in terms of a defence of the status of the Spirit as fully divine. The Bishop of Thmuis, Serapion, had asked for Athanasius's thoughts on a group of Egyptian Christians Athanasius called *Tropici* because of their figurative teaching on the Spirit. These *Tropici* argued that the Spirit was an angel, superior to other angels in rank, but nonetheless to be classified among the ministering spirits mentioned in Hebrews 1:14.

Athanasius's response to Serapion, in which he sets out his understanding of the Spirit's status, was given whilst in hiding in the desert during his third exile. His response comes in the form of four letters and is typical of his style in general. He shows what is at stake with the Arians, and their desire to depict God not as a Triad, but either as Dyad, or, as their stated aim says, as a Monad (1:2). Athanasius then examines the Scriptures to see what they say about the status of the Spirit. Nowhere in Scripture is the Spirit simply "the spirit" without being either the Spirit of God, or of the Lord, or of Christ or simply the Holy Spirit. These descriptions indicate that in Scripture the Spirit is part of the Godhead. Athanasius argues cogently that if not part of the Godhead how can the Spirit renew us in the image of the Son who also is fully God (1:9)? Having surveyed Scripture in relation to the Spirit's occurrence, Athanasius's first letter to Serapion moves towards an emphatic conclusion. Thus, he writes:

> For the holy and blessed Triad is indivisible and one in itself. When mention is made of the Father, there is included his Word, and the Spirit who is in the Son. If the Son is named, the Father is in the Son, and the Spirit is not outside the Word. For there is from the Father one grace which is fulfilled through the Son in the Holy Spirit; and there is one divine nature, and one God "who is over all and through all in all" (1:14).

This first letter to Serapion is very much the foundation of his defence of the Spirit's divine status against the claims of the *Tropici*. For Athanasius, the Spirit is fully divine, consubstantial with the Father and the Son. And the argument which Athanasius frequently deploys in summary is that the Son and the Spirit have the closest of relationships, just as the Son does with the Father. Indeed, in Scripture the Holy Spirit is frequently called the Spirit of the Son (John 14:26; 16:14,15b) and as such enlightens, illuminates and sanctifies, and is bestowed by the Son (1:20). "For the Spirit is inseparable from the Son, as the Son is inseparable from the Father" (1:33). It is a powerful case, but by the end of this first letter, he is not above confessing the weakness of his writing and asks Serapion to "amend it" because it may be feebly written due to his present circumstances in exile (1:33). This is Athanasius at his most compelling: allowing the truth to speak for itself but expressing his own shortcomings with humility and grace.

The first letter from Athanasius to Serapion, the bedrock of his teaching on the Holy Spirit, makes the case for the Spirit's full inclusion in the Godhead. The second letter, rather than being about the Spirit, is in fact for the most part a restatement of arguments against the Arians and their belittlement of the Son. Athanasius seeks "to refute the impiety of those who say the Word of God is a creature" (2:6). Although not restating his position on the Spirit in his second letter to Serapion, Athanasius makes good this omission in his third. He excuses his focus on the Son in the second, adding ironically that he was moved by the Spirit to write about the Son, "for it is natural that I should have spoken and written first concerning the Son, that from our knowledge of the Son we may be able to have true knowledge of the Spirit" (3:1).

Athanasius once again speaks about the Spirit in his third letter, and summarizes his argument succinctly, so that it can be more easily shared with others:

> Throughout divine Scripture you will find that the Holy Spirit, who is said to belong to the Son, is also said to belong to God. This I wrote in my previous letter. If therefore the Son, because of his proper relationship with the Father and because he is the proper offspring of his essence, is not a creature, but is one in essence with the Father, the Holy Spirit likewise, because of his proper relationship with the Son, through whom he is given to all men and who is all that he has, cannot be a creature, and it is impious to call him so (3:1).

Once again Athanasius's central argument about the Spirit, as previously with the Son, is that neither he, nor they, are creatures, but existed from the beginning as part of the Godhead. "If the Son cannot be a creature because he does not come from nothing, but from God, then of necessity the Spirit is not a creature, for we have confessed that he comes from God. It is creatures that come from nothing" (3:2). Athanasius then gives reasons why the Spirit cannot be a creature (reasons that may be more or less convincing to us), as follows: because he is unction, anointing the Son and then the believers; because he confers on us the other members of the Godhead so that "he who has seen the Son sees the Father, so he who has the Holy Spirit has the Son, and, having him, is a temple of God" (3:3). One who confers the Godhead on a creature (i.e., a disciple) cannot himself be a creature but is part of the Godhead. Thus, the Spirit is not created, but is of divine substance, and as he is everywhere, he cannot be of the created order (3:4).

In the fourth and final letter to Serapion, Athanasius is concerned that each member of the Trinity is properly described, for Arians mock the Trinity by giving its members tendentious titles. Thus, the Arians, or the Holy Spirit-deniers, suggest that if the Spirit is begotten by the Son, the Son too must be a father and the Father a grandfather! Athanasius outlines this Arian argument in these terms: "If the Son is an image of the invisible Father, and the Spirit is an image of the Son, then according to this, the Father is a grandfather" (4:3). Athanasius was having none of this. He taught instead the complete interdependence of Father, Son and Spirit in which each was fully active with the others. This is well expressed in the quotation:

> The Son is an offspring proper to the essence and nature of the Father; that is the sense the term bears. The Spirit, who is said to be of God and is in God, is not alien to the nature of the Son nor to the Godhead of the Father. Therefore, there is in the Triad—in the Father and in the Son and in the Holy Spirit himself—one Godhead and in the same Triad there is one baptism and one faith. Thus, when the Father sends the Spirit, it is the Son who by breathing upon them gives him to the disciples (4:3).

This, then, was the essence of Athanasius's defence of the Spirit's full divinity against the Arians. It was a position he would maintain for the remaining years of his life (356–73). His *Letters to Serapion* stand as his most developed understanding of the matter, and form part of his most polemical and definitive teaching about the Trinity in the face of Arianism. Athanasius makes it clear that far from having anything in common with the creatures, the Spirit "belongs to and is one with the Godhead which is the Triad . . . Thus, while creatures come from nothingness, are recipients of sanctification and life, and are mutable, circumscribed and multiple, the Spirit comes from God, bestows sanctification and Life, and is immutable, omnipresent and unique."[6] It was in this period of his third exile that he also wrote his sweeping condemnation of Arianism in *Historia Arianorum* and in particular of their attacks on him. He let rip his full vilification of Constantius in this work also.[7] But as we have seen, far from being a single entity or the work of one man, as a philosophical and theological movement, Arianism manifested as a many-headed hydra, such that if a head was decapitated in one place, it would not be long before it re-emerged elsewhere. This was the case in the matter of the divinity of the Spirit.

Basil of Caesarea

As we have already seen, the Cappadocians took on the defence of the Trinity in their different ways in the middle and late fourth century. All of them had to contend with various group of heresiarchs, who, in different ways and to varying degrees, questioned the full divinity of the Spirit. Just as with the Son or *Logos* there were varying ways of defining closeness to the Father (like in substance, *homoiousios*, or like in will but unlike in substance, principally *homoian*), so too there were different ways of describing the Spirit's closeness to the Father and the Son. By 380, a group had emerged opposed to the full deity of the Spirit, known as the Macedonians or Pneumatomachians (Spirit-fighters). The former name, Macedonians, was derived not from Macedonia the place, but from the Bishop of Constantinople in 360. Macedonius was a moderate Arian deposed by those more extreme. These so-called "Spirit-fighters" were themselves divided into two groups. The more moderate of them accepted the consubstantiality of the Son, if not the Spirit, while the more radical, led by Basil's old friend and later theological rival, Eustathius of Sebaste, taught that the Spirit was unlike the Father and in a similar category as the Son.[8] By 375, Basil had clearly broken with Eustathius, who had accused him of writing to Apollinaris, the heretic, 25 years before, and of being close to him.[9] Partly in response to this rift with Eustathius and the other "Spirit-fighters", Basil wrote the first full-length book on the Holy Spirit.

Basil's approach to advocating the full divinity of the Spirit was initially cautious. His fellow Cappadocians, Gregory of Nazianzus and Gregory of Nyssa, were much more forthright. When preaching in 372, Basil had studiously avoided fully acknowledging the Spirit's deity.[10] This may well have been tactical, in that he was trying to win over the more moderate Spirit-fighters by not stating too unequivocally that the Spirit was consubstantial with the Father and the Son. It could also be that he was simply theologically more cautious about declaring the Spirit coequal to the Father and the Son. However, as the policy did not bear fruit and Eustathius and the Spirit-fighters did not come around, Basil gradually adopted a clearer position on the divinity of the Spirit. He also increasingly adopted an understanding of the Trinity in which each member of the Godhead shared inseparably in a common *ousia*. Each was described as a *hypostasis* in which none were subordinate to the others, but where the Father was the source of the other two.[11]

On the Holy Spirit was dedicated to a younger bishop and mentee of Basil's: Amphilochius of Iconium. In some ways, the work is an extension of Basil's *Against Eunomius* and in its earlier part it denigrates the methods of Eunomius and Aetius in literally subordinating the Spirit and Son to the Father. In the matter of creation, the Spirit or Son are said to be described by Scripture as instruments of God "by whom" or "through whom" what is has come into existence. For Basil this is "logic-chopping".[12] Much attention is given to refusing to allow these prepositions of creation to give rise to a subordinated role in creation for the Son or the Spirit. Then, after dealing with the false inferences that the Spirit was no more than the Father's instrument of creation, Basil moves to a more positive description of the Spirit and the Spirit's relationship with the Father and Son.

Midway through *On the Holy Spirit*, Basil begins a felicitous survey of the work and being of the Spirit in Scripture, saying: "Let us examine now our general ideas about the Holy Spirit, those that are gathered about him for us from the Scriptures together with those that we have received from the no-scriptural tradition of the Fathers."[13] Basil marvels at the ubiquity and particularity of the Spirit:

> He is simple in substance, but manifold in powers. He presents as a whole to each and wholly present everywhere. He is portioned out impassibly and participated in as a whole. He is like a sunbeam whose grace is present to the one who enjoys him as if he were present to such one alone, and still he illuminates land and sea and is mixed with the air. Just so, indeed the Spirit is present to him alone, and still, he sends out grace that is complete and sufficient for all.[14]

Again, Basil writes wonderfully of the Spirit's work:

> The Spirit illuminates those who have been cleansed from every stain and makes them spiritual by means of communion with himself. When a ray of light falls upon clear and translucent bodies, they are themselves filled with light and gleam with a light from themselves. Just so are the Spirit-bearing souls that are illuminated by the Holy Spirit: they are themselves made spiritual, and they send forth grace to others. Thence comes foreknowledge of the future, understanding of mysteries, apprehension of secrets, distributions of graces, heavenly citizenship, the chorus with angels, unending joy, remaining in God, kinship with God, and the highest object of desire: becoming God.[15]

Having garnished the dish of the Spirit's work and set forth "his greatness, his dignity and his energies",[16] Basil returns to the more prosaic work of refuting those who subordinate the Son and the Spirit to the Father, through a kind of pecking order in the Trinity with regard to the divinity of each of the three persons. Basil's main point will be that the work of the Spirit is inseparable from the Father and the Son and that this deeply affects how the work of sanctification is understood.[17] Furthermore, Basil insists that the disciple is baptized in the name of Father, Son and Spirit, and that each of them will play their part in the life of the disciple.[18] So, Basil asserts, "For as we believe in the Father, Son, and Holy Spirit, so also, we are baptized in the name of the Father, Son, and Holy Spirit. The confession that brings salvation comes first and there follows baptism that seals our assent."[19]

Basil then comes to the assertion that the Holy Spirit is indivisible from the Father and the Son.[20] There is one source, the Father, who creates through the Son and perfects through the Spirit. Furthermore, Basil says, like the Son and the Father, the Spirit is beyond comprehension,[21] is glorified,[22] alone can search the deepest places of the Godhead (1 Corinthians 2:10) and be called Lord. But for all his assertion of the Spirit's coequality with the Father and the Son, his fellow Cappadocians, Gregory of Nazianzus and Gregory of Nyssa, would have had him go further in making it unmistakeable that the Spirit was God sharing the same substance as Father and Son. Basil had begun to make this clear in *Contra Eunomius* 3.1, but in *On the Holy Spirit* the Spirit is seen as the perfecter of what the Father and Son have begun, and Basil is a little more reserved about affirming the Spirit's divinity. It would take Gregory of Nazianzus six years, a year after Basil's death, to make what had been inferred explicit, namely that the Spirit was fully God.

Gregory of Nazianzus

Gregory's fifth and last Oration, No. 31, given in the Chapel of Anastasia, was on the Holy Spirit, and broadly aimed at the so-called Spirit-fighters or Pneumatomachians who were a strong force, even among the bench of bishops in the area. Indeed, a contingent of 36 bishops at the council held in Constantinople "were agreeable to a broadly Nicene Christology but stoutly resisted the theology of the Spirit".[23] If Basil's exegesis of the Spirit was cautious, even reserved, and if he was slow to name the Spirit as God in the same way as the Father and the Son, Gregory of Nazianzus was not so circumspect, saying: "For our part we have such confidence in the Godhead of the Spirit, that, rash though some find it, we shall begin our theological exposition by applying identical expressions to the Three." He goes on to say that each person of the Godhead was "the true light that enlightens every man coming into the world".[24]

Gregory of Nazianzus then comes to the age-old Arian assertion that there can only be one ingenerate God (i.e., one God without generation and thus eternally existing) and therefore the Son and Spirit must be subordinate to the Father since he gave them existence. Gregory of Nazianzus is pleased to use the terms "begotten of the Son" and "the procession of the Spirit" to ensure that they are seen as eternally part of the Godhead, although coming from a common source. Thus, Gregory of Nazianzus says, "The Holy Spirit proceeds from the Father (John 15:26). In so far as he proceeds from the Father, he is no creature; inasmuch as he is begotten, [the Spirit] is no Son; and to the extent that procession is the mean between ingeneracy and generacy, he is God."[25] He goes on to say we are not competent to fathom this mystery of being or origin, but must accept what is taught in the Scriptures. And then, in answering in what way the Spirit is different from the Son, Gregory of Nazianzus comes to a kind of apotheosis of his exposition:

> The very facts of not being created, of being begotten and of proceeding, give them whatever names are applied to them—Father, Son and Holy Spirit respectively. The aim is to safeguard the distinctness of the three hypostases within the single nature and quality of the Godhead. The Son is not Father; There is one Father, yet he is whatever the Father is. The Spirit is not Son because he is from God; there is one Only-begotten. Yet whatever the Son is, he is. The three are a single whole in their Godhead and the single whole is three in personalities.[26]

And in a final swipe at his opponents at the end of this paragraph, Gregory of Nazianzus says this teaching is not Sabellianism. It is not proclaiming a single God manifest in three forms. Nor is it proclaiming three Gods, but one Godhead with three hypostases. Emboldened by his statement, Gregory of Nazianzus answers his own questions:

"Is the Spirit God? Certainly."

"Is he consubstantial? Yes, if he is God."[27]

A declaration of the Spirit's divinity comes more unequivocally after this high point in his Oration. Gregory of Nazianzus returns to answering oft-repeated objections to the Spirit's full divinity. Is there evidence of the Spirit being worshipped as God? How can plurality in the Godhead exist, if both the Son and Spirit are fully God? And if there are three *hypostases*, is there numerical distinction between them? Gregory of Nazianzus argues that individuated existence does not mean that they cannot be of the same substance.[28] He maintains that these truths are to be found in the Bible, but the Bible must be rightly interpreted.[29]

All in all, Gregory of Nazianzus discerns a progressive revelation of the Trinity to humanity: first the Father, then the Son and finally the Spirit. All were from the beginning but were progressively revealed through the two covenants:

> God meant it to be by piecemeal additions, "ascents", as David called them, by progress and advance from glory to glory, that the light of the Trinity should shine upon more illustrious souls. This was, I believe the motive for the Spirit's making his home in the disciples in gradual stages proportionate to their capacity to receive him—at the outset of the Gospel when he performs miracles, after the Passion when he is breathed into the disciples, after the Ascension when he appears in fiery tongues. He was gradually revealed by the Spirit.[30]

And then in a cascade of biblical texts, in a way which is typical of him, Gregory of Nazianzus seeks to show the divinity of the Spirit.[31] Curiously, after such a resounding affirmation of the Spirit's divinity from the Bible, Gregory of Nazianzus then considers and discards an analogy of the Trinity with the sun (the sun itself, its beam and light). He discards the analogy because of insufficient substance given to the beam and the light. And in this vein, Gregory of Nazianzus turns his back on "images and shadows", calling them deceptive and utterly inadequate to express reality. Instead, using the Spirit as his guide, and presumably the biblical texts as his foundation, he seeks to "persuade all men to worship Father, Son, and Holy Spirit as the single Godhead and power, because to him alone belong all glory, honour and might for ever and ever. Amen."[32]

With this, Gregory finished his last Oration on the Godhead in the Chapel of Anastasia. A surer commendation of the divinity of the Spirit could not be found in the eastern Church, building as it did on the most reserved work on the Spirit of his friend, colleague and sometimes sparring partner, Basil, and in turn upon the beginning made by Athanasius in his letters to Serapion. The third Cappadocian, Gregory of Nyssa, would be responsible for promulgating this full Trinitarian faith to the churches.

Gregory of Nyssa

The Council of Constantinople began in May 381, with Gregory of Nazianzus temporarily president after the sudden death of the previous president, the saintly bishop of Antioch, Meletios. Gregory himself resigned the post in frustration with the bench of bishops and was replaced by another, appointed by the new Emperor Theodosius. Gregory of Nazianzus had little good to say about the council, which he considered a mass of fractious and unruly bishops, and he records as much in his autobiographical poem, *De Vita Sua*.[33] Still, Gregory of Nyssa and his brother Peter of Sebaste (both brothers of Basil of Caesarea) arrived in Constantinople for the council and to lend support to Gregory of Nazianzus. Despite its difficulties for Gregory of Nazianzus, the council produced a creed in which there was slightly more recognition of the Holy Spirit than in the Nicene Creed. Gregory of Nazianzus nevertheless fought hard for a more comprehensive definition of the Spirit's divinity (*homoousios* with the Father and the Son), and this was one of his sticking points with the council.

The creed did contain this statement of belief about the Spirit: "We believe . . . in the Holy Spirit, the Lord and Life-giver, who proceeds from the Father who is worshipped and glorified together with the Father and the Son, who spoke by the prophets . . . "[34] Everything after the words "the

Holy Spirit" was an addition to the Nicene Creed, which had the barest minimum, simply "We believe in the Holy Spirit".[35]

Both Gregory of Nazianzus and Gregory of Nyssa had wanted a much more comprehensive definition of the Spirit's divinity and of being *homoousios* with the Father and Son, but it was not forthcoming from a council influenced by Arian thinking and by general reticence in the matter. On the other hand, there is an argument that the wording of the creed was left ambiguous with regard to the Spirit, so as to draw in as many of the *homoiousian* and ex *homoiousian* bishops as possible.[36] Indeed, Gregory of Nyssa had been invited to Constantinople by Gregory of Nazianzus and others in the spring of 381 to give a series of talks, probably also at the Anastasia Chapel, about his newest work, *Contra Eunomium*, a sequel to Basil's own work *Against Eunomius* to which Eunomius had given a blistering response in his *Second Apology*, produced after Basil's death.[37] These talks were attended by a cluster of influential theologians and thinkers, including Evagrios of Pontike, Jerome and possibly Diodore of Tarsus, as well as Gregory of Nazianzus and Peter of Sebaste. Here was the future of the orthodox Church; although at the time defining such orthodoxy was tough going and was proceeding slowly.[38]

Being a little younger than Gregory of Nazianzus, and less pessimistic about the possibility of progress in rightly rendering the Trinity, Gregory of Nyssa brought to the table strong credentials on the Holy Spirit as well as fresh energy. He was regarded with affection by his older brother Basil, but at the same time considered a bit suspect, because in 371 he had forged a letter from their uncle with the worthy but misguided intention of patching a quarrel with Basil.[39] Steeped in Platonic thought and in the teaching of Origen, Gregory of Nyssa was nevertheless thoroughly orthodox in his understanding of the Trinity in the sense that Father, Son and Spirit were *homoousias*. (When it came to the doctrine of final judgement he followed Origen as a universalist, believing all would finally be reconciled.) Nevertheless, Gregory of Nyssa's beauty was that on the one hand he held to the truth of the Trinity firmly, yet used the tools of contemplation and *epinoia* to explore the mystery of the Godhead through *askesis* (ascetic self-denial) on the other. He did this in a deeply mystical way, using texts like the Song of Songs and the Beatitudes. Only such a discipline could yield a true understanding of God, "since there is no faculty in human nature adequate to the full comprehension of the divine essence".[40]

We have already considered Gregory of Nyssa's important work *Ad Ablabium: Not Three Gods*, which was a defence of the Trinity. However, Gregory was to make other important contributions to the orthodox position following the Council of Constantinople in 381. In combating the idea that the Nicene position leads to the conclusion there are three Gods, Gregory of Nyssa makes a distinction that became common with the Cappadocians: the nature or substance of the Father, Son and Spirit is indivisible and cannot be known, but the *hypostases* of Father, Son and Spirit may be discerned in their energetic activity, and indeed in creation itself. Far from each person of the Trinity being independent in their activity, they work together. The analogy he used was that of the rainbow, a single bow made up of discernible colours.[41]

Further important contributions by Gregory of Nyssa to the Trinitarian debate, and the notion of the divinity of the Spirit, were his *De Spiritu sancto, adversus Macedonianos*, his *Against Eunomius Books 1–XII* (c.382), his *Answer to Eunomius's Second Book* (c.384), and *On the Holy Trinity, and of the Godhead of the Holy Spirit.* While the *Answer to Eunomius's Second Book* is largely taken up with maintaining the ingeneracy of the Only Begotten, the short work *On the Holy Spirit Against the Followers of Macedonius* is much more illustrative of Gregory of Nyssa's understanding of the Spirit.

At the outset, he is unequivocal: "We, for instance confess that the Holy Spirit is of the same rank as the Father and the Son, so that there is no difference between them in anything, to be thought or named, that devotion can ascribe to a Divine nature."[42] Gregory of Nyssa answers the naysayers on the subject of the Spirit's divinity thus: "We shall fall back upon the testimony in Holy Scripture about the Spirit, whence we learn that the Holy Spirit is divine, and is to be called so."[43] Once again he emphasizes the complete interdependence and unity of Father, Son and Spirit, saying, "We are not to think of the Father as ever parted from the Son, nor to look for the Son as separate from the Holy Spirit. As it is impossible to mount to the Father, unless our thoughts are exalted thither through the Son, so it is impossible also to say that Jesus is Lord except by the Holy Spirit."[44] Indeed, the indivisibility of the three cannot be broken and they share a common kingship.[45] It was typical of him to stress that "the power which gave rise to them is the same and the ineffable divine nature in which that power is inherent must also be one. Thus, the divine nature remains unknown but shared, but its power is revealed to be one."[46] Gregory of Nyssa is not speaking about three Gods but a divine unity.

At the Council of Constantinople over which Gregory of Nazianzus temporarily presided and at which Gregory of Nyssa was present, there were some further elaborations of the role of the Spirit in our salvation compared with Nicaea. It was he, the Spirit, it was stated, who enabled the incarnation through the Virgin Mary, and it also expanded the simple subclause on the Spirit in the Nicene Creed to say:

> We believe in the Holy Spirit, the Lord, the giver of life
> who proceeds from the Father.
> With the Father and Son, he is worshipped and glorified
> He has spoken through the Prophets.

As the fourth century drew to a close, Gregory of Nyssa, who died in *c.*395, provided a mature, well-founded and sophisticated doctrine of the Trinity, and in particular of the Spirit's divinity. As he said in response to Eunomius in his long work *Contra Eunomius*, "The peculiarity (*idiótēs*) of the hypostases renders the distinction of the persons (*prosopon*) clear, and unconfused and one Name (God) of the statement of faith presented to us indicates plainly the singleness of the *ousia* of the Persons in our belief: I mean the Father and of the Son and of the Holy Spirit."[47] At the end of this century of the Cappadocians, the *ousia* theology prevailed as a means of describing the single nature of the Godhead. It had first made its appearance in a creed at Nicaea, was later adopted more fully by Athanasius, and then later defended and advocated by him, and now, by the end of the century, and with the support of imperial power once again (Theodosius also died in 395), was in the ascendancy again.

Notes

1 G. W. H. Lampe, *The Seal of the Spirit* (London: SPCK, 1976), p. 103.

2 Henry Chadwick, *The Early Church* (Harmondsworth: Penguin, 1993), p. 85.

3 J. N. D. Kelly, *Early Christian Doctrines* (London: Adam Charles Black, 1960), p. 255.

4 Kelly, *Early Christian Doctrines*, p. 256.

5 Kelly, *Early Christian Doctrines*, p. 256.

6 Kelly, *Early Christian Doctrines*, p. 257.

7 Athanasius, *Historia Arianorum* §8, in *Nicene and Post-Nicene Fathers: Second Series, Vol. IV Athanasius: Selected Works and Letters*, ed. Philip Schaff (Edinburgh: T&T Clark, 1987), pp. 68–74.

8 Kelly, *Early Christian Doctrines*, p. 259.

9 Basil, Letters 125 and 223 (to Eustathius), in Basil, *Letters* II, pp. 259ff. and Vol. 243, pp. 287ff.

10 Kelly, *Early Christian Doctrines*, p. 260.

11 Hanson, *The Search for the Christian Doctrine of God*, p. 698.

12 Basil, *On the Holy Spirit* (Yonkers, NY: SVS Press, 2011), §3, p. 31.

13 Basil, *On the Holy Spirit* §9, op. cit., p. 52.

14 Basil, *On the Holy Spirit* §9, op. cit., p. 53.

15 Basil, *On the Holy Spirit* §9, op. cit., p. 54.

16 Basil, *On the Holy Spirit* §9, op. cit., p. 54.

17 Ayres, *Nicaea and its Legacy*, p. 217.

18 Basil, *On the Holy Spirit* §12, op. cit., pp. 58–9.

19 Basil, *On the Holy Spirit* §12, op. cit., p. 59.

20 Basil, *On the Holy Spirit* §16, op. cit., p. 69.

21 Basil, *On the Holy Spirit* §16, op. cit., p. 91.

22 Basil, *On the Holy Spirit* §16, op. cit., p. 84.

23 McGuckin, *St Gregory Nazianzus*, p. 381.

24 Gregory of Nazianzus, Or. 31.3, *On God and Christ*, op. cit., p. 118, citing John 1:9.

25 Gregory of Nazianzus, Or. 31.8, *On God and Christ*, op. cit., p. 122.

26 Gregory of Nazianzus, Or. 31.9, *On God and Christ*, op. cit., p. 123.

27 Gregory of Nazianzus, Or. 31.10, *On God and Christ*, op. cit., p. 123.

28 Gregory of Nazianzus, Or. 31.18, *On God and Christ*, op. cit., p. 130.

[29] Gregory of Nazianzus, Or. 31.1ff., *On God and Christ*, op. cit., pp. 133ff.

[30] Gregory of Nazianzus, Or. 31.26, *On God and Christ*, op. cit., p. 137.

[31] Gregory of Nazianzus, Or. 31.29, *On God and Christ*, op. cit., pp. 139–40.

[32] Gregory of Nazianzus, Or. 31.33, *On God and Christ*, op. cit., p. 143.

[33] *De Vita* §v, line 1525, and McGuckin, *St Gregory Nazianzus*, p. 350.

[34] Cited Ayres, *Nicaea and its Legacy*, p. 255, using Hanson's translation from *The Search for the Christian Doctrine of God*, p. 816.

[35] Kelly, *Early Christian Doctrines*, p. 232.

[36] Ayres, *Nicaea and its Legacy*, p. 258.

[37] McGuckin, *St Gregory Nazianzus*, p. 349.

[38] Ayres, *Nicaea and its Legacy*, pp. 257ff.

[39] Basil, Letter 58, in Basil, *Letters* I, ed. Roy Defferari, Loeb Classical Library, Vol. 190 (Cambridge, MA: Harvard University Press, 1926), p. 357.

[40] Gregory of Nyssa, *Answer to Eunomius's Second Book*, in *Nicene and Post-Nicene Fathers: Second Series, Vol. V Gregory of Nyssa: Dogmatic Treatises* (New York: Cosimo, 2007), p. 257.

[41] Hanson, *The Search for the Christian Doctrine of God*, p. 724; see also Basil's Epistle 38 on the Trinity, *Letters* I, Loeb Classical Library, Vol. 190, pp. 197ff.

[42] Gregory of Nyssa, *On the Holy Spirit*, in *Nicene and Post-Nicene Fathers: Second Series, Vol. V*, p. 316.

[43] Gregory of Nyssa, *On the Holy Spirit*, op. cit., p. 316.

[44] Gregory of Nyssa, *On the Holy Spirit*, op. cit., p. 319.

[45] Gregory of Nyssa, *On the Holy Spirit*, op. cit., p. 321.

[46] Ayres, *Nicaea and its Legacy*, p. 355.

[47] Hanson, *The Search for the Christian Doctrine of God*, p. 725, citing Gregory of Nyssa, *Contra Eunomium* 12.

CHAPTER 12

Athanasius and his legacy

Athanasius has remained a pivotal and controversial figure in Church history: pivotal because he stemmed the tide of Arianism, laying a bulwark of truth for the future when Arianism was in full flood (curiously the threat was greatest in the years following Nicaea when Constantius was the emperor); and controversial because the methods or stance he adopted in defending his cause combined great intransigence and a tone that was sometimes interpreted as high handed, especially by his theological opponents. Theologically the stakes could not have been higher; the actions against him drove him into exile five times, and on several occasions, it was touch-and-go whether he would succeed in his endeavours.

Estimations by his contemporaries and by historians over the years have varied greatly. Gregory of Nazianzus, who probably never met him, said, "He was sublime in action, lowly in mind; inaccessible in virtue, most accessible in intercourse; gentle, free from anger, sympathetic, sweet in words, sweeter in disposition, angelic in appearance."[1] In 1898, Adolf von Harnack, the liberal German scholar of religion, wrote, "by the standards of his time, we can discover nothing ignoble or mean about him".[2] Gibbon wrote admiringly of him in his great work in the eighteenth century: "Amidst the storms of persecution, the archbishop of Alexandria was patient of labour, jealous of fame, careless of safety; and although his mind was tainted by the contagion of fanaticism, Athanasius displayed a superiority of character and abilities which would have qualified him, far better than the degenerate sons of Constantine for the government of a great monarchy."[3] And more recently, Timothy Barnes wrote, "[Athanasius] exercised power more efficiently (than other later Coptic Patriarchs) and ... was successful in presenting himself to posterity as an innocent in power, as an honest, sincere and straightforward 'man of God'".[4] In some ways, Athanasius was not unlike Martin Luther, 12 centuries later, who also faced an emperor: In his case Charles V, at the Diet of Worms. Both used language or actions which could be construed as extreme; both saw that this was necessary to combat the falsehoods of either powerful men or institutions.

Athanasius: *Contra Mundum* (Against the World)

There is no doubt that Athanasius's greatest legacy was the record of his life and its privations in the cause of the incarnation, and his writings, which ranged from profound reflection on the emptiness of paganism and the truths of the incarnation to a history of the Arian controversy in his lifetime. The understanding he gave and an understanding of the development of the latter were not fully evaluated until the advent of modern scholarship in the twentieth century.

What has hopefully been clear in this book is that Arianism was the product of a rationalist frame of mind, beloved of logicians, with logic itself strong in Greek culture, and the premium placed on reason. The overriding conclusion of Arianism was that there was only one true God, who was himself ingenerate, and from whom all other beings were generated in a sequence of seniority. Thus, the Son and the Spirit were generated by the Father and were his creations and were themselves generated by him and subordinate to him. Not being fully God, the Son and the Spirit could not fully and eternally redeem or sanctify respectively. If this were the line of argument of the so-called Ariomaniacs, as Athanasius called them, they passionately thought they were defending the Godhead from any degradations and believed there was one Almighty God and all else were his creations.

In the end, and to put it simply, Arianism was a view of God moulded and shaped by Greek philosophy and Middle Platonism with its love of reason and purely logical view of the Scriptures. Wherever a text in the Scriptures could be pressed into Arian service it was. The profound irony was that far from defending the Godhead from degradation, the Arians were in fact degrading the richness, diversity, wisdom and power of the Godhead: one substance (being/*ousia*) but three persons with energy and roles that could be severally but uniformly experienced, discerned and known on earth to a degree (1 Corinthians 13:12b). For the Cappadocians such knowing was through *epinoia*.

Arianism was the name that Athanasius gave to this movement within the Church, but it was a broad trend in philosophical and theological interpretation of the Bible with its particular interpreters or advocates. It provided one answer to questions that had been surrounding the exposition of the Godhead since the second century, the Monarchist controversy in Rome and the teaching of Sabellius (*c*.215—we do not know his dates) and Paul of Samosata (200–75). Arius was the first of many advocates of this broad movement. His personal appeal was great, and he had wide-ranging support among fellow theological travellers—the Eusebians and teachers such as Lucian and Iamblichus of the neo-Platonist school. There were many others in his lifetime like them, while others, e.g., Eunomius, arose after his death. Furthermore, Arianism gained particular traction among the Goths and with several of the emperors, e.g., Constantius and Valens (364–78), until the emergence of the pro-Nicene Theodosius in 380.

Not only was Arianism a broad theological and philosophical movement, but in seeking to defend a Trinitarian understanding in which there was a single Godhead revealed in three persons, each of whom were eternal, from the beginning, a new vocabulary was minted. This vocabulary had its own pedigree and background (sometimes carrying baggage which had to be re-examined) and attracted or repelled others. The terms which both defined and divided Church leaders in the fourth and early fifth centuries were *homoousios* and the associated *ousia* words. *Homoousios* was adopted into the Nicene Creed to describe the common identity of Father and Son, especially that they were of the same substance. Of course that begged further questions about what this novel word actually implied. (In what ways were they of the same substance?) It was a word that had its advocates and detractors, and for many Arians, including the Eusebians, it was rejected because not biblical, although, ironically, it was intended to defend the biblical doctrine of the Trinity.

Athanasius did not pitch his tent on the word *homoousios* for some time. Indeed, he did not start using it until about *c*.353 and his work *De*

Decretis (355–6).[5] Until then he was content to explain the doctrine of the incarnation as God becoming man, so that we might become as he is and share in his defeat of death (*De Incarnatione*), and to argue against the Arian distortion of particular Scriptures (see *Orationes contra Arianos*, c.340–6; *Apologia contra Arianos*). Only by 335 had Athanasius begun to map out the existence and development of something called Arianism and give a framework to the polemic which became long-lasting.[6] *Homoousios* became something of a benchmark position in a single word. It was then subdivided in the Greek language by the word *homoiousios*, meaning "like in substance". Retaining the *ousia* concept of shared being gave new theological territory to the debate. There were then shades of *ousia* meaning, and by 360, according to his work *De Synodis*, Athanasius was willing to accept there was only a sliver of difference between himself and those like Basil of Ancrya who accepted *homoiousios* and in so doing agreed that the Son came from the essence or *ousia* of the Father.[7] In this way, Athanasius laid the groundwork and theological trajectory for the future, which the Cappadocians would ably and imaginatively take up.

Athanasius's legacy in the west

The division between west and east was based on the administrative, political and linguistic division in the Roman empire. Since the days of Diocletian, two emperors ruled east and west respectively, although there would be a few exceptions, such as Constantine and later Theodosius who briefly ruled both parts of the empire. Furthermore, the division was cultural and linguistic: the *lingua franca* of the eastern empire was Greek while in the west it was Latin. This cultural and linguistic division spilled over into theology as well, with the Greek or Latin terms used by one half not understood by the other. Relatively few of Athanasius's Greek words were widely read or even translated into Latin.[8] If Origen, Athanasius and the Cappadocians proved seminal in eastern theology in framing the terms of the debate, together with those who opposed them, contrastingly, in the west Justin Martyr, Tertullian and later Jerome were the Latin writers or theologians to establish the terminology of western theology, and who with others framed the exposition of the

Trinity in the west. Others, whom we will refer to, and who especially shaped the western understanding of the Trinity, were Hilary, Ambrose and Augustine: these were the advocates of mature Trinitarian theology expressed in western terms and in Latin.

Athanasius's own influence in the west was in part due to the periods he spent in exile there. As a young bishop (consecrated in 328) he was exiled by Constantine to Trier in 335–7, and it is quite possible that while there he began to write *Contra Gentes* and *De Incarnatione*. His presence there may well have had a lasting influence, not so much for his theology as inspiring a monastic lifestyle which we hear of later from one Ponticianus, who was an inspiration to Augustine of Hippo.[9]

Indeed, it was Athanasius's *Life of Antony*, more than his theological or historical works on the development of Arianism, that gained traction in the west. And the writer on asceticism, Rufinus of Aquileia (345–410), who spent time in Jerusalem and Alexandria, had further influence on monastic practice in the west. Rufinus wrote an extension of Eusebius's history of the Church and in Book X offers a clear appreciation of Athanasius's struggles and endurance.[10] Still, theological terms like *homoousios* were relatively unknown in the west, along with the entire *ousia* theology and the Nicene Creed.

Athanasius's second exile after the Council of Tyre, in which the Eusebians were able to manipulate the outcome of his deposition as bishop, took place from 335 to 337 and was mostly spent in Rome where he received warm support from Pope Julius, and where a council declared him innocent of any charges of heresy. This was then communicated to the bishops at Antioch who had recently debarred him—an early sign of a growing breach between west and east. The subsequent western council at Serdica in the Balkans once more upheld Athanasius because the eastern bishops refused to participate, as with the later council at Arminum (Rimini) in 359 with 300 to 400 bishops which overwhelmingly supported the Nicene position.

The principal western theologian of the Trinity in this period was Hilary (*c.*315–67), Bishop of Poitiers. A clear theological follower of Tertullian (*c.*155–220), he believed in the eternal generation of the Son (i.e., that the Son was ingenerate). There is no unmistakeable sign of Athanasius's influence, although Hilary did spend several years in exile in the east for an unknown misdemeanour. In fact, it was only shortly before his exile (*c*.356) that he learnt of the existence of the Nicene Creed.[11] Nevertheless, his stay in the east did give him some familiarity with eastern theological terms.

A few years later, he wrote his great work *De Trinitate*, in which he clearly accepted the eternal generation of the Son. At the outset of this work he writes, "Jesus Christ is to be confessed as nothing else than God in the fullness of Godhead."[12] He asserts that the union of Father and Son is one in nature and that they share a common *essentia* (essence or *ousia* in the Greek). In fact, in *De Trinitate*, he records the Nicene use of the word *homoousios.*[13] This unity of substance or essence reflects the Nicene theology at the root of Athanasius's Trinitarian theology and was clearly held by Hilary as well. In his later work, *De Synodis*, written for the most part to inform the Gallic bishops of previous Church councils, Hilary is more comfortable in recording the terms *ousia* and *hypostasis.* And, on hearing of Basil of Ancyra and the position of *homoiousios* which Basil upheld, Hilary was willing to countenance his inclusion within orthodoxy.

Yet Hilary had not yet come to the point, reached by the Cappadocians, of holding to a single substance in the Godhead while sharing three *hypostases*. The Latin equivalent to *hypostasis* might well have been *persona*, which was used by Tertullian, but Hilary was shy of it.[14] Thus, Hilary is clear on the Father, Son and Spirit as being of the one essence, but their individuated roles have still to be clearly expressed by him. His doctrines of the incarnation and the Holy Spirit remained slight.

He upheld the full divinity of Jesus on earth, saying, "when Christ was born as a man, he introduced to himself a new nature, not by the loss of divinity and power, but by change of condition".[15] Jesus emptied himself of the form of God but did not thereby destroy his divine nature. Yet in upholding Christ's divinity, Hilary advocated the impassibility of God, thus denying that Jesus actually "thirsted, hungered or mourned".[16] Surely here Hilary had overstepped the mark, compromising the humanity of Christ in the attempt to maintain his divinity. He could be accused of Docetism, of holding that Jesus had not really come in the form of human flesh that feels pain, suffers and truly dies (see 2 John 7). It would be years before the true expression of Christ's humanity and divinity would be found, in part at the Council of Chalcedon in 451.

Finally, Hilary had a very limited understanding of the Holy Spirit's work. Like most theologians of the period, little space was given to the Spirit till the latter part of the fourth century. He saw the Spirit as a "distinct manifestation of the divine nature",[17] but had little understanding of the Spirit's role outside of inspiring the prophets and law makers of the Old Covenant, helping our understanding of the incarnation through intercession, and helping disciples recognize the truth. Although stressing the Spirit's closeness to the Father and Son, Hilary nevertheless wrote: "It is the height of impiety for him to be described as ingenerate who was sent by the Son for our comfort."[18] In other words, the Spirit was not considered fully divine and part of the Godhead.

Theology in the west was innately more cautious, not as reflective, and it did not have to be hammered in the heat of powerful and acrimonious controversy, which created a furnace in which terms and teaching were beaten out, examined, cast aside or adopted. Hilary's Trinitarian theology, which owes a little to Nicene and Athanasian theology, was comparatively undeveloped. Further impetus would be given in the west by two Fathers of the Church: Ambrose and Augustine of Hippo. Ambrose was the executive bishop, *par excellence*, with a clear mind, strong gifts of communication and firm views. Augustine was in a sense made to be the explicator of the Trinity—his biblical faithfulness and philosophical mind attached to a deeply reflective nature made understanding the Trinity both a delight and a magnetic attraction.

Ambrose was consecrated Bishop of Milan by popular acclaim in 374, the year after Athanasius's death. Milan had replaced Rome as the capital of the western empire, and the imperial family lived there or at Ravenna. Ambrose had carefully nurtured the young western emperor, Gratian, who was later assassinated in Lyons (Lugdunum) in 383. Theodosius took over the eastern empire after the disaster of Adrianople and succeeded in pacifying the Goths. In succession to Gratian, his younger brother Valentinian II became emperor in the west at just 12 years of age and went on to be deeply influenced by his mother, Justina, who was a convinced Arian of the *homoian* kind. A struggle ensued between the court and

Ambrose, over the use of Milan's churches for Arian worship, in which Ambrose resolutely resisted imperial power.[19]

Ambrose would not yield any churches for Arian worship in the city, and hence into the hands of Justina or the boy emperor, Valentinian II. Two mobs, one supporting Ambrose and the other the Arians, threatened bloodshed in the churches, but in the end the emperor withdrew in a stand-off. Ambrose pursued a strongly anti-Arian policy and was in part nerved for this by the Cappadocians, and in particular, Basil of Caesarea. In a letter written to Ambrose in Milan in 375, a year after Ambrose became bishop, Basil called him to the fight against Arianism:

> Come then, O man of God—since not from men have you received or been taught by the Gospel of Christ, but the Lord himself has transferred you from the judges of the earth the seat of the Apostles—fight the good fight; correct the infirmities of the people, in case the disease of the Arian madness has indeed touched any; renew the ancient footsteps of the Fathers; and hasten to build upon the foundation which you have already laid of your love for us by the continuance of your salutations.[20]

Ambrose was to pursue a policy of no tolerance of the Arians in his restrictions of their use of churches in Milan, in his opposition to the Arian Palladius at the Council of Aquileia, in the instruction he gave to the young emperor Gratian in *De Fide* and *De Spirito Sancto*, and in his powerful sermons, encountered by Augustine of Hippo. Although there was no direct influence of Athanasius on Ambrose, because he died a year before Ambrose's episcopacy, his influence was nonetheless strong. Ambrose was well aware of the terms of Nicaea. He was encouraged by the Cappadocians, who themselves looked to Athanasius, and he modelled his work on the Spirit on that of Didymus the Blind (313–98), a contemporary of Athanasius teaching also in Alexandria. There can be little doubt that Athanasius's great struggle was an inspiration to Ambrose.

The final figure in western theology to shape our understanding of the Trinity from among the Church Fathers was Augustine of Hippo. Written between the years 400 and 419, *De Trinitate* became a seminal text in the west. Much discussion since has centred on the extent of Platonic influence in what is a clear biblical description of the Trinity, embracing both the unity of the Godhead and the inseparable operation of the Father, Son and Holy Spirit and their individuated roles.[21] Augustine especially loved triads, personally experienced in Platonic fashion as a means of fathoming the Trinity. Thus, the notion of lover, love and the bond of love would admirably reflect the Trinity by analogy.

But it was now 25 years since the death of Athanasius, whose works, apart from *The Life of Antony*, were little known in the west. Augustine certainly knew of Athanasius's heroic stand for the Nicene description of the Trinity, however undeveloped it may have been in 325. In a letter of instruction to Fortunatianus in 413/14, he referred to Athanasius as one of the theologians he read from the east, along with Gregory of Nazianzus. However, his limited knowledge of Greek and the probable patchy availability of Athanasius's writings curtailed his influence on Augustine. There is no mention of Athanasius in *De Trinitate*, but texts that Augustine, Ambrose, Rufinus and Jerome knew well were his *Life of Antony* and *De Virginitate*. Jerome gave Athanasius the sketchiest of biographies in his account of important Christians titled *De Viris Illustribus*.[22] For the west, it is probably fair to say Athanasius's ascetic writings became more influential than his narrative or theological writings.

Much later, and probably in the Middle Ages in the west, Athanasius became best known for the Athanasian Creed, sometimes called the *Quicunque Vult* from its opening Latin words. But it was probably not written by Athanasius himself,[23] being instead post-Athanasius, as it includes the doctrine of the double procession of the Spirit from the Father and the Son, a great bone of contention between east and west, and never adopted by Athanasius. Most likely the creed was composed in southern Gaul by Caesarius, Bishop of Arles, in the sixth century and used in catechumenate instruction, with its dire warnings that unbelief led to eternal damnation found in its opening and close.[24] Furthermore, the Christology found in the later part of the creed, while developing, was not so much of a focus in the fourth century, although it did become front and centre in the lead-up to Chalcedon in 451.

In short, in the west Athanasius was a heroic example of someone contending for the faith, to the extent that he was most probably plagiarized in the *Quicunque Vult*. But even so, his life was only partially known, as the records from Jerome and others are very sketchy. Better known, and probably more influential, were his ascetic writings and particularly his *Life of Antony*, at least until the nineteenth century, when his writings became widely influential in framing the Arian controversy.

The east

Athanasius's legacy in the Byzantine part of the empire and in the eastern churches was and is understandably more widespread. First and foremost, he left an enduring and powerful legacy in Egypt in the Coptic Church, which is still fresh and deeply influential today. On a recent visit to Heliopolis, effectively part of greater Cairo, I listened to teaching sessions of Daoud Lamei, presiding priest and pastor of the Coptic Orthodox church of St Mark in Cleopatra Street in Heliopolis, on salvation. (Incidentally, the church was heavily guarded against attack with a fence and guards.) Lamei referred extensively to Athanasius and quoted from the main principles of *De Incarnatione*. There can be no doubt that Athanasius in particular, and later Bishop Cyril of Alexandria, remain seminal to the self-understanding of the Coptic Church. If Athanasius gave the Egyptian Church a long-lasting exposition of the reasons for and reality of the incarnation, Cyril explained why they are a Monophysite or Miaphysite Church, one that stresses the single overarching nature of Christ as divine, or in the case of the Miaphysites, a single nature of Christ which is human but also chiefly divine.

Furthermore, Athanasius is one of the founding fathers in the Coptic tradition, providing an inspiring model of a pastoral bishop, teaching as well as guiding his flock. In the *History of the Patriarchs*, he is not only presented as a close associate and indeed protégé of Bishop Alexander, his predecessor and mentor, but as a model of ascetic living and one who left an enduring example of suffering for his faith. As such, he is a pattern and model for the Coptic Church today (and indeed the entire international Church), which is often called upon to suffer. That he is a continual inspiration to the monastic tradition in the Coptic Church is still evident today in its monasteries in Wadi El Natrun and elsewhere.

He is venerated as a saint and as a pastoral leader. Indeed, John of Niku, a late-seventh-century bishop and chronicler of the Coptic Church—as Bede (*c*.673–735) was of the Anglo-Saxon Church and at a similar time—wrote of Athanasius's characteristics in a way that Bede would have quickly recognized:

> In those days [the reign of Emperor Valens], there appeared a miracle through the intervention of the apostolic Saint Athanasius, the father of faith, patriarch of Alexandria. When the sea rose against the city of Alexandria and, threatening an inundation, had already advanced to a place called Heptastadion, the venerable father accompanied by all the priests went forth to the borders of the sea, and holding in his hand the book of the holy Law he raised his hand to heaven and said "O Lord, Thou God who liest not, it is Thou that didst promise to Noah after the flood and say: 'I will not again bring a flood of waters upon the earth"'. And after these words of the saint the sea returned to its place and the wrath of God was appeased. Thus, the city was saved through the intercession of the apostolic saint Athanasius, the great star.[25]

Elsewhere Athanasius figured strongly in the Syriac, Armenian and Orthodox Churches. The Orthodox Church, represented by national churches, is spread through eastern Europe, including Russia and the Ukraine, the Balkans and especially Greece. And of course, they have their outposts in western Europe and North America. The Syrian churches, which include the Chalcedonian Church, the Church of the East (sometimes wrongly called the Nestorian Church) and the Miaphysite churches, although divided in their understanding of the nature of Christ, are united in their admiration of Athanasius, in that he pre-dated the Chalcedonian division of 451. They are found in the Middle East in Syria and Iraq with patriarchates in Seleuchia-Ctesiphon and Baghdad, Iraq, and other centres in Kirkuk, Arbela, Mosul, Nisibis and Urfa (Edessa), Damascus and Jerusalem.[26] In recent years in Syria, Iraq and southern Turkey, however, war has threatened their existence.

Syriac, Armenian, Nestorian and Orthodox Churches all looked and look to Athanasius as a true defender of the faith. Since he defended the Nicene Creed, which is common to all these churches, he is fundamental to their faith-understanding. Indeed, in November 1994, when Pope John Paul II sought a new rapprochement with the Church of the East, led then by Mar Dinkha IV, the declaration was developed from a Christological statement based around the Nicene Creed.[27] Many of Athanasius's works were handed down in Syriac to some of these churches, and this corpus of Athanasius's works is in fact the oldest collection now extant. However, it does not include his major polemical and doctrinal works.[28] As in the west, many of the texts transmitted were his teaching on asceticism as well as his Festal Letters.

The Armenian Church was predominantly Miaphysite, believing the human and divine were combined in a single will in Christ, with the divine predominating. Although Athanasius is not recorded in the great eighth-century Armenian work, *History of the Armenians* by Moses Khorenats'i, a number of references to Athanasius were taken from the historian Socrates and are found in an Armenian edition of Socrates's work.[29] Some of these references are anachronistic, as Athanasius is credited with teaching a Miaphysitic view of Christ's nature, when in fact he could not have done so. He was long dead at the time of the Christological issues that led to Chalcedon in 451. As with the Syrian record of Athanasius, many of the polemical and doctrinal works were not conveyed to the Armenian Church, only parts that had been redacted to help support and define Armenian Christological beliefs. It was another case of picking out of context parts of the teaching of former authorities that agree with a position now held, or of making up teaching that upholds your own. What is clear is that Athanasius was very much a figure worth quoting, or attributing teaching to, such was his stature in the Church at large.

The legacy of Athanasius in the Church

There can be little doubt that after the Apostolic era, Athanasius was one of the few to help shape the faith of the Church and retain biblical Christianity. Among the Church Fathers, I would suggest only Irenaeus and Augustine of Hippo were as, or more, influential: the former in combating Gnosticism and restating the gospel, and the latter in stressing the teaching of grace. Later, during the Reformation, the two great teachers of the faith were Luther and Calvin, not that they were perfect. Indeed, Lyndal Roper in her book on Luther shows his real shortcomings.[30] They nevertheless rediscovered that salvation was through grace and by faith in the God-Man Jesus Christ, the Jewish Messiah, through whom atonement was made for human sin by his vicarious death and resurrection.

What was at issue during the fourth century especially was our very understanding of God, indeed our definition of the Godhead. In the east and in imperial circles, the Church was in grave danger of subscribing to a notion of God deeply affected by reason and logic, in which it was only possible for there to be one ingenerate and eternal being. In light of this presupposition, advocated by a whole range of influential and powerful figures, Christianity and biblical teaching were in the process of being recast. The Father alone was truly God and not the Son or the Holy Spirit, thus placing in jeopardy our eternal redemption and sanctification, and depriving Christianity of the glorious Trinity. It was a case of another thought structure diminishing biblical Christianity and remaking it in a rational, philosophical image.

Modern scholarship, and in particular Maurice Wiles and Young Kim, tend to emphasize the manner in which Athanasius framed the Arian controversy in order to demonstrate the way he polemicized the debate. As with most controversies, sound bites and epithets help to fix the issues in the common mind, without necessarily doing justice to the nuanced theological thinking. If Athanasius framed the debate in this way in his later writings, then it was with the central purpose of maintaining the full divinity of the Son as an uncreated being who shared the substance of the Godhead. And this was at the heart of the dispute.

Nor would this be the last time such a thing would happen. During the Middle Ages, in the European universities and in the Church, a blend of philosophy and Christianity would predominate in what was called scholasticism. A mix of Aristotelianism and Christianity resulted in a synthesis that ultimately found its expression in Lombard's *Sentences*. Add to this corruption of the Church and virtual ignorance of the Bible, and orthodoxy once again needed rescuing. The printing press, new translations of the Bible from Erasmus, Luther and Tyndale, and a reformation of the Church, not without its blemishes, rescued the essence of the faith.

Once again in the eighteenth century, a blend of rationalism, adherence to classical virtues and humanism swept the European nations, not least in revolutionary France but also in the elite in many nations, including England, where the likes of John Wesley would raise a challenge. More recently, at the end of the nineteenth century the scientific, liberal and humanist movements of the west once again recast Christianity, shorn of its supernatural power and its indictment of humankind, as a handmaid of progress. Until, that is, the First World War and then the Second. The writings of P. T. Forsyth and Karl Barth would help bring us back to our senses.

And now we face a world in which once again humans creep back to place themselves unremittingly at the centre of the universe: whether cloaked in authoritarian power and military adventurism, whether shrouded in ever more strident claims of new human rights like choosing our own sex, or whether in a return to paganism and the dark arts of magic. Perhaps it is time for another Athanasius?

Notes

1 David M. Gwynn, *Athanasius of Alexandria: Bishop, Theologian, Ascetic, Father* (Oxford: Oxford University Press, 2012), p. 160, citing Gregory of Nazianzus, Oration 21, §9.

2 Cited by Gwynn, *Athanasius of Alexandria*, p. 195.

3 Gwynn, *Athanasius of Alexandria*, p. 196, citing Edward Gibbon, *Decline and Fall of the Roman Empire*, Chapter 21.

4 Timothy D. Barnes, *Athanasius and Constantius: Theology and Politics in the Constantinian Empire* (Cambridge, MA: Harvard University Press, 1993), p. 33.

5 Lewis Ayres, *Nicaea and its Legacy: An Approach to Fourth-Century Trinitarian Theology* (Oxford: Oxford University Press, 2006), p. 140.

6 Gwynn, *Athanasius of Alexandria*, p. 77.

7 *De Synodis* §41, see also Ayres, *Nicaea and its Legacy*, p. 172.

8 Gwynn, *Athanasius of Alexandria*, p. 173.

9 Augustine of Hippo, *Confessions* VIII.14, tr. Henry Chadwick (Oxford: Oxford University Press, 2008), pp. 142–4.

10 Gwynn, *Athanasius of Alexandria*, p. 176.

11 Hanson, *The Search for the Christian Doctrine of God*, p. 473.

12 Hanson, *The Search for the Christian Doctrine of God*, p. 477, citing *De Trinitate* I.13.

13 Hanson, *The Search for the Christian Doctrine of God*, p. 489.

14 Hanson, *The Search for the Christian Doctrine of God*, p. 486.

15 Hanson, *The Search for the Christian Doctrine of God*, p. 493, citing *De Trinitate* IX.38.

16 Hanson, *The Search for the Christian Doctrine of God*, p. 499, citing *De Trinitate* IX.25.

17 Hanson, *The Search for the Christian Doctrine of God*, p. 503.

18 *De Trinitate VIII.39*; cited by Hanson, *The Search for the Doctrine of God*, p. 503.

19 Patrick Whitworth, *Constantinople to Chalcedon: Shaping the World to Come* (Durham: Sacristy Press, 2017), pp. 36ff.

20 Basil, Letter 197, in Basil, *Letters* III, ed. Roy Defferari, Loeb Classical Library, Vol. 243 (Cambridge, MA: Harvard University Press, 1926), p. 93.

21 Ayres, *Nicaea and its Legacy*, pp. 366 ff.; Henry Chadwick, *Augustine of Hippo* (Oxford: Oxford University Press, 2009), pp. 118ff.

22 Gwynn, *Athanasius of Alexandria*, pp. 177–8.

23 See Appendix for the Athanasian Creed.

24 Gwynn, *Athanasius of Alexandria*, p. 183.

25 John of Niku, Chronicle 82.21–3; cited by Gwynn, *Athanasius of Alexandria*, p. 193.

[26] Christoph Baumer, *The Church of the East* (New York: I. B. Tauris, 2016), pp. 269ff.

[27] Baumer, *The Church of the East*, p. 280.

[28] Gwynn, *Athanasius of Alexandria*, p. 185.

[29] Gwynn, *Athanasius of Alexandria*, p. 186.

[30] Lyndal Roper, *Living I Was Your Plague: Martin Luther's World and Legacy* (Princeton, NJ: Princeton University Press, 2021).

Chronological Table

199–217 Outbreak of the Monarchist (Trinitarian) Controversy in Rome

*c.***295** Birth of Athanasius

303 Great Persecution begins in Nicomedia under Diocletian

306 Constantine declared emperor in York by the Praetorian Guard

312 Battle of Milvian Bridge; Constantine takes Rome; The Conversion of Constantine

313 Edict of Milan: Constantine and Licinius (Eastern Emperor) grant toleration to Christians in the empire

318 Council of Alexandria called by Bishop Alexander to condemn Arius

321 Dispute between Arius and Bishop Alexander of Alexandria

324 Defeat of Licinius by Constantine; founding of Constantinople at Byzantium

325 Council of Nicaea

328 Athanasius consecrated Bishop of Alexandria

335 Council of Tyre; Athanasius deposed

335–7 Athanasius's first exile (Trier, Germany)

336 Death of Arius in Constantinople

337 Death of Constantine the Great; accession of Constantine II

337–50 Constans Emperor in the West (337–50); Constantius (337–61)

338 Council of Alexandria; Antony (the monk) visits Alexandria

339 Athanasius's second exile (339–46) (Gregory appointed bishop)

341 Dedication Council of Antioch, called by Constantius

343 Council of Serdica (Sofia), called by Constans

346–56 Athanasius's golden decade in Alexandria

356 Attack on the church at Theonas and flight of Athanasius

359 Councils of Ariminum and Seleucia

356–62 Athanasius's third exile (Bishop George of Alexandria)

361 Accession of Emperor Julian the Apostate (361–3)

362–3 Athanasius's fourth exile

364 Accession of Valens as emperor in the east (364–78)

364 Basil of Caesarea ordained priest

365–6 Athanasius's fifth exile

372 Basil consecrated archbishop of Caesarea

373 Death of Athanasius

374 Basil writes *On the Holy Spirit*

379 Gregory Nazianzen preaches *Five Theological Orations* at the Anastasia Chapel in Constantinople

379 Accession of Emperor Theodosius

381 Council of Constantinople: Nicene-Constantinopolitan Creed

381 Ambrose of Milan calls Council of Aquileia to condemn the Arians

382 Gregory of Nyssa preaches the Nicene-Constantinopolitan Creed

419 Augustine of Hippo completes *De Trinitate*

Dramatis Personae

Alexander, *c.*250–328 Bishop of Alexandria and Patriarch of the Coptic Church 312–28. He followed Achillas and Peter the Martyr, Patriarch 300–11. During his episcopacy, Alexander was opposed by the Melitians who sought harsher treatment of the lapsed, as the Donatists did in the west. He led the opposition to Arius, locally convening a Council in Alexandria in 318 and then later at Nicaea. His secretary and successor was Athanasius.

Ambrose of Milan, *c.*339–97 Ambrose was born in Trier into the ruling class. After training in law, he became Prefect of Liguria and Emilia in 372. He was forcibly made bishop in 373 by the crowd. He challenged Arianism especially in the court led by the Empress Justina, mother of Gratian. He condemned Arianism at the Council of Aquileia in 381. His preaching was instrumental in the conversion of St Augustine of Hippo.

Antony, *c.*251–356 He was a hermit, mystic and ascetic. Born in Lower Egypt to well-off parents who died while he was young, he was left to care for his sister. He took literally Jesus's injunction to sell all. He lived as a hermit in the Nitrian Desert west of Alexandria, then in Middle Egypt before moving to the east beyond the Nile to Mount Coizim, and to a monastery that still bears his name, *Der Mar Antonios*. He formed a close bond with Athanasius, who wrote his life which became the standard text in the west on the ascetic life before the Rule of Benedict.

Apollonaris of Laodicea, d. 382 His strongly anti-Arian teaching slipped into an equal and opposite heresy called Apollinarianism. This theology taught that in the incarnation Jesus took on human flesh, but the soul of Jesus was divine and likewise his mind, compromising his full humanity. It tended towards Docetism, a Gnostic heresy that denied that Jesus *really* came in the flesh. It was condemned at the Council of Constantinople in 381. Athanasius did not condemn him outright in his fight with Arianism, but Basil of Caesarea broke with him.

Arius, *c*.250–336 Heresiarch and priest from Libya. He taught in Alexandria that Jesus was not fully God, that he was a created being and that "there was a time that he was not". His most notable work was the *Thalia*, quoted against him by his chief opponent Athanasius. He was excommunicated by Bishop Peter of Alexandria in 311, but after reinstatement was excommunicated again by Bishop Alexander. The Emperor Constantine summoned the Council of Nicaea in 325 which anathematized Arius's teaching, but he had powerful support for his teaching from Eusebius of Caesarea and Eusebius of Nicomedia. His teaching and party were consistently opposed by Athanasius. Arius was effectively reconciled to Constantine on news of a partial recantation. Arianism remained a disruptive force in the Church for many decades after his death in 336.

Athanasius, *c*.296–373 Consecrated Bishop of Alexandria in 328. Attended the Council of Nicaea as Bishop Alexander of Alexandria's secretary. In *c*.328 he wrote his best-known work *Contra Gentes—De Incarnatione* which laid the theological basis for his opposition to Arianism. After Nicaea, ironically, the Arian party grew in strength and Athanasius was deposed. In all he suffered five exiles, the longest from 356–62 when he wrote his very influential work, *A Life of Antony* (the monk/hermit). He also wrote over many years the history of the Arian dispute, forming a comprehensive view of the heresy and its political and ecclesiastical backers. He supported the *homoousian* view expressed in the Nicene Creed. He became probably the most influential Father of the Coptic Church along with Cyril of Alexandria (378–444). Resolute, outspoken and brave, he resisted all political and ecclesiastical pressure and championed the Incarnation of the Divine Word in Jesus Christ.

Augustine, Bishop of Hippo, 354–430 Born in North Africa at Thagaste and a Berber. Taught at Carthage University when a Manichee and then in Milan as Professor of Philosophy. Converted while in Milan in 386. Baptized in Milan 387. 395 became Bishop of Hippo and lived in a small monastic community, wrote *Confessions.* Among numerous writings about grace and against the Donatists, he wrote *De Trinitate (On the Trinity)* from 398–419 and *De Civitate Dei* (The City of God) between 413 and 426. He became one of the chief proponents of the Trinity in the western Church. His book on the Trinity took 20 years to write. His method was to begin with Scripture but end with philosophical reflection on the nature of things, which also demonstrates the Trinity and the triad nature of human experience and the creation. He defends the one-substance theology of the Nicene Creed. He died while the Vandals were destroying Carthage.

Basil of Ancyra, *c.*310–64 Bishop of Ancyra and theologian of a compromise party between the Nicene position wedded to *homoousios* and the full Arian position suggesting that Jesus was a creature of the Father. He espoused the position that "the Son was of like essence to the Father" in his Synodal Letter of 358. Athanasius conceded in his *De Synodis* of 359–61 "that they are not far from accepting even the phrase *homoousios*". It was sign of rapprochement. For a time, Basil was in high favour with Constantius II.

Basil of Caesarea, *c.*329–79 One of three Cappadocian Fathers. Member of a land-owning Cappadocian family with a reputation for piety. Brother of Gregory of Nyssa and St Macrina. Ordained in 364 after education in Athens, took vows of chastity and poverty as a monk and pursued an ascetic lifestyle. He founded the monastic order and hospital called the Basiliad in Caesarea after becoming Archbishop of Caesarea in 370, writing both longer and shorter monastic rules. He wrote extensively, including *Against Eunomius* the Arian in 364, *On the Holy Spirit* in 374. He had an extensive correspondence and formed an Orthodox Nicene party. With his fellow Cappadocians he cautiously formulated an orthodox Trinitarian position in which each person of the Trinity shared the same substance (*ousia*) but were distinct hypostases. His care of the poor and for social justice, devotion to the ascetic life and Nicene orthodoxy gave him a unique place in the Church.

Constantine the Great, *c*.272–337 First Christian emperor of the Roman empire. Son of Constantius I, emperor of the west. Constantine proclaimed *augustus* of the west by his troops in Eboracum (York) in 306. Only in 312 did Constantine move against the usurper emperor in the west, Maxentius, defeating him and taking Rome after the Battle of Milvian Bridge after a vision of Christ before the battle and fighting under a Christian banner (the *Labarum*, see Glossary). In 312, Licinius, the eastern emperor, and Constantine published the Edict of Milan giving Christians freedom to worship in the empire. A Church council was called at Arles to deal, unsuccessfully, with the Donatist Controversy. Churches were founded by the emperor at the Lateran in Rome and worship at pagan temples was neglected. In 324, Constantine defeated Licinius and ruled the whole empire, east and west. A new city at Constantinople was founded on the site of Byzantium. In 325, the Council of Nicaea was called with Constantine opposing Arianism, but his opposition was tempered later by influential bishops like Eusebius of Nicomedia who were not supporters of the Nicene Creed. Constantine's mother Helena founded several churches like the Church of the Holy Sepulchre in Jerusalem and the Church of the Nativity in Bethlehem. Constantine died in 337 and was succeeded by his sons by his wife, Fausta: Constantine II, Constantius II and Constans. He was buried in the Church of the Apostles in Constantinople. A man of exceptional ability and military prowess who desired as a Christian the unity of the Church and had formidable power to pursue it.

Constantius II, *c*.317–61 Second son of Fausta and Constantine the Great. Emperor in the east from 337 and became *augustus* of the empire after the death of his brother Constantine II and his other brother Constans who became *augustus* in the west until 350. Much of his energy was spent campaigning against the Quadi and Sarmatians in the Danube region, the Persians in the east and a usurper, Magnentius, in the west whom he defeated. Paganism was largely suppressed in his reign, but he adopted a compromise position on the issues of Arianism agreeing with creeds which said that the Son was of like substance (*homoiousios*) with the

Father. This was strongly opposed by Athanasius who was deposed by Constantius and exiled. Athanasius increasingly criticized Constantius in his writings.

Constans, *c*.320–50 Youngest son of Constantine the Great. He defeated his eldest brother, Constantine II, and took control of the western empire including Italy, Gaul, Britain and North Africa. He was defeated and killed by the usurper Magnentius in 350. He was a supporter of Athanasius and his cause. The last Roman emperor to have visited Britain.

Cyril of Jerusalem, 313–86 Became Bishop of Jerusalem in AD 350. Cyril is best known for his Catechetical Lectures which prepared catechumenates for baptism in Jerusalem, probably in 348–50. Cyril is an example of a bishop who moved over time to the *homoousion* position, but who had not originally been a supporter of Athanasius. He was appointed bishop by the Arian Archbishop of Caesarea Maritima in Palestine who succeeded Eusebius. He was deposed during his episcopacy by the Arian Emperor Valens in 367 and accused and deposed by Archbishop Akakius of Caesarea for selling church furniture to feed the poor in 358–60!

Diocletian, *c*.242–312 Reforming Roman emperor (284–305) who re-established stability but began a violent persecution of the Church in pursuance of conservative paganism. He divided the empire into east and west with their own *augustus* and *caesar* (a tetrarchy). He promulgated unsuccessful economic reforms to standardize prices (the Edict on Prices, 301). The Great Persecution began at the Temple of Apollo in Didyma from 303–12. It was the most systematic attack on the Church: destroying buildings, confiscating books, martyring leaders and imprisoning and torturing Christians. In turn this led to divisions in the Church about treatment of the lapsed (Donatists in the west and Melitians in Egypt). Ironically Diocletian's reforms stabilized the empire for 150 years after the mayhem of the late third century, but within a year of his death, despite the persecution, Christianity became the religion of the empire.

Eunomius, *c*.335–93 Arian bishop of Cyzicus. He studied in Alexandria under Aetius, a fellow Arian. He was ordained by

Eudoxius, the Arian Bishop of Antioch. He took the extreme Arian position in which the Son was said to be unlike the Father (*homoian*). He was a brilliant logician and applier of Greek philosophy, especially Aristotelian theory, to theology. Both Basil of Caesarea and Gregory of Nyssa wrote lengthy works against him in 364 and 382 respectively. He was twice deposed from his bishopric by Constantius II (a semi-Arian by comparison) and by the Emperor Theodosius.

Eusebius of Caesarea, *c.*260–338 Church historian and bishop. He became Bishop of Caesarea in 313, which was a notable centre of scholarship following Origen's teaching there (231–51) in the third century. A prolific author, he was best known for his *Ecclesiastical History*, our main source of early Church history. He refused to accept *ousia* language in the creeds, rejecting *homoousios* in the Nicene Creed as unbiblical. Together with his namesake Eusebius of Nicomedia, he resiled from Nicaea and was opposed by Athanasius and Eustathius of Antioch. A conservative bishop, he found the language of Nicaea hard to swallow. He stood on the shoulders of Origen who remained suspect to those opposed to Arianism. He was more a historian than a theologian, despite writing many commentaries.

Eusebius of Nicomedia, *c.*280–341 Bishop of Nicomedia and essentially the court bishop of Constantine the Great and characterized as being a consummate political bishop. Although he signed the Nicene Creed, he resiled from its use of *ousia* language. He opposed the anti-Arians, especially Athanasius, Eustathius of Antioch and Marcellus of Ancyra, eventually getting them all deposed. He was sent into exile by Constantine but made his way back. He persuaded Constantine to accept Arius back into fellowship by arguing that Arius's views and the Nicene Creed could be squared. He baptized Constantine shortly before his death in 337.

Eustathius of Antioch, *c.*290–*c.*355 He was the revered Bishop and Patriarch of Antioch in succession to the Apostle Peter, Ignatius and other distinguished predecessors. He became increasingly critical of Origen whom he saw as the father of Arianism, and was opposed, as a pro-Nicene theologian, to Eusebius of Nicomedia. He was falsely accused at a synod in Antioch in 330 for adultery and deposed. He was exiled. A group of Christians continued in their allegiance to him. This schism confused and divided the Church in Antioch for the next 50 years.

Gregory of Nazianzus, *c*.326–90 One of the Cappadocian Fathers, along with Basil of Caesarea and Gregory of Nyssa. He was brought up at Nazianzus in Cappadocia, Turkey where his family owned estates and his father was bishop. He was a reluctant priest and was ordained by his father in 361, whereupon he fled to the Black Sea or Pontus. Educated in Athens with Basil he was a literary stylist and later convert to Christianity. In 372, Basil consecrated Gregory Bishop of Sasima, which Gregory regarded as a backwater. His moment in the limelight came when invited to give a series of addresses in Constantinople in the Anastasia Chapel by the Nicene party. These five Theological Orations given in 379 became elegant expositions on the Trinity from the Nicene position. He briefly led the Council of Constantinople and expected to be affirmed as archbishop, but another was appointed by Theodosius. Sensitive, introverted and fastidious, he was not suited to the rough and tumble of ecclesiastical politics in the fourth century. He retired to his estates, polished his Orations and wrote a full-length autobiography in verse called *De Vita Sua* (Concerning his own life).

Gregory of Nyssa, *c*.334–95 One of the Cappadocian Fathers, and a younger brother of Basil of Caesarea. He became Bishop of Nyssa in Cappadocia in 372. His theology and spirituality were a unique combination of orthodox Nicene theology and Platonic mysticism. In the former he followed Athanasius and in the latter Origen. An example of his orthodox theology is his long work *Contra Eunomius* (382), but his spirituality is displayed by his conversation with his dying sister Macrina called *On the Resurrection*, *The Life of Moses* and his *Commentary on the Song of Songs*. He was present at the Council of Constantinople in 381 and preached Nicene orthodoxy following it, and in particular the divinity of the Spirit.

Hilary of Poitiers, *c.*310–*c.*367 Bishop of Poitiers in western France and sometimes called the Athanasius of the west. He campaigned against the Arian party and in particular against Valens of Mursa and Ursacius of Singidunum, who opposed Athanasius, as well as later Bishop Auxentius of Milan in 363. He was exiled in Phrygia by Constantius II. He held out for the Nicene position on the Trinity although he also sought reconciliation with the *homoiusios* party and wrote extensively on the Trinity and Scripture.

Julian, 331–63 A nephew of Constantine, he survived the purges of that part of Constantine's family at the accession of Constantius II. He succeeded Constantius II as emperor in 361 and was himself succeeded briefly, for eight months, by Jovian. Educated in Athens at the same time as Gregory Nazianzen and Basil of Caesarea, he was a devotee of the classics and Plato. He espoused traditional paganism in 351 and sought to revive the empire's fortunes thereby. He proved an able military commander and administrator, dealing with corruption at court. He restored deposed bishops like Athanasius, did not so much persecute the Church as advocate paganism. He died while fighting the Persians in Mesopotamia. His brief rule meant that his reforms were not entrenched.

Julius, *c.*290–352 Pope from 337 until his death. Following the backlash after Nicaea in which the Arian party gained the upper hand, Julius and Rome proved a safe haven for Athanasius in his second exile. Tertullian (155–220) had been the first to express the Trinity as three persons but a single substance, although he was still weak on the eternal generation of the Son. Julius used the Arian dispute to suggest the primacy of Rome in establishing teaching and questioned the authority of the eastern bishops. It was he who set the date of Christmas as being 25 December.

Marcellus of Ancyra, d. *c.*374 Attended the Council of Nicaea and was a strong opponent of Arianism. Indeed, his opposition led him to a mild form of Sabellianism (see below) which emphasized the unity of the Godhead at the expense of the hypostasis of each member and each person being ingenerate, like the Father. He was exiled in 336 at an earlier Council of Constantinople when the Anti-Nicenes, i.e., the Eusebians, held sway. Basil of Ancyra (see above) succeeded him. He sought support from Pope Julius but was not wholly endorsed by either Athanasius or Basil of Caesarea, who wrote warning of his teaching.

Meletius of Lycopolis, d. 327 Founder of the Meletian Church in Egypt in 305 in opposition to the bishops of Alexandria including Athanasius. Like the Donatists in North Africa (i.e., Carthage and Punic North Africa), they refused to have communion with lapsed members and leaders of the Church. In Egypt, they combined with the Arians at the Councils of Nicaea and Tyre (337) against the patriarchs of the Egyptian Church. Eventually, they survived only as a monastic movement.

Meletios, d. 381 The saintly archbishop of Antioch (360–81) was a firm supporter of Nicaea and the *homoousios* position but was repeatedly exiled (361–2, 365–6, 371–8). He was opposed by a more hard-line rival Nicene bishop of Antioch, Paulinos, with whom he was reconciled. He most probably ordained John Chrysostom as deacon, making him his close assistant. In 381, Meletios chaired the Council of Constantinople until his untimely and sudden death when Gregory Nazianzen briefly took over. He was a much-loved leader of the Church in Antioch.

Origen, *c.*185–253 A colossus in early Christian theology although also controversial, as he was heavily influenced by Platonism. He taught in Alexandria and Caesarea and was martyred under the Emperor Decius, dying in *c.*253 from the effects of torture and imprisonment. His thinking influenced the trajectories of Trinitarian thought. Although in his *On First Principles* he maintains that there was never a time when God was not a Father, the theological tools for defining this further were not developed. In particular, he was not yet ready to use *ousia* language to describe the unity of the Father and the Son for fear of being seen to be materialistic. He was still searching for language to denote the unity of the Godhead and their individuated existence and activity. He was a remarkable exegete and spiritual writer on asceticism but his cosmology that all material beings have a prior existence as souls, and his teaching on universal salvation, led to his later excommunication in the sixth century.

Ossius, *c*.256–359 Bishop of Cordoba. Ossius had an extraordinarily long life and ministry. He presided at the Council of Nicaea and the abortive Council of Serdica (Sofia, modern-day Bulgaria) in 343, called by Constans I and Pope Julius. He later objected to imperial interference in the Church's affairs in 353 and was exiled. He was pressured to agree the Homoean formula of 357 at the Council of Sirmium and returned to die in Spain two years later.

Sabellianism, *c*.220 A heresy about the Trinity which bears the name of its founder Sabelius, an early-third-century priest and theologian working in Rome. None of his writings are extant so what is known is from the polemical writings of his opponents. His views are described as Modalism, meaning the One God and Father expressing himself as also Son and Spirit, so jeopardizing their individual existence or hypostasis. Thus, the Trinity for Sabelius was three modes of one being. Some thought that the *homoousios* clause of the Nicene Creed played into the hands of the Sabellians since it did not distinguish sufficiently between the individuated beings of the members of the Trinity and used an unscriptural term. He was opposed by Tertullian and Hippolytus, and in particular Tertullian's work *Adversus Praxeas.*

Tertullian, *c*.155–220 Often called the father of Latin Christianity, was quite possibly a lawyer and a prolific author. Most famously he wrote a defence of Christianity called *Apologeticum* in *c*.197. He wrote extensively about Christian practice such as the veiling of women, modesty and attitude to the games, as he also did against Gnosticism in his *Against Marcion.* He responded to the Sabellian (see above) and Monarchist (the idea that there is only one sovereign God, the Father, to whom Son and Spirit are subordinate in status) controversies in Rome and wrote an important tract, *Adversus Praxeas.* Arianism, as such, was unknown at the time, but he held to the notion of a single substance and three persons as being fundamental to the doctrine of the Trinity.

Theodosius, 347–95 Emperor 379–95. A Spanish general, he was appointed *augustus* in the east by Gratian, the western emperor, after the death and defeat of Valens (see below) at the Battle of Adrianople. An Orthodox Christian who supported Nicaea, he was determined to stamp out paganism by decree, and force if necessary. He appointed orthodox bishops, called the Council of Constantinople in 381 which issued an expanded Nicene Creed (see Appendix 1) and issued laws against pagan sacrifice. He briefly ruled the whole empire as senior *augustus* from 388. He was reproved by Ambrose of Milan for the massacres caused by his troops in Thessalonica in 390. Regarded as a great Christian leader by the Church, he was buried in the Church of the Apostles in Constantinople, his body being taken there after dying in Milan.

Valens, 328–78 Emperor or *augustus* of the east 364–78. He died fighting the Goths at the Battle of Adrianopolis, 9 August 378. He was the brother of the western emperor Valentinian I and uncle of Valentinian's successor Gratian. He continued the policy of Constantius of supporting the Arian or *Homoian* positions. He succeeded Julian the Apostate and Jovian—who was briefly emperor for eight months—and reverted to Christianity. He was frequently petitioned by Basil of Caesarea over caring for the poor and orthodoxy. His death, in a devastating defeat for Roman arms at Adrianopolis (modern-day Edirne, Turkey), precipitated a great change of policy towards the Church under Theodosius.

Glossary of Terms

agennētos Greek for "without beginning". An important term in the Trinitarian debate for establishing the divinity of the Son, who was without beginning.

anomios A term used to describe the Son and Holy Spirit as being unlike in substance to the Father. An Arian heresy, espoused by Eunomius.

Apollinarianism Based on teaching of Bishop Apollinaris of Laodicea (*c.*320–*c.*382) in which it was taught that, in the incarnation, the human body of Jesus had a divine mind. Declared a heresy in 381 at Constantinople.

apologia A work written in defence of Christianity or any subject. For instance, Justin the Martyr wrote two *apologias* defending Christianity in the second century.

apophatic The understanding of God as being beyond knowing and expressed in negative terms, e.g. invisible, immortal, inscrutable, inexpressible etc.

Arianism The teaching and heresy that broadly followed Arius who taught that the Word or Son was a creature with a beginning and that "there was a time when he was not". In compromising his divinity, it jeopardized the eternal nature of the salvation he procured.

divi filius Son of God. Title taken by Roman emperors following Augustus.

Docetism An early heresy which stated that Jesus did not really take on human flesh, but that it only *seemed* like he did. The word is taken from the Greek word *dokeīn,* to seem. The Apostle John wrote against these ideas in his First Letter (see 1 John 1:1–4) and it was condemned by the Council of Nicaea AD 325.

Donatism Donatism was not so much a doctrinal heresy as a false view of the Church. It was given its name by a North African Bishop Donatus (*c*.290–*c*.355) who argued that those who had lapsed (i.e., given in to persecution and either worshipped the emperor as god by burning incense to him or handing over (*traditores*) church books and sacred objects to authorities) should not be readmitted to Church fellowship. Others like Cyprian maintained that the lapsed could be readmitted after time, and public penance. The Donatist movement split the North African Church for centuries until the arrival of the Muslims in the seventh century, and led Augustine to argue seminally that the efficacy of clergy's ministry did not depend on their blamelessness.

epinoia Contemplation or meditative reflection. Used by the Cappadocians as a means of gaining understanding of the substance or being of the Godhead, apart from their activity.

Gnosticism A complex heresy which became extremely influential in the second century onwards in which followers sought revelatory knowledge/gnosis to give them salvation. It became deeply rooted in the Church. It created an overall religious system in which there were several mediators or intermediaries from a single God. Matter was thought to be corrupt, and salvation meant escaping its influence or being unaffected by fleshly desires. The result was that followers oscillated between asceticism and indulgence.

homoousios of the "same substance", used in the Nicene Creed to denote the Son as being of the same substance as the Father.

homoiousian "like in substance", used of the Father and the Son, i.e., "not of the same substance". Also ***'omoios kat' oùsian***.

hypostasis an important term in the Trinitarian debate, initially meaning exact likeness or representation, but increasingly, with the Cappadocians, meant the individuated being of each member of the Trinity.

idios often used by Athanasius to denote the idea of something being proper to (meaning belonging to) another and hence sharing common characteristics.

labarum Latin term with Gallic origins which describes the symbol on a military standard or shield. The symbol included the first two letters of the Greek alphabet, Chi-Rho, denoting Christ. Constantine's soldiers were the first to use it in battle.

Melitians The Melitians, like the Donatists above, were schismatics and rigorists in the Egyptian Church who refused to readmit to fellowship or acknowledge clergy or laity who had lapsed by worshipping the emperor as a god, handing over sacred books or things, or had gone into hiding during the Great Persecution (303–13). On account of Archbishop Peter of Alexandria's flight in 304, Melitius, Bishop of Lycopolis, began ordaining new bishops and formed a breakaway rigorist Church. He was excommunicated by Archbishop Peter, who was in fact later martyred in renewed persecution under Maximin in 311. The Melitians opposed the Archbishops of Alexandria, including Athanasius, and allied themselves with Arius and the Arians against both Alexander and Athanasius.

Modalism is a heresy akin to Sabellianism (see below) in which the Trinity is described as one God expressing himself sequentially in three ways: as Father, Son and Spirit. Although ensuring the unity of the Godhead it does so at the cost of there being three individuated beings or hypostases (Father, Son and Spirit) sharing the same substance.

Nestorianism is a later heresy (a century after Nicaea) of the Church following the teaching of Nestorius (*c.*386–*c.*450), Archbishop of Constantinople (428–31). Having settled how to express the divinity of the Son and Spirit as being of the same substance as the Father, the issue of how Jesus was both God and Man now came into sharp focus. Nestorius maintained the separateness of the divinity and humanity of Christ, while Cyril Archbishop of Alexandria stressed the singleness of Jesus's will and nature as being fundamentally divine. The Council of Chalcedon (451) defined Jesus's nature as being both human and divine mixed together, but this was insufficient for Cyril of Alexandria who, with the Egyptian (Coptic) Church, seceded. Nestorius was exiled in 435 by Theodosius II (Emperor 408–50), but his theology was taken up especially by the Eastern Chaldean churches.

ousia important Greek word in the Trinitarian debates referring to the Aristotelian or Stoic idea of substance or essence. It was used to describe the essence of the Godhead.

Patripassianism used to describe the Father (pater) suffering (passus/patior) in the Son; often associated with Sabellius. Contrariwise, others maintained that God was impassable and so subject to no change and therefore could not himself suffer in the Son's passion. Nevertheless Paul teaches that God was in Christ "reconciling the world to himself" (2 Corinthians 5:19).

persona Latin term which signifies a person. Used by Tertullian to describe the three persons of the Trinity.

Pneumatomachians in Greek literally means the Spirit fighters. In other words, those who would not ascribe full divinity to the Spirit. This included the Arians and the semi-Arians led by Archbishop Macedonius of Constantinople (Archbishop 342–60). The Council of Constantinople defined the full divinity of the Spirit in the Niceno Constantinopolitan Creed of 381.

Sabellianism a heresy named after Sabellius, a North African who taught theology in Rome in the third century. Most of his writings have not survived, but he is believed to have taught that there is one God with three names: Father, Son and Holy Spirit. Also called modalism (see above).

theosis theological term used by Athanasius and the Cappadocians to describe the process of becoming like God.

The Creeds

The Nicene Creed, as adopted in 325

We believe in one God, the Father Almighty, Maker
of all things visible and invisible.
And in one Lord Jesus Christ, the Son of God, begotten of the Father, the only-begotten; that is, of the essence of the Father, God of God, Light of Light, very God of very God, begotten, not made, being of one substance (ὁμοούσιον) with the Father; by whom all things were made both in heaven and on earth; who for us men, and for our salvation, came down and was incarnate and was made man; he suffered, and the third day he rose again, ascended into heaven; from thence he shall come to judge the quick and the dead.
And in the Holy Ghost.
But those who say: "There was a time when he was not;" and "He was not before he was made;" and "He was made out of nothing," or "He is of another substance" or "essence," or "The Son of God is created," or "changeable," or "alterable"—they are condemned by the holy catholic and apostolic Church.

The Niceno-Constantinopolitan Creed of 381

I believe in One God,
the Father Almighty,
Maker of Heaven and Earth,
and of all things visible and invisible.
And in one Lord Jesus Christ,
the Son of God,
the Only-Begotten, begotten of the Father before all ages;

Light of Light;
True God of True God;
begotten, not made;
of one essence with the Father,
by Whom all things were made;
Who for us men and for our salvation
came down from Heaven,
and was incarnate of the Holy Spirit and the Virgin Mary,
and became man.
And He was crucified for us under Pontius Pilate,
and suffered, and was buried.
And the third day He arose again,
according to the Scriptures,
and ascended into Heaven,
and sits at the right hand of the Father;
and He shall come again with glory to judge the living and the dead;
Whose Kingdom shall have no end.
And in the Holy Spirit, the Lord, the Giver of Life,
Who proceeds from the Father;
Who with the Father and the Son together is worshipped and glorified;
Who spoke by the prophets.
And in One, Holy, Catholic, and Apostolic Church.
I acknowledge one baptism for the remission of sins.
I look for the resurrection of the dead,
and the life of the world to come.

The Athanasian Creed

Attributed, probably wrongly, to Athanasius (probably originating in the Christian west in the twelfth century)

Whosoever will be saved, before all things it is necessary that he hold the catholic faith. Which faith unless every one do keep whole and undefiled, without doubt he shall perish everlastingly. And the catholic faith is this: that we worship one God in Trinity, and Trinity in Unity; neither confounding the Persons, nor dividing the Essence. For there is one Person of the Father; another of the Son; and another of the Holy Ghost. But the Godhead of the Father, of the Son, and of the Holy Ghost, is all one; the Glory equal, the Majesty coeternal. Such as the Father is; such is the Son; and such is the Holy Ghost. The Father uncreated; the Son uncreated; and the Holy Ghost uncreated. The Father unlimited; the Son unlimited; and the Holy Ghost unlimited. The Father eternal; the Son eternal; and the Holy Ghost eternal. And yet they are not three eternals; but one eternal. As also there are not three uncreated; nor three infinites, but one uncreated; and one infinite. So likewise, the Father is Almighty; the Son Almighty; and the Holy Ghost Almighty. And yet they are not three Almighties; but one Almighty. So, the Father is God; the Son is God; and the Holy Ghost is God. And yet they are not three Gods; but one God. So likewise, the Father is Lord; the Son Lord; and the Holy Ghost Lord. And yet not three Lords; but one Lord. For like as we are compelled by the Christian verity; to acknowledge every Person by himself to be God and Lord; So are we forbidden by the catholic religion; to say, there are three Gods, or three Lords. The Father is made of none; neither created, nor begotten. The Son is of the Father alone; not made, nor created; but begotten. The Holy Ghost is of the Father and of the Son; neither made, nor created, nor begotten; but proceeding. So, there is one Father, not three Fathers; one Son, not three Sons; one Holy Ghost, not three Holy Ghosts. And in this Trinity, none is before, or after another; none is greater, or less than another. But the whole three Persons are coeternal, and coequal. So that in all things, as aforesaid; the Unity in Trinity, and the Trinity in Unity, is to be worshipped. He therefore that will be saved, let him thus think of the Trinity.

Furthermore, it is necessary to everlasting salvation; that he also believe faithfully the Incarnation of our Lord Jesus Christ. For the right Faith is, that we believe and confess; that our Lord

Jesus Christ, the Son of God, is God and Man; God, of the Substance [Essence] of the Father; begotten before the worlds; and Man, of the Substance [Essence] of his Mother, born in the world. Perfect God; and perfect Man, of a reasonable soul and human flesh subsisting. Equal to the Father, as touching his Godhead; and inferior to the Father as touching his Manhood. Who although he is God and Man; yet he is not two, but one Christ. One; not by conversion of the Godhead into flesh; but by assumption of the Manhood into God. One altogether; not by confusion of Substance [Essence]; but by unity of Person. For as the reasonable soul and flesh is one man; so, God and Man is one Christ; Who suffered for our salvation; descended into hell; rose again the third day from the dead. He ascended into heaven, he sitteth on the right hand of God the Father Almighty, from whence he will come to judge the living and the dead. At whose coming all men will rise again with their bodies; And shall give account for their own works. And they that have done good shall go into life everlasting; and they that have done evil, into everlasting fire. This is the catholic faith; which except a man believe truly and firmly, he cannot be saved.

Bibliography

Anatolios, Khaled, *Athanasius* (London: Routledge, 2004).

Annas, Julia, *Plato: A Very Short Introduction* (Oxford: Oxford University Press, 2003).

Athanasius, *Contra Gentes* and *De Incarnatione*, tr. Robert W. Thompson, Oxford Early Christian Texts (Oxford: Oxford University Press, 1971).

Athanasius, *The Life of Antony* (London: HarperCollins, 1980).

Athanasius, *On the Incarnation,* tr. John Behr (Yonkers, NY: SVS Press, 2011).

Ayres, Lewis, "Not Three People: The Fundamental Themes of Gregory of Nyssa's Trinitarian Theology as Seen in To Ablabius: On Not Three Gods", in Sarah Coakley (ed.), *Re-thinking Gregory of Nyssa* (Oxford: Blackwell, 2003).

Ayres, Lewis, *Nicaea and its Legacy: An Approach to Fourth-Century Trinitarian Theology* (Oxford: Oxford University Press, 2006).

Bardill, Jonathan, *Constantine: Divine Emperor of the Christian Golden Age* (Cambridge: Cambridge University Press, 2015).

Barnes, Timothy, *Constantine and Eusebius* (Cambridge, MA: Harvard University Press, 1981).

Basil of Caesarea, *Letters,* Loeb Classical Series Vols I, II, III and IV (Cambridge, MA: Harvard University Press, 1926).

Baumer, Christoph, *The Church of the East* (New York: I. B. Tauris, 2016).

Birley, Anthony (transl. and intr.), *Lives of the Later Caesars: the first part of the Augustan history, with newly compiled Lives of Nerva and Trajan* (Harmondsworth: Penguin, 1976).

Bowman, Alan, "Diocletian and the First Tetrarchy", in Alan K. Bowman, Peter Garnsey and Averil Cameron (eds), *The Cambridge Ancient History, second edition, Vol. XII: The Crisis of Empire, A.D.*

193–337 (Cambridge: Cambridge University Press, 2005), pp. 67–89.

Brakke, David, *Athanasius and Asceticism* (Baltimore, MD: John Hopkins University, 1995).

Cameron, Averil, "The Reign of Constantine", in Alan K. Bowman, Peter Garnsey and Averil Cameron (eds), *The Cambridge Ancient History, second edition, Vol. XII: The Crisis of Empire, A.D. 193–337* (Cambridge: Cambridge University Press, 2005), pp. 90–109.

Campbell, Brian, "The Severan Dynasty", in Alan K. Bowman, Peter Garnsey and Averil Cameron (eds), *The Cambridge Ancient History, second edition, Vol. XII: The Crisis of Empire, A.D. 193–337* (Cambridge: Cambridge University Press, 2005), pp. 1–27.

Chadwick, Henry, Hobbs, Edward C. and Wuellner, Wilhelm (eds), *The Role of the Christian Bishop in Ancient Society: protocol of the thirty-fifth colloquy, 25 February 1979* (Berkeley, CA: Center for Hermeneutical Studies, 1980).

Chadwick, Henry, *The Early Church* (Harmondsworth: Penguin, 1993).

Chadwick, Henry, *Augustine of Hippo* (Oxford: Oxford University Press, 2009).

Chitty, Derwas, *The Desert a City* (Yonkers, NY: SVS Press, 1999).

Clarke, Graeme, "Third-Century Christianity", in Alan K. Bowman, Peter Garnsey and Averil Cameron (eds), *The Cambridge Ancient History, second edition, Vol. XII: The Crisis of Empire, A.D. 193–337* (Cambridge: Cambridge University Press, 2005), pp. 589–671.

Clement of Alexandria, *The Instructor* (Lighthouse Publishing, 2014).

Clement of Alexandria, *Stromata* (Beloved Publishing, 2014).

Coakley, Sarah (ed.), *Re-Thinking Gregory of Nyssa* (Oxford: Blackwell Publishing, 2003).

Daniélou, Jean and Musurillo, Herbert, *From Glory to Glory: Texts from Gregory of Nyssa's Writings* (Yonkers, NY: SVS Press, 1979).

Davis, Stephen J., *The Early Coptic Papacy* (Cairo: The American University Press, 2004).

Davis, Stephen J., *The Early Coptic Church* (Cairo: The American University in Cairo Press, 2017).

Drinkwater, John, "Maximinus to Diocletian and the 'crisis'", in Alan K. Bowman, Peter Garnsey and Averil Cameron (eds), *The Cambridge Ancient History, second edition, Vol. XII: The Crisis of Empire, A.D. 193–337* (Cambridge: Cambridge University Press, 2005), pp. 28–66

Edwards, Mark J., *Culture and Philosophy in the Age of Plotinus* (Cambridge: Duckworth, 2006).

Edwards, Mark J., *Religions of the Constantinian Empire* (Oxford: Oxford University Press, 2015).

Eusebius of Caesarea, *Life of Constantine* (Limovia.net, 2017).

Eusebius of Caesarea, *History of the Church* (Harmondsworth: Penguin Classics, 1989).

Fowden, Garth, "Public religion", in Alan K. Bowman, Peter Garnsey and Averil Cameron (eds), *The Cambridge Ancient History, second edition, Vol. XII: The Crisis of Empire, A.D. 193–337* (Cambridge: Cambridge University Press, 2005), pp. 553–72

Fox, Robin Lane, *Pagans and Christians* (Harmondsworth: Penguin, 1986).

Grillmeier, Alois, *Christ in Christian Tradition,* tr. John Bowden, Vol. I from the Apostolic Age to Chalcedon (451) (London: Mowbray, 1975).

Gwynn, David M., *Athanasius of Alexandria: Bishop, Theologian, Ascetic, Father* (Oxford: Oxford University Press, 2012).

Hanson, R. P. C., *The Search for the Doctrine of God: The Arian Controversy 318–381* (Edinburgh: T&T Clark, 1988).

Heine, Ronald E., *Origen: Scholarship in the Service of the Church* (Oxford: Oxford University Press, 2010).

Hunt, David, "The Successors of Constantine", in Averil Cameron and Peter Garnsey (eds), *The Cambridge Ancient History, Vol. XIII, The Late Empire, AD 337–425* (Cambridge: Cambridge University Press, 1997).

Kelly, J. N. D., *Early Christian Doctrines* (London: A. & C. Black, 1960).

Kim, Young Richard, The Cambridge Companion to the Council of Nicaea (Cambridge: Cambridge University Press, 2021).

Lampe, G. W. H., *The Seal of the Spirit* (London: SPCK, 1976).

Ludlow, Morwenna, *The Early Church* (London: I. B. Tauris, 2009).

Mansell, Philip, *The Levant: Splendour and Catastrophe on the Mediterranean* (London: John Murray, 2011).

McGuckin, John, *Saint Gregory of Nazianzus: An Intellectual Biography* (Yonkers, NY: SVS Press, 2001).

Musurillo, Herbert, *From Glory to Glory: Texts from Gregory of Nyssa* (Yonkers, NY: SVS Press, 1979).

NAPNF Second Series, Vol. V and VII, eds Philip Schaff and Henry Hardcastle (New York: Cosimo Classics, 2007).

Opitz, Hans-Georg, *Urkunden zur Geschichte des arianischen Streites III* (Berlin: de Gruyter, 1934).

Origen, *On First Principles*, tr. G. W. Butterworth (Notre Dame, IN: Ave Maria Press, 2013).

Osborn, Eric, *Clement of Alexandria* (Cambridge: Cambridge University Press, 2005).

Plato, *Timaeus and Critias*, tr. Desmond Lee and T. K. Johansen (Harmondsworth: Penguin Classics, 1977).

Potter, David, *Constantine the Emperor* (Oxford: Oxford University Press, 2015).

Roper, Lyndal, *Living I Was Your Plague: Luther's World and Legacy* (Princeton, NJ: Princeton University Press, 2021).

Rousseau, Philip, *Basil of Caesarea* (Berkeley, CA: University of California Press, 1998).

Russell, Bertrand, *The History of Western Philosophy* (London: Routledge, 2007).

Shaw, B. D., "Rebels and Outsiders", in Alan K. Bowman, Peter Garnsey, Dominic Rathbone (eds), *The Cambridge Ancient History, Vol. XI: The High Empire, AD 70–192, second edition* (Cambridge: Cambridge University Press, 1993), pp. 361–414.

Socrates Scholasticus, *The Ecclesiastical History* (Aeterna Press, 2016).

Stark, Rodney, *The Rise of Christianity* (London: HarperCollins, 1997).

The Apostolic Fathers, Vols I & II, Loeb Classical Series, Vols 24 and 25 (Cambridge, MA: Harvard University Press, 2003).

Trigg, Joseph W., *Origen* (London: Routledge, 1998).

TANF Vol. I *Apostolic Fathers, Justin Martyr, Irenaeus*, eds Roberts and Donaldson (Grand Rapids, MI: Wm. B. Eerdmans, 1975).

TCAH Vol. XII *The Crisis of Empire AD 193–337* (Cambridge: Cambridge University Press, 2005).

TCAH Vol. XIII *The Late Empire AD 337–425* (Cambridge: Cambridge University Press, 2009).

White, Carolinne, *Gregory of Nazianzus: Autobiographical Poems* (Cambridge: Cambridge University Press, 1996).

Whitworth, Patrick, *Three Wise Men from The East: The Cappadocian Fathers and the Struggle for Orthodoxy* (Durham: Sacristy Press, 2015).

Whitworth, Patrick, *Constantinople to Chalcedon: Shaping the World to Come* (Durham: Sacristy Press, 2017).

Whitworth, Patrick, *Suffering and Glory: The Church from the Apostles to Constantine* (Durham: Sacristy Press, 2018).

Wiles, Maurice F., *The Remaking of Christian Doctrine* (London: SCM Press, 1974).

Williams, Rowan, *Arius* (London: SCM Press, 2001).

Williams, Stephen, *Diocletian and the Roman Recovery* (London: Routledge, 1997).

Index

Printed in Great Britain
by Amazon

0b0e819a-8c15-4cce-8a72-4fcd5beb908bR01